ECONOMIC TRANSITION IN HISTORICAL PERSPECTIVE

Economic Transition in Historical Perspective

Lessons from the history of economics

Edited by

CHARLES MICHAEL ANDRES CLARK
St John's University, USA

JANINA ROSICKA
Jagiellonian University, Poland

LONDON AND NEW YORK

First published 2001 by Ashgate Publishing

Reissued 2018 by Routledge
2 Park Square, Milton Park, Abingdon, Oxon OX14 4RN
711 Third Avenue, New York, NY 10017, USA

Routledge is an imprint of the Taylor & Francis Group, an informa business

Copyright © Charles M. A. Clark and Janina Rosicka 2001

All rights reserved. No part of this book may be reprinted or reproduced or utilised in any form or by any electronic, mechanical, or other means, now known or hereafter invented, including photocopying and recording, or in any information storage or retrieval system, without permission in writing from the publishers.

Notice:
Product or corporate names may be trademarks or registered trademarks, and are used only for identification and explanation without intent to infringe.

Publisher's Note
The publisher has gone to great lengths to ensure the quality of this reprint but points out that some imperfections in the original copies may be apparent.

Disclaimer
The publisher has made every effort to trace copyright holders and welcomes correspondence from those they have been unable to contact.

ISBN 13: 978-1-138-73549-1 (hbk)
ISBN 13: 978-1-138-73544-6 (pbk)
ISBN 13: 978-1-315-18652-8 (ebk)

Contents

List of Contributors		vii
Acknowledgements		ix
Preface		x
1	Plato on *Topos*, Economy and Transition Janina Rosicka	1
2	Karl Polanyi's *Great Transformation* and the Current Transformations in Central Europe Eric R. Hake and Walter C. Neale	27
3	On Building up a Market Society: Lessons from the Wealth of Nations and The Great Transformation António Almodovar and Maria de Fátima Brandão	43
4	Groundwork for an Institutional Economic Approach to 'Transition': Smith and Polanyi Reconsidered Eyüp Özveren	63
5	The Money Fiction and Central Banking William C. Schaniel	79
6	Labour: A Fictitious Commodity Needs Instituted Power Dell Champlin and Ann Jennings	85
7	Three Paths to Capitalism: An Agenda for Research Ana Bela Nunes and Nuno Valério	101
8	Friedrich von Hayek's Idea of Spontaneous Social Order and Transforming the Socialist Economy Janina Godłów-Legiędź	115
9	Worldly Advice from Other-Worldly Philosophers: Catholic Social Thought and the Problem of Economic Transition Charles M. A. Clark	123

10 The Promotion of National Prosperity: The Case of Industrial   141
    Activities in Portugal in the Transition to Liberalism
    Pedro Nuno de Freitas Lopes Teixeira

List of Contributors

António Almodovar is associate professor at the Faculdade de Economia of the Universidade do Porto (Portugal), where he has been teaching History of Economic Thought. He co-authored *A History of Portuguese Economic Thought* (Routledge), and has several works published in Portuguese on the history of economic thought. He is a member of the Advisory Board of the *European Journal of the History of Economic Thought*.

Dell Champlin is an Associate Professor of Economics at Eastern Illinois University. She has also taught at the University of Nevada, the State University of New York, College at Fredonia, the University of Tennessee and the University of Dallas. Prior to completing her PhD at the University of Utah, she worked for eight years as an economic analyst for the US government and in the private sector. Her primary research interests are labour issues, corporate power, and social economics.

Charles M. A. Clark is Professor of Economics and Senior Fellow, Vincentian Center for Church and Society, at St. John's University, New York. His past positions include Visiting Professor, University College Cork, Ireland. His most recent book is *Basic Income: Economic Security for All Canadians* (1999) (with Sally Lerner and W. Robert Needham).

Maria de Fátima Brandão is Associate Professor at the Faculdade de Economia of the Universidade do Porto (Portugal), where she has been teaching Economic History. She has several works published, mainly in Portuguese, on the history of rural communities in western Portugal and on the history of Portuguese economic thought.

Janina Godłów-Legiędź is Associate Professor of the History of Economic Thought at Uniwersytet Lodzki (University of Łótź), Poland. She is the author of one book and over 40 articles.

Eric R. Hake is an assistant professor at Eastern Illinois University. After receiving his doctorate in 1994 from the University of Tennessee at Knoxville, he taught in Slovakia and the Czech Republic for three years. His research has dealt with the evolution of financial institutions and ownership structures in an historical and comparative context.

Ann Jennings currently teaches in the Economics and Management Department at DePauw University, Greencastle Indiana. She has published extensively on the economic thought of Thorstein Veblen and on the relationship between feminist thought and economics. Her current research interests focus on problems in theorizing the commodification of labour, particularly as related to units of measurement and standardization.

Walter C. Neale is Professor of Economics, Emeritus, at the University of Tennessee-Knoxville. He was a student of Karl Polanyi's in the late 1940s and a colleague of Karl Polanyi in the project at Columbia University that produced *Trade and Markets in the Early Empires*. He has done research on economic and social change in rural India and has published frequently on India, in economic anthropology, and on the welfare state.

Ana Bela Nunes is Professor of History at the Institute of Economics and Management of the Technical University of Lisbon and director of the Research Centre of Economic and Social History of the same institute. She worked on general and Portuguese history, mainly in the fields of education and human capital history and retrospective national accounts, and theory of economic systems.

Eyüp Özveren is in the Department of Economics, Middle East Technical University & Boaziçi University. He has a Ph.D. in Sociology from the State University of New York. His research fields include: political economy, history of economic thought, Middle East.

Janina Rosicka is Chair of the History of Economic Thought at Jagiellonian University, Krakow, Poland. She is the author of three books and over 50 articles and over 50 reviews.

William C. Schaniel is Professor of Economics at the State University of West Georgia, Carrollton, GA, USA.

Pedro Nuno de Freitas Lopes Teixeira is Assistente Estagiário at the University of Porto. His research interests include: the economics of education, History of Economic Thought and Economic History.

Nuno Valério is Professor of History at the Institute of Economics and Management of the Technical University of Lisbon and President of the Portuguese Association for the History of International Relations. He works on general, Portuguese and colonial history, mainly in the fields of monetary and financial history and retrospective national accounts, and theory of economic systems.

Acknowledgements

In 1997 the editors of the book presented here were lamenting the lack of an historical perspective in most of the work on the problem of economic transition. Rather than merely complain about the problem, we did what every self-respecting academic does when they see a problem – we organized a conference. Thus on September 17-19, 1998, in Cracow, Poland, the *Economic Transition in Historical Perspective: What can be learned from the history of economics* conference was held, co-sponsored by Jagiellonian University, Cracow Academy of Economics and St. John's University, New York. We would like to thank each of these institutions for their generous support, especially the Cracow Academy of Economics, which provided the meeting place for conference. And we must thank the Rector of the Cracow Academy of Economics Prof. Jerzy Mikulowski Pomorski, who was also a co-organiser of the conference. Without his help and efforts our conference would never have gone beyond being an interesting idea. We also need to thank Dariusz Grzybek and Marek Jarzebinski who acted as our guides and generally kept the vistors to Cracow from getting too lost.

Our conference benefited from the wisdom of many guest speakers: Prof. Dr. Jerzy Mikulowski Pomorski; Prof. Dr. Tadeusz Kowalik; Dr. Ewa Miklaszewska; Prof. Dr. Stanislawa Surdykowska; who together gave the conference participants great insight into the economic reality of transition from many (and very different) perspectives. A special mention of gratitude must be made for Prof. Dr. Kurt Rothschild whose considerable experience, intelligence and presence left all inspired and enlightened.

Preface

While few economists would dispute the claim that the economic transition that the Eastern and Central European have been going through since the late 1980s is one of the most important developments in economic history, surprisingly few analysts of this phenomena have looked to the past for assistance in understanding this process. This is particularly surprising due to the fact that the problem of transition has been central to the history of economic thought. Most of the 'Worldly Philosophers,' to use Robert Heilbroner's term, wrote during periods of economic transition, and their work reflects this fact. Yet there has been very little written on the current economic transitions from the perspective of the great economists. It is this glaring omission that is the inspiration for this volume of essays. Too often the recent transformation of post-communist countries has been seen solely through the lens of numbers and tables, percent changes in GDP, share of economy in the private sector and other economic statistics. This approach is much like a report card from school, with the aim being to grade the leaders of a country. This book invites you to take a different – historical – perspective, to see the past, as Zygmunt Lempicki, a Polish intellectual from the early 20th Century, suggested, as a 'store of psychic and spiritual energy.' In this book we present this sort of energy as contained in Plato, Adam Smith, J.S. Mill, Karl Polanyi, John Paul II's writings and show not only their economic attitudes towards transition, but also their moral perspectives. The subject of these papers is the connection between moral values and economic activities, and this 'psychic and spiritual energy' should supply us with a more complex and complete picture of the problems of economic transition.

The insights of the great economists on the question of economic transition are important for the simple fact that their ideas form the foundations of what we now call economics. Although many of these insights, particularly those that relate to economic transition, may now be rejected or forgotten, these insights were in many ways fundamental to the parts of their economic theory that has been incorporated into economic orthodoxy. Furthermore, although the current economic transition is new, and to a certain extent, unique, as are all such transitions, there is much more that is in common with past transitional periods than there are differences. This is particularly the case when we look at what the great economists of the past emphasized in their analysis of economic transition, and compare it with the current approach. Looking at the economists considered in this volume, an admittedly small sample of the history of economic thought, one clearly sees that two of the most important aspects of economic transition are the problem of institutional adjustment and change, and the central role of historical and social context in understanding economic transition. These two facets of economic transition are exactly what the current crop of economic analysts and policy advisors seem to leave out of the picture. They tend to look at the problem of economic transition as one of merely obtaining the correct macro-economic and micro-economic policy mix, and that, along with the one institutional change they consider, the establishing of property rights, all these countries need to do is step back and let the 'invisible hand' carry out the process. This book informs us that this is not how the great economists of the past would have addressed this issue.

The collection of essays in this book starts off with probably the first serious student of the economy, Plato. In Janiana Rosicka's chapter we see that the problem of transition is fundamental to understanding both Plato's economics and his critique of his contemporary Athens. Here the transition is the movement from an abundant, but stable and limited, society and economy to one of unlimited wants, greed and overabundance. In this essay we see that Plato has much to say to 'Affluent Societies' of the West.

The 'Worldly Philosopher' who dominates this volume, for he dominates the topic, is Karl Polanyi. This is due to his critically important book *The Great Transformation*. Five of the ten chapters in this book relate in some way to Polanyi's ideas. In chapter 2 we have an introduction to *The Great Transformation* and its relevance to the transition going on in Eastern and Central Europe, written by Eric Hake and Walter Neale (a former student and colleague of Karl Polanyi, and a contributor to *Trade and Markets in the Early Empires*. This chapter is followed by an excellent comparison of Polanyi and Adam Smith (the founder of modern economics) by António Almodovar and Maria de Fatima Brandao. The Almodovar and Brando chapter is particularly important for it shows how institutionally based Adam Smith's analysis was. One of the main limitations of how orthodox economists have looked at the problem of economic transition is that they seem to have only read chapter 7 of *The Wealth of Nations*. A more attentive reading of Smith yields much greater insights. This comparison of Smith and Polanyi is extended in Eyüp Özveren's chapter. The Polanyi section of this book is completed with two chapters, 'The Money Fiction and Central Banking' by William Schaniel and 'Labour: A Fictitious Commodity Needs Instituted Power' by Dell Champlin and Ann Jennings. These two chapters are import because they apply Polanyi's insights to actual economic issues raised during periods of economic transition. One has to go beyond the grand scope of Smith and Polanyi and get into the specifics if one is to fully come to grips with the enormity of economic transition.

The last four contributions to this volume bring the insights of other strains in the history of economic thought. Ana Bela Nunes and Nuno Valerio review the various approaches to economic history. Janina Godłów-Legiędź brings out the role of Hayek in the transition from central planning to a market economy. Charles Clark raises the role of values and the conception of a 'good society' in his chapter on what Catholic social thought has to say about economic transition. Finally, Pedro Nuno Teixeira discusses the economic transition that took place in Portugal during the 19th century and the discussions on transition that this prompted.

Studying the history of economic thought is a necessary part of a useful education in economics. Besides the time saved in reinventing the wheel, the history of economic thought teaches us to look at the economy, any economy, differently than an unhistorical understanding of economics provides. It teaches us that social and historical context are important. It also teaches us that the philosophical preconceptions of economic theorists greatly shape their analysis, and that these 'value judgements' must be made more transparent. But mostly, it teaches us to be humble, that what economists do not know is usual greater than what they do, and what they do know will eventually be wrong. This should be kept in mind when we are designing policies that will affect the lives of millions of fellow citizens of the Earth.

Chapter One

Plato on *Topos*, Economy and Transition

Janina Rosicka

Introduction

Prior to the Enlightenment, most economic theorizing centred on abundance. The world of agrarian economies was described using terminology that suggested that the coexistence of wealth and poverty lead to an undesirable state of the economy; and that abundance, coupled with moderation, meant a desirable state of the economy. Within this view, economic man was seen mostly as a consumer. Although all agreed that everyone was dependent upon the gods or Fortune or Providence or Grace, as they determined the success or failure of the crops, man was still perceived as a 'joint' producer or creator of the state of economy. When man did not violate the eternal order he could reckon on the powers above. On the other hand, when he violated that order he could be sure of some sort of punishment. Thus economy and morality (in this case pleasing the gods) were closely interrelated. Generosity was connected with moderate consumption, and both of these features characterize good patterns of behaviour. Avarice was the central feature of bad behaviour. The recommended pattern of behaviour was that of those who lived in the country estates, whereas less than reputable behaviour was typified by those who lived in towns. Hence the common fears of commerce and town, and simultaneously, the praise of country and land. Myths, religion, theatre and *belles letters* all reinforced this manner of thinking.

Plato took part in this discussion, creating a theory which I would like to call the 'philosophy of economy space'. Living during a crisis of the Greek institution of the *polis,* Plato experienced first-hand the period of the transition, and an important part of his philosophy was dedicated to the transition. He combined cosmological, anthropological, historical, economical and psychological arguments in order to show regularities in the history of human race. These arguments were arranged by him to answer mainly two questions: 'what is the proper order of civilisation?' and 'what is disorder?' The proper order was described by him, in the *Republic* and the *Laws*, as the two models of the ideal state. Disorder was understood by Plato as the transition - a period full of chaos caused by commercial behaviours.

Based on the number pages Plato devotes to the problem of order in the *Republic* and the *Laws*, he clearly paid more attention to order than disorder. This part of

Plato's thinking has been recognised as an important part of Plato's overall thought, and has been carefully examined by historians both of economic and political thought. In our century, because of the experience with fascism, Nazism, and Stalinism, Plato's social ideas are interpreted as totalitarian. In the history of economic thought Plato is presented as a philosopher who denied the importance of the economy; as a theorist who wanted to eliminate the influence of economic goals over people; and as an adherent of the total intervention of the state in the economy. In this way, the economic image of Plato was generally accepted as a philosopher who interpreted economic questions only in the context of moral discourse, and demonstrated his aristocratic distance from the economy, especially from trade. Because of this image, there has been a tendency to forget Plato's long-lasting impact on European economic ideas, and to neglect the fact that for more than two thousands years his instructions concerning economic behaviour have been accepted, analysed, and enriched by the Church writers, and then by the political thought of the old republicanism in the Baroque and the Enlightenment periods and later by German cameralism and the 'Hausevater-literatur'.[1]

My starting point is different. I am interested in Plato's understanding of transition, that is to say, the period between two different kinds of economic orders. So I am forced to put stress on Plato's understanding of disorder. This point of view provides an interesting, to my knowledge unknown, connection between Plato's cosmology expounded in the *Timaeus*, and the description of Atlantis and old Athens in the *Critias*, namely the connection between space and society. As understood by Plato, this connection involved a close relationship between the state of the human and social environment and that of the state of society, and in particular - in the economic dimension - the relationship between the economic efficiency of the human environment, and the stage of economic welfare of society. We can say, using modern economic terminology, that as Adam Smith created a modern economics connected market, division of labour and wealth, Plato created a theory of agrarian or traditional economy demonstrating a relationship between, on the one hand: both space and place, and on the other: wealth, division of labour and consumption.

Plato saw this relationship as a source of social disorder. This disorder was described by him as a growing discrepancy between the commercial goals of society and a way in which the space - the *topos* existed. He understood the transition as a period full of economic and social chaos, during which people's elementary practices - especially commercial behaviours and luxurious consumption - violated the physical, biological, and human spaces. We are accustomed to think about space and place in the economy as a market - this perfect flexible place. Plato thought about the *topos* of the economy as flexible, although not as flexible in comparison with man's growing needs.

From his theory of the transition, Plato appears as a very interesting economist. He differentiates his 'economics' on micro- and macro-levels; he employs four theoretical models: two of man's existence: social and in isolation, and two of the states; he considers the relation between population and the efficiency of the economy.

We can find in his writings pre-Malthusian statements, a pre-Veblenian understanding of competition, and a pre-Hirschian idea of congestion.

Plato describes a cycle of the development of the human race from deluge to deluge and from surviving in mountains to a rise of civilisation in lowlands. Transition - according to Plato - is a period between two ways of human existence: in isolation and in community, the first takes place in the mountains, the second in lowlands. I will refer to these two different modes of existence further on as the Mountain and the Lowland. In fact there are two kinds of transition. First between the Mountain and the Lowland, after a deluge, during this period people try to overcome their isolation and establish a community; and the second between the end of welfare of the Lowlands civilisation, and the total disaster of this civilisation caused by a deluge. This deluge ended the second transition. The possibilities of the Lowland resources became exhausted and the people of Lowland were drowned. At that time only the Mountain people remained safe. Plato is not very interested in the first period of transition, however, the next period he studies very carefully. His goal is to describe the menaces of the Lowlands civilisation in order to admonish contemporary Athenians, and he wants to show activities that delayed or prevented this sinister transition. Plato's recipe is similar to recipes written by economists in the twentieth century, he wants to flatten a period of transition and to sustain as long as possible the period of true abundance.

Two notions: space and place; play a crucial part in the transition. The main human activities in the Lowland consist of bringing the Lowland space into cultivation. The economic space, according to Plato, appears only in the social space of the *polis*. People penetrate the whole space and their efforts result in a growth of the division of labour, which is accompanied by a growing population. These processes persist as long as the Lowland abundance can satisfy the needs of the growing population. However, once population has outgrown the abundance, that is all the space of the Lowland is filled, there will be not sufficient space for the growing population. This day of reckoning can be delayed by conquering new pieces of land, and thus wars become the main means of survival, but this is merely a delaying action.

According to Plato, the *topos* of the Lowlands are the source of abundance, and thus the transition emerges as a lack of possibilities for development. The result of economic growth is an overgrowth of economic and commercial space, provoking a shrinkage of human and physical spaces. The transition is a process of destruction, or corruption, of the true Man in man, and of the true *Topos* in *topos*. Plato elucidates why the transition came into being and what we can do in order to prevent the catastrophe.

To understand Plato's economic theory we should remember two things: first, he wants to find out the relationship between the general and the particular, and second, in his 'economics' there exists a basic relationship between space and economy. In the first part of this paper I intend to present Plato's main economic assumption, that the *topos* is a room for abundance (*Topos* and Abundance). Next I will try to reconstruct Plato's macroeconomic thinking about the social behaviour patterns in the

Mountain (Mountain *Topos*) and in the Lowland (Lowland *Topos* and Transition). Then Plato's microeconomics will be described. Here we see Plato's view that limited consumption is an economic virtue (Man and Economic Virtue). Afterwards I will bring forward Plato's arguments of the relationship between consumption, overabundance and the transition (Consumption and Transition; Plenty Supports Transition). In the final section of this chapter Plato's general philosophy of economy, and the new economy will be presented together with his suggestion of how to prevent the transition (Philosophy of Economy Space; The New Economy a Contrivance of Transition).

Topos and Abundance

For Plato, a history of the macrocosm is a zigzag line leading from overabundance to harmony. At the beginning there were the absolute 'being and space and generation' (*Timaeus* 52d). Then, the Creator filled the space by means of the four elements: fire, water, land and air. There was chaos, and the elements were in overabundance. The wrestling of the elements in search of measure became a prelude to the emergence of the macrocosm. Each of the elements was supplied in abundance, 'all without reason and measure' however, the creator has written, by means of 'form and number', the macrocosm as perfect as possible: 'as far as possible the fairest and best, out of things which were not fair and good' (*Timaeus* 53b). The elements subjugated their local excess and the macrocosm found their global measure and balance. The state of global measure means that there is not a vacuum. The macrocosm rotates and this rotation 'compresses everything' within the macrocosm and 'will not allow any place to be left void', so every bit of space is occupied by things (*Timaeus* 58b).

All places within the macrocosm are filled by a form made from the elements. There are three kinds of beings: no born and not perishable ideas, being object of mind perception only; sensible things born, being always in motion, and perceived by sense; and the third kind (the most interesting for us), space - the ***topos***.

> 'And there is a third nature, which is space and is eternal, and admits not of destruction and provides a home for all created things, and is apprehended, when all sense is absent, by a kind of spurious reason, and is hardly real -- which we, beholding as in a dream, say of all existence that it must of necessity be in some place and occupy a space, but that what is neither in heaven nor in earth has no existence' (*Timaeus* 52b).

The *topos* is imperishable and it offers some space (a 'home' or a 'stay within itself' [Siwek's trans., Timajos, Kristias, 1986] to all beings that are born. The *topos* is invisible and we can perceive it only in an extra-sensory manner. It possesses no form itself, due to its role of giving a place to stay for all possible forms. The *topos* is the 'mother and receptacle of all created and visible and in any way sensible things is not to be termed earth or air or fire or water, or any of their compounds, or any of the elements from which these are derived, but is an invisible and formless being which receives all things and in some mysterious way partakes of the intelligible, and is most incomprehensible' (*Timaeus* 51ab).

Within the *topos* the elements are 'shaken by the receiving vessel, which, moving like a winnowing machine, scattered far away from one another the elements most unlike, and forced the most similar elements into close contact' (*Timaeus* 53a) and – in Siwek's translation– 'they rendered blows to the *topos* which returned the blows with the same intensity'. The *topos* brings things into existence because everything has to be in its own place. The thing which has no place does not exist. The *topos* is a 'shelter' and 'seemingly a host' [Siwek's trans. Timajos, Kritias, 1986], 'the receptacle, and in a manner the nurse, of all generation' (*Timaeus* 49b), it gives a 'shelter' - the place of safety and it nourishes the born things.

So we can say that in its physical and biological dimension, the Earth embraces all the elements of the macrocosm, it has its own space in the macrocosm and it is able to offer places to others, especially to people. That means it provides shelter and is a host for people, and, like a mother, it offers its abundance to man. Man should worship his part of the Earth and revere her even more than his own mother. The Earth is a goddess and a sovereign of all mortals (*Laws* V 740a). Because of the Earth, man, in his turn, has received his place. The human *topos* is a seat of values which supply man's biological needs and gives him a sense of safety. Yet, not every place on the Earth is suitable for man. The Earth's area is marked by lowlands and mountains. The lowlands are fertile and there is space for life in community. The mountains are not fertile and cannot support communities, however it is possible for individuals to survive in such a place (*Critias* 110a). Only the lowlands part of the *topos*, which is a meeting spot of man and fertility, can create the possibility to establish a society. Thus, the external feature of the *topos* that makes it suitable for people is abundance.

This seemingly banal statement leads Plato to some unusual reflections concerning a good state of the Lowland's economic possibilities, and to his crucial question about the possible threats to these possibilities. He examines this question using two methods of analysis. In the first, he gives a historical and bucolic description of Old Athens and Atlantis, and contrasts it with his contemporary Athens (*Timaeus* 20e-26c, *Critias* 110a-121c). In the second, he develops generalisations based on two theoretical models, known as the 'City of Pigs' and the 'Luxurious City', and he again sets these models in contrast against each other (the Second book of the *Republic*).

Mountain *Topos*

Though the macrocosm has found its perfect measure, there is still the possibilities of local disasters, mainly deluges. Civilisation is created by the people living in the Lowlands and they, and their fortunes, are wiped out by the deluge. The story of the survivors of a deluge gave Plato the starting point for his economic and historical deliberations. Two similar versions of this story can be found in *Critias* and *Laws* (*Critias* 109e, 111ab; *Laws* III 677bc). Plato's circular view of human history supposes the rise and fall of cities and civilizations over the ages, frequently wiped out by a deluge (flood) or some other form of natural disaster.[2] Plato's starting point for explaining the origins of civil society is the period immediately after one of these events, when the cycle starts again. In the story the only people that survived the deluge are those who live in the Mountains. Though these people have a vague idea about the civilisation of the Lowland people, they are 'ignorant of the art of writing' (*Critias* 109d). Their efforts are concentrated mainly on the procurement of food and basic necessities, and they communicate with others in order to speak on this subject (*Critias* 110a). Man, faced with the limited biological possibilities of the Mountains, is forced to perpetual hard work. This coercion deprives man of freedom, which is understood by Plato as: time for seeking knowledge and for leisure. This lack of freedom prevents the Mountain people from developing intellectually, however they do not become corrupted (*Laws* III 678, 679).

The *topos* of the Mountain is described in a few sentences laid down in *Laws*, *Republic*, *Critias* and *Timaeus*. It is evident that Plato does not pay much attention to this case. The Mountain people are - in their physical and biological beings - doubly safe. They do not violate their *topos*: firstly, because they cannot do it; and secondly, because their environment's configuration counteracted its congestion. The Mountain people always remain primitive and due to this feature they will be spontaneously moral and enjoy a successfully life (*Laws* III 679abc). They do not have either good or bad knowledge. And only they, 'who are destitute of letters and education' *(Timaeus* 23a), will survive deluges. These people never endanger their place, and perhaps, that is the reason that they are practically imperishable. The *topos* of the mountains is the shelter of human race.[3]

Lowlands *Topos* and Transition

Plato's reflections on the Lowlands *topos,* and the transition, is based on the conviction that the present can only be understood by looking to the past. The Atlantis story forms one full circle of the human history circles; the Old Athens case, acts as an example of the transition in early stage, and Plato's analysis of his Athens demonstrates the last phase of the transition, a period just before a deluge.

In the beginning the narrative of the Lowland people was a happy story. In Old Athens people had preserved by maintaining an equal balance (measure) between overabundance and humiliating poverty. Athenian farmers and artisans create an autarkic society, abiding by the rules of simple reproduction. Generation after generation, the Athenians lived in houses with furnishings completely unchanged, living a simple life, and owning no silver or gold. The population was stabilised at a level of twenty thousand, with a balance between the number of men and women.

Describing Athenian welfare, Plato emphasised the need to preserve autarky in spite of the land's overfertility. There were only two rules: to keep population and consumption stable. 'They aimed at the mean between splendour and meanness, dwelling in decent houses where they grew old, themselves and their children's children, each succeeding generation leaving them to another like itself' (*Critias* 112c). ... [T]he number of both sexes already qualified and still qualified to bear arms they were careful to keep, as nearly as possible, always the same, roughly some twenty thousand' (*Critias* 112d).

The civilisation of Atlantis enjoyed an even more fruitful economy; 'that sacred island, which then lay open to the sun, in marvellous beauty and inexhaustible profusion [abundance]' (*Critias* 115b). In his tale of Atlantis, Plato took pleasure in a numeral 'two' which was, together with twins, considered as a mythical symbol of fertility.[4] The beginning of the Atlantis tribe starts with Poseidon, who generated 'five pairs of twin male children' (*Critias* 113e). Two fountains of cold and hot water gave fertility, resulting in a double harvest (*Critias* 113b, 114b). Plato wrote about an 'abundance' of rare resources, such as 'orichalcum' (not identifed metal, probably brass), copper or zinc. Atlantis forests were will stocked with big game and deer, and even a 'great number' of elephants. Corn and pulse (a fertilizer) were found in an 'infinite abundance' and crops were perfect and various. There was enough water for swimming pools for people and cattle. Atlantis walls were coated with copper, zinc, and with *orichalch* ('which gleamed like fire' *Critias* 116c). The ruler's palace was golden and Poseidon's silver shrine was set with ivory. Two harbours were roofed with stone. Canals were set in the mountains in order to carry wood to the lowlands and return to the mountains with fruits from lowlands, and pool water was utilized to irrigate Poseidon grove. This all testifies to their expanded division of labour and advanced systems of transportation and communication. Atlantis houses were roomy and beautiful (*Critias* 115c-117e). Although the Atlantis economy was supported by subordinated provinces, Plato puts stress on its self-sufficient economy.

The discontinuous description of Atlantis in *Critias* is cut short after an episode showing growing turmoil (*Critias* 117e). It is the first symptom of Atlantis's corruption. The entire area 'was completely filled by a multitude of closely set houses, and the large harbor and canal were constantly crowded by merchant vessels and their passengers arriving from all quarters, whose vast numbers occasioned incessant shouting, clamour, and general uproar, day and night' (*Critias* 117e). Atlantis did not manage its fortune. 'But when the god's part in them began to wax faint by constant crossing with much mortality, and the human temper to predominate, then they could no longer carry their fortunes, but began to behave themselves unseemly. To the seeing eye they now began to seem foul, for they were losing the fairest bloom from their most precious treasure, but to such as could not see the happy life, to appear at last fair and blessed indeed, now that they were taking the infection of wicked coveting and pride of power' (*Critias* 121b).

In the Second Book of the *Republic* we are acquainted with the sequel to the Atlantis story - a description of the transition. The 'luxurious city' requires 'couches and tables and every other article of furniture, as well as viands, and fragrant oils, and perfumes, and courtesans, and confectionery; and all these in plentiful variety' (*Republic* II 373a). The town becomes richer and richer, ever more populated. These processes are accompanied by diminishing space.

> [Socrates] Then we shall also have to enlarge our city, for our first or healthy city will not now be of sufficient size, but requires to be increased in bulk, and filled out with a multitude of callings which do not exist in cities to satisfy any natural want; for example, the whole class of hunters, and all who practise imitative art, including many who use forms and colours, and many who use music, poets [...], rhapsodists, actors, dancers, contractors (*Republic* II 373b).

We see 'congestion', and decreased fertility, and there appeared a new, unknown formerly, state of poverty. There is no poverty in the Mountain, and in the period of abundance. The first is a period of heroic efforts, however there is no poverty because there are no differences among people. The abundance period introduces no social differences as well. It is in the period of overabundance when people start to experience social differences, and instead of the single state, in fact, there appears two states: the rich state and the poor state: 'a city must necessarily lose its unity and become two cities, one comprising the rich and the other the poor; who reside together on the same ground, and are always plotting against one another' (*Republic* VIII 551d).

Turmoil and congestion appear parallel with this 'bad understanding' of wealth. The Atlantis harbour becomes noisy and crowded with people (*Critias* 117e). The existing area of the state is not sufficient for the increasing number of habitants. As Atlantis was losing its divine element, and allowed itself to be possessed by turmoil, so this 'healthy town' became the 'luxurious town'. The town in the transition exists in a way which is truculent and prerequisite to conquest. The result is a war for land.

> [Socrates] The country too, I presume, which was formerly adequate to the support of its then habitants will be now too small, and adequate no longer. ... Then must we not cut ourselves a slice of our neighbour's territory, if we are to have land enough both for pasturage and tillage, while they will do the same to ours, if they, like us, permit themselves to overstep the limit of necessaries and plunge into the unbounded acquisition of wealth?
> Shall we say so?
> Certainly.
> It must inevitably be so, Socrates.
> Will our next step be to go to war, Glaucon, or how will it be? (*Republic* II 373de).

The state in transition steers all of its energy towards conquering space and resources, namely to things which it lost and which it will lose and lose again. In addition this process will be accelerated for two reasons: a growing population, especially of artisans, traders, and plebs (who are dangerous to the order of the town); and increasing expenditures on the continuously enlarging army (*Republic* II 374).

Plato uses the bare rock of the Acropolis contemporary to him, (*Critias* 111abcd, 112b), to visualise this idea of a shrinking physical and biological space. Plato notes that the output of the Old Athens was more abundant than it is presently. Because of the soil erosion caused by the 'many formidable deluges in the course of the nine thousand years – that is the interval between the date we are speaking of and the present' the land has been made a 'skeleton of a body wasted by disease' (*Critias* 111c). Just as the overpopulation increased, the fertility of land and water - two main resources of an agrarian economy - were diminished, and the economy became a wasteful exploitation. Not utilised springs water flowing down into the sea; bare rock of Acropolis as 'human bones' instead forest hill; these show that Athens has already reached this stage of development. The Lowlands *topos* becomes overcrowded in relation to its fertility and physical space. This overpopulation resulted in a transgression of the natural barrier of the Lowland fertility. According to Plato, the *polis* should not go over this barrier. The *topos* is an eternal and not annihilated being (*Timaeus* 52b). This seemingly optimistic statement in fact means that people cannot create the *topos* by themselves; they can only adjust to its finite fertility.

The contraction of physical space generates congestion and lack of resources; and then subsequently it produces wars. The congestion results not exactly from the bare number of people, but from the covering of the Lowland human *topos*, by exploiting all of its resources. This congestion around resources negates the way which both fertility and human beings work. The friendly balanced relationship between people and their *topos* transforms into the chaos of congestion and in this way it starts to be corrupted. The economic activity cannot recognise its natural limits and it cannot stop by itself, because it cannot control itself. Economic processes, within the *polis*, are spontaneous and impetuous; their nature is elementally. They do not cement the state, contrary they split the state into two different spaces: the *topos* of wealth and the *topos* of poverty. The area of wealth has to defend itself against the area of poverty. As the area of poverty may want to change the internal order of the *polis*, the wealthy part of Lowland has to focus on its defence and on gaining more resources. Plato believes the earth is fully populated: 'The fact is that wherever the extremity of winter frost or of summer does not prevent, mankind exist, sometimes in greater, sometimes in lesser numbers' (*Timaeus* 22e). To gain the resources means the necessity to wage wars against ones neighbours. Plato emphasises that once initiated, social-economic movements can only intensify and provoke wars, and they will endure permanently till the global catastrophe - a deluge. Winning a war does not restore the old balance, because the enlarged area of the state will demand more people in the state economy and army. The wars can delay, for a time, the economic and ecological catastrophe. Only a deluge can restore the lost balance of the Lowlands societies and then people again go down the mountain, and take up once more their efforts. And it will last until people are taught how they should recognise the possibilities of their *topos*, and afterwards, to arrange a peaceful co-existence within the *topos*.

In the *Timaeus* Plato says the process of the stabilisation of the four elements has been accomplished within the macrocosm. He permits the possibility of local disasters caused by local imbalances. For him, such a disaster, specific for some parts of the Earth, namely the Lowlands, is the deluge. Economic activities lead people to a drastic violation of the Lowland *topos* and the way in which the *topos* demonstrates itself. The fertility ceases and the Lowland *topos* does not tolerate people, and for people's violence it answers by striking back, and using the coercion of a deluge, earthquake, or other cosmic disaster. Plato mentions mainly deluges, which he considered as historical turning points (in this way he describes the disappearance of Atlantis). For him the deluge is not a notion that perceived as an unfavourable aspect of the stars or gods, it is rather a way of the Lowland *topos* reaction to a thoughtless and wasteful economy. The macrocosm is perfect; its parts, as the Earth, are regionally not perfect; nevertheless everywhere are the *topos* and it operates in the same fashion, namely in relation to the Lowlands people, by means of fertility and deluge. From the history of Atlantis we know that those who wasted their chance for safe and healthy life given them by the *topos*, should be afraid of this sort of punishment. Only shepherds and peasants do not waste their chance and they remain in the Mountain (*Timaeus* 22de).

Plato's macroeconomic assumptions are derived from his cosmology. The Earth *topos* has a limited capacity for supporting people. It offers safety to the Mountain people, and a relative abundance to the Lowland people, though the latter have to pay the high price of annihilation of their civilisation due to their abuse of this *topos*. The amount of space is finite and will not increase, according to Plato, thus the macrocosm is shaped and people have to accept this fact. The limitations of the Earth *topos* force autarky; people must and can make a proper use of accessible means and they do not have not to cross their own Lowlands to renew resources. This last statement is very important. Plato understands the economic dimension of the Lowland *topos* as a space limited to the physical and biological possibilities of the Lowland. So the clue to macroeconomic practice is in adjusting to these limits. What is needed is to find the positive solution in two rules: economic autarky, understood as an adjustment to the Lowland physical possibilities; and consequently, as a limitation of the Lowland population by the product of the economic autarky. For Plato, the Mountains *topos* is a case study of the period when real scarcity existed. The Lowlands *topos* is a case study of two periods: the abundance-welfare, and the overabundance or false scarcity (scarcity created by luxury). Both these examples show Plato's macroeconomic ideas.

Man and Economic Virtue

In *Critias*, Plato sets up a more picturesque description of the social and macroeconomic features of abundance - welfare. In the *Laws* and in the *Republic* he is more occupied by the microeconomic sphere and he tries to establish the limits of human needs. In his macroeconomic thinking he emphasises the importance of water and land resources, and the optimal number Lowland inhabitants. In his microeconomic thinking - analogous to these macroeconomic topics - he is interested in three main human needs, namely: drink; food; and propagation (*Laws* VI 782e). He investigates the issues of consumption, nature of wealth; and he investigates the relationship between wealth and poverty; and he tries to discover the most favourable human economic behaviours.

In the Second Book of the *Republic* Plato sets up a mental experiment where he builds up a state consisted of individuals immunised against economic passions (*Republic* II 369d - 374e). The inhabitants of this hypothetical town possess houses, clothes and boots, though they use them only in winter. In the summer they work and sleep with no clothes on; sleep on willow brake, myrtle and bindweed, and eat wheat or barley cakes served on leaves, and 'not begetting children beyond their means'. They practise all these functions under their 'prudent fear of poverty and war' (*Republic* II 372bc). This not very refined consumption ensures that 'Living in peace and health, they will probably die in old age and hand on a lie life to their offspring' (*Republic* II 372d). An elder brother of Plato, Glaucon revolts against this diet, so Plato added extra figs, peas, broad beans, and acorns to this menu. Plato's generosity becomes a futile gesture and Glaucon names this town the 'City of Pigs'. The Platonic diet is similar to a description of the Orifice life (*Laws* VI 782c). In others fragments of the *Republic* Plato is not so rigorous, he wants to eliminate a mysterious 'Athenian confectionery' (*Republic* III 404e), or limiting himself to a comparison of a lack of modesty in eating to too big sails for ship (*Laws* III 691e). This diet, dated back to the period when humans were gatherers, becomes, next to both postulates from *Critias*; autarky, and effectively restrict population; hence the third condition of keeping the 'abundance-welfare' period.

Analysing consumption becomes Plato's starting point for defining true wealth. Lust for wealth corrupts man's spirit, causing of 'an incessant hunger gnawing at their souls' (*Laws* VIII 832a). This corruption manifests itself in aggression; Plato gives the example of an innkeeper who treats his clients as 'enemies' and wants a 'ransom'(*Laws* XI 919a). Man does not know what 'wealth' means, because he does not know himself. Non-reflective compliance with his passions, meaning a lust for wealth, kills the man in a man by focusing his attention on things not worth troubling with. In the *Gorgias* Plato named such a man a 'duck' which eats a lot and excretes a lot (*Gorgias* 494b). Wealth, and not the abundance-welfare, is followed by laziness, and supports the careless practising of professions and can even hinder work. We are able to 'put golden coronets' on the cultivator's head, however this stops him from working as a cultivator (*Republic* IV 420e). A newly rich potter becomes lazy and he too stops being a potter (*Republic* IV 421d). Poverty breeds unemployment, humiliation and crime. Poor man cannot afford to buy tools and they stop practising their profession. Both poverty and wealth promote subversive behaviours. In stating why wealth and poverty need to be kept out of the city, Socrates says: 'Wealth and poverty, said I, since the one brings luxury, idleness, and innovation, and the other illiberality and the evil of bad workmanship in addition to innovation' [in Grube's translation 'innovation' is translated as 'revolution' (Grube, 1992)] (*Republic* IV

422a). A rich man immorally conquers wealth, and his expenses are different from expenses of a moral man. By taking away wealth from others he creates a space of poverty. The nearness of poverty and wealth render envy and aggression and breeds insatiability and revolt.

This abnormal situation of man concentrating on his alimentary canal must be altered. Even in our body, the stomach (compared by Plato with a 'crib') is situated far away from our soul, in order to make 'as little noise and disturbance as possible, and permitting the best part to advice quietly for the good of the whole and the individual' (*Timaeus* 70e). Man should work to improve his life. He can do it even in the unfavourable conditions in Athens. In the First Book of the *Republic* Plato pays a 'wise and sensible' man from Piraeus, Cephalus, a visit. Cephalus' style of life is a compromising solution between the simplest life in the 'City of Pigs', and the luxurious life in the Glaucon's town. 'In the conduct of money' Cephalus stands 'midway' between his grandfather and his father, and he intends to leave to his sons 'not less but if anything rather more' (*Republic* I 330b). He makes good use of his property, so he knows his estate helped him to avoid temptations of 'deceit or falsehood', and supports him as an old-age insurance (*Republic* I 330e).

Plato expresses in many places (mainly the *Gorgias*, the *Republic*, and the *Laws*) his advice concerning a successful life. In his writings we can find a description of something like the 'four steps' way to the economic virtue, called by him 'to set his house in order' (*Republic* IV 443d) or in Witwicki's translation: the 'inward household'(Panstwo, 1958). He distinguishes four 'good' types of life: healthy, well considered, brave, and wise, and in contrast to these good lives, are four 'bad' lives: sick, foolish, cowardly, and licentious (*Laws* V 733e). In accordance with these styles of the good life, Plato formulates four rules: to exercise restraint in consumption (*Laws* IV 710a, V 729a); to keep in mind the importance of correspondence between individual and the external world (*Timaeus* 88c), to support harmony between quantity and quality (*Gorgias* 508a, *Republic* IV 441e, 443d); and the last, to compete in virtue (*Laws* V 731a). His counsels, concerning how to enjoy the healthy and well-considered life, and how to avoid the sick and foolish one, have a high economic content.

For him economic virtues are an important precondition for virtues of courage and the mind; and consequently, are a means to enjoy the most desired state of balance. The initial step consists in the subduing of an individual's temperament and passions. The next step is very important and it consists in the establishment of a harmony between the 'inward household' and the 'external household'. The external household embraces a whole social system understood as a place of man in his *polis*. After tidying himself up, man should be interested in state affairs. However, he is limited in the effect he can have on state affairs, so this task becomes a duty of politicians. With regard to a size of the Lowland supply of resources, the rulers have to establish the limits of the *polis* demand. They have insure the compliance with these limits and, if necessary, they should confiscate estate excess (*Laws* V 744de). These two steps: within man; and within society; in building the economic virtue mean a necessity of a perpetual adjustment to the Lowland possibilities and limits. The Lowland economy establishes the limits of both individual and social behaviours. The success of these stages relies upon a flexible control performed by both the individual on himself and by the politician on society. Wealth still remains a quantitative ('arithmetic') wealth, though it, due to the limitations and the laws, brings near the perfect state of the qualitative ('geometric') wealth. The third step consists in the subordination of the arithmetical wealth to the geometric one (*Laws* V 744c, VI 757a). For the economy, this is once more establishing a relationship between fertility and restraint in order to subdue quantity to quality. Economic activities must be ruled by the virtues; noble goals achieved by noble means, for example we should hunt for animals face to face, without snares, or nets (*Laws* VII 823-4). In fact, Plato's sentences lose their chivalrous context if we see them as ecological postulates for the elimination of wasteful economic activity. At last, the fourth step - the creation of community, which competes in virtue, and does not participate in the race for resources. Practising the virtue of restraint, man gradually builds his own virtue, in order to use his highest possible freedom, which allowed him to enjoy individual and social profits. His microcosm becomes reconciled with the macrocosm.

The economic virtues refers to the biological and physical sphere of life. Practising this virtue man can achieve a satisfaction of his biological and physical needs. The economic and biological balance of man characterises a symmetry: how much he wants, thus he gets in return. Moderate needs are satisfied by the Lowland nature. Plato shows man as an economic being depending on nature; however this dependence is not very burdensome. Two natural borders mark it: possibilities of the Lowland nature, and consumer possibilities of man.

Dominated by a lust for wealth, man remains in a nasty asymmetry. His wants are beyond measure, so he never attains fulfilment. Instead of emancipation he is troubled with his body diseases and he is tortured by insatiability. Man, being in the first stage of balance, lives a moderate life, not much troubled by economic things. His way of life will be honest because he does not contribute to the war or future catastrophe of deluge. Man, being in the total balance (a man of the geometric wealth), will be richer by the time, free from the lust for wealth, allowing him to practice wisdom and he will enjoy freedom for self-improvement.

We can clearly see Plato's idea of replacing the commercial understanding of scarcity and plenty with a fuller understanding of the ecological, political and economic consequences of man's economic practices. To live a beautiful (it means happy and fair) life, man's estate and his bodily needs must be subordinate to his soul. It is good that man wants scarce things, he has only to understand that virtue is the unique scarce thing. The majority of people do not know what true virtue is. The Athenian says in the *Laws* that 'not many of us who remain sober when we have the opportunity to grow wealthy' (*Laws* XI 918d). To practice the Platonic virtue is similar to going into a circle, the Ancient symbol of perfection. The nearer you are to the centre of the circle, the more you possess the virtues, and you are at a shorter distance from the centre and perfection. The centre is a point of both your perfection and your satiation. You have to seek and to conquer the moral good by means of exceptional efforts. Material goods possess quite opposite features. They are outside the circle, they have no limits, and by its elemental character they can without difficulty take control of man. Outside the circle there is no possibility, by means of the element and of the infinity, to reach freedom and wisdom. Both, the lack of chaos and finite, are understood as an approval of limitations, and are the proper means to realise the Man in man.

Plato proposes the way for the full perfection of an elite only and he is well aware of the impossibility to create an entire community of men of virtue. His reflections on the economic and total balance, and about citizenship, and his models of ideal states, indicate that he preserves for the majority of the Lowland people the task of the first step - to make economic order within himself. It is significant that Plato starts the *Republic* with the description of a meeting with Cephalus, who is not only a positive example but something more. Plato teaches by Cephalus' example that the practice of virtue is not so difficult as it seems to most people. All can follow these steps along with the elite. The ruling elite has to provide the harmony between individuals and the Lowland fertility. They are given the higher consciousness of a choice - on the social level - between living in peace and war.

The scarcity of noble (virtuous) men caused both the need to control a society, and to proclaim laws. The control of society and the laws act as a substitute for the spontaneous reactions called for true virtue. The legislator has to fight on two fronts protecting his society from poverty and from wealth. The members of the wholesale trades are the most disturbing people in the Lowland. This is the part of society in need of the most moral tutelage, their attitudes are the most susceptible to corruption, and - in addition - their population increased the fastest during the transition.

Consumption and Transition

The precondition for economic virtue, according to Plato, is the establishment of restrictions on individual consumption. Plato defines restraint by drawing an analogy to 'rhythm' and 'harmony' (*Timaeus* 47e). Rhythm and harmony should mark the limits of individual consumption, bringing order to our 'irregular and graceless ways'. Plato proposes a simple vegetarian diet due to its social and healthy good points (*Republic* II 372abcd). This is a universal diet, equally useful both during the period of abundance-welfare, and during the Mountain period or the first period after the deluge. This is the consumption of a man who is aware of the consequences resulting from different diets. The practice of a Platonic diet supports courage and wisdom in the individual. In the social dimension this diet does not demand too much of the state's land; does not subordinate citizens to foreigners; and does not provoke: aggression, congestion, turmoil, and noise. On the contrary, this diet allows for the autonomy of both the individual and the state. Man ceases being a 'duck' and can return to his uncorrupted nature. The limited consumption results in a limited, but autonomous, economy. In the pursuit of a growing economy the Lowlands may lose its autonomy. Plato wants to show harmony between man and his surrounding. Man's lust for abundance, health and fortune, is in fact, a wish full of harmony co-existence with the World. Experience of the abundance-welfare is a true man's acceptation of himself. Submission to the Lowland *topos* and acceptation of limitations mean liberation and emancipation of these limitations. These are the social rhythm of economic activities and the individual harmony of the good life. Even in Plato's Athens it is possible to enjoy such a life. The success of a such way of life is recounted by a wise man from Piraeus - Cephalus, who is an owner of a middle estate (*Republic* I 331ab).

Plato's general thesis is: the most desirable economic state of society is a balance between what nature has to offer and human needs, therefore we must come back to the macroeconomic level to investigate further the conditions for such a balance. The economy, in which individuals consume in a manner similar to the gather's diet, must be autarky resting on recognisable and renewable resources. Plato comes to a conclusion that there is a stable number of people who can live in the Lowlands without breaking this balance. Plato respects nature's capacities. We should not replace the fertility of nature with scarcity and congestion. Nature marks the borders to the division of labour and the specialisation of labour. The breaking of these borders creates an avalanche of the most unfavourable social phenomena. On the surface, in the transition, the welfare increases; there are more commodities, more wealth, and more satisfaction. However there is a growth in population as well. The new social phenomena's are: crowds and diseases. Starting with and concentrating in the wealthy, society falls into the trap of spiralling needs. A new need means a new profession, the new profession adds to society a new man, and this new man has to eat. Once stimulated, human needs grow and grow. This infinite chain of human needs may be satisfied only by war and the deluge.

Plato's point is that we should not forget the behaviour and lifestyle of the Mountain period in the Lowland period and enjoy, with restraint, things given by nature. Plato's argument is sophisticated; he takes differentiation of consumption into account. According to him, in the town there will be enough luxury goods, though there will be not enough food for the people who produced and deal in these luxury goods, and for the 'guardians'. The food and a lack of the main resources - land - are the main barriers of the demographic growth. So, the true wealth of the *polis* is land and water, and then people. The wealth of nations rests in a society having modest requirements and being content with its own resources.

Plenty Supports Transition

So far we have investigated the transition of the economy from abundance to scarcity. Plato does not stop at this point; he is more interested in the battle with plenty in itself. The main weapon, employed by him in this battle, becomes the measure. In Plato's dialogue *Symposium*, Socrates tells a story, told him by a priestess Diotima, about Abundance [Resource], the son of Restraint [Craft]. Abundance took part in a banquet on the occasion of Aphrodite's birthday. He got drunk with the ambrosia and went to sleep. His lamentable situation was not wasted by begging Poverty [Need] and she, taking advantage of the situation, became pregnant with Eros [Love]. Being a son of such parents, Eros is an eternal 'poor fellow', tossed between a wise and rich father, and poor and uneconomical mother (*Symposium* 201D).[5] The moral of the story is clear: only the restraint - a measured life - provides the protection from poverty and excess which are close friends. Abundance should not get drunk with the ambrosia; it must be vigilant in order to avoid a transition to the overabundance. The overabundance breeds devastating insufficiency.

Plato thinks about the measure as a manager of virtue.[6] The task of philosophy is to investigate and to show a proper use of the measure. According to Plato, the measure is not only a norm, or logical criterion, or a sort of yardstick in order to define the states of plenty or scarcity. Platonic measure is in itself the true abundance, and everything beyond this measure is overabundance. First of all, he considers it as the border; outside of which there is a an area of danger. So, the economic part of the Platonic measure is not only a kind of an arithmetic mean between a number of people and quantity of products, in fact it is the safe area for human economic activities. Plato is not afraid of true scarcity and the period after the deluge. It is easy to deal with scarcity and it is easy to get some abundance, even if it takes generations. The Mountain period employs only the physical power of man, thus increasing output takes time. However, their efforts do not create any threats for their personality due to a lack of overabundance. What we have to be afraid of is the overabundance.

Written in this way, Plato expresses a fear of overabundance common in all agrarian cultures. This fear had prompted the Normans to bury their hoards of silver and gold, and customs of surfeit gorging and 'aggressive generosity' among the people of the Middle Ages. It would be visible even in mercantilist fear of surplus that does not find either a domestic or export market. The fear of plenty has organised a hierarchy of tribal and agrarian community values. The recommended activity was to give, not to take. Melville J. Herscovits named this economy the 'prestige economy'. This was a system in which gain comes through expenditure rather than through saving, and the highest position is reserved for those who most conspicuously spend the contributions of the less privileged [Guriewicz, 1976, pp. 220-44, Herscovits, 1955, p. 164].

Philosophy of Economic Space

Compared with the macrocosm, a human civilisation is situated in the initial stage. The chaos is produced by the clashing human passions taking devious paths between overabundance and scarcity. In general the macrocosm has overcome the general transition. However there are still possibilities for the local transitions. On Earth there is a particular place, namely the Lowland. The Lowland develops from disaster to disaster caused by deluges. Between disasters there are - according to Plato - three stages of economy marked by a supply of the *topos*: scarcity, abundance, and overabundance. From these three stages the most beneficial for man is the shorter period of the abundance. People in their history learned to use land fertility in order to overcome scarcity. Then they created a civilisation offering wealth, which was not secure. Their wealth is a liability and they must pay a high price for it.

The price of this wealth depends on the place occupied by the people during the transition. Nearer the final catastrophe of the deluge the price is higher. However even in the very beginning of the transition, there is always the price of man's life. During the transition, man, seduced by verisimilitudes, lives a life of misery. As long as people do not learn how to avoid scarcity and overabundance, they can not enjoy abundance.

The macrocosm is a self-sufficient entity. Plato understands this self-sufficiency in a peculiar way. He writes in *Timaeus* that for the macrocosm to feed itself has to destroy itself; '... there was nothing which went from him or came into him, for there was nothing beside him. Of design he was created thus – his own waste providing his own food, and all that he did or suffered taking place in and by himself' (*Timaeus* 33cd). The macrocosm destroys one of its parts if within this particular part there appears a lack or an excess of the elements. In a similar way Plato thinks about the Lowland. The Lowland is self-sufficient when it is populated by the proper number of people in relation to its resources. Under theses conditions people consume their natural part of the *topos*, and while there is no breaking other people's *topos*, there is no poverty. When the Lowlands borders becomes disturbed, the process of destruction begins. The Lowland starts to eat itself. In the very beginning there is not enough land and water. According to their physical and social possibilities, people take the *topos* away from others, or they are deprived of their *topos*. The area of poverty becomes wider and wider. The transition is the people's self-destruction.

Plato claims the human *topos* exists by its fertility. On the economic level the fertility is a class of resources. On the human value level the fertility is a class consisting of health and safety. So the human *topos* is a hotbed of human values, its space is marked by these values. Speaking Einstein's language, these values produce the *topos* space and bend it back. If some parts of the values are gone, the space of *topos* will lose some of its energy and it starts to diminish. The Lowland fertility supplies the pragmatic (biological and economic) part of the human *topos*. The economy in itself is not enough for the stability of the human *topos*. To prevent the self-destruction of the *topos* we have to try and establish a harmony between the *Topos* and people by filling the *topos* with human values. It means the reconciliation between the fertility of nature and human behaviour. History tought that people might replace the mythical order of things with the order of commercial values. This is due to the lack of serious reflection, and due to their society popularising bad patterns of behaviours by various means: myths, poetry, music, theatre. It is due too to the

Lowland features: its soft limits, and flexibility. Plato states that there was about nine thousand years between the Atlantis deluge and his contemporary time. Nine was a magic Pythagorean number and plausibly Plato wants to suggest that the end of the circle is near and there is a possibility of a similar catastrophe in Athens, and we may read his theory as the writing on the wall to Athenians.

According to Plato, people as a society enjoy some freedom of manoeuvre both in time (these 9000 years!) and in the space. Plato understood human history in being non-linear; he stresses this feature when he considers different forms of government. The history of macrocosm teach us that the establishing of balance is possible, and the period of chaos is a period of the transition, which means it may come to an end. There are three positive solutions possible: 1) evolutionary, leave the overabundance and go towards the abundance; 2) once to establish and then to keep with the abundance; and 3) to try to stay between scarcity and abundance. In the *Republic* Plato chooses the last solution to propose to all of the population – the Mountain diet plus the Lowland's knowledge. In the *Laws* he considers the second variant as the holding of a balance between population and resources. Why he does not choose the easiest of these variants and even he does not discuss them? There is not a satisfactory answer. We can interprets the solution presented in the *Laws* as leading towards the *Republic* solution and say, follow Popper, that this was the totalitarian project. However we know from his letter (the *Letter* vii) Plato was an adviser to the Syracuse tyrant, and he recommended him to be a master of his passions. It seems he had tested this evolutionary solution and this test came off not very well for him. The tyrant used his authority for his own aims. Maybe this personal experiences could explain Plato's position.

Changes in the Lowland *topos* are elementally, meaning, in general, they do not repeat and are directed in different ways. The economy is wasteful and people competed aggressively for resources. Popper said that Plato first of all wanted to stop any change. However, it seems that Plato's goal is to give a new quality to change. He wants to guide social energy in order to reconcile the economic space with the mythical space. The new economic *topos* should be safe and create a base for the further self-improvement of man. So far, neither the Mountain nor the Lowland have created such a base. The Mountain people have no time to think about higher values. The Lowland people have no time too, because of their commercial activities left no time for other activities. On the one hand the Mountain isolation prevents the establishing of a society contrary to man's needs. Man has a lot of wants, and thus requires, in order to supply them, institutions of society, namely division of labour and specialisation (*Republic* II 369bc). On the other hand, society, which is so desirable to man's development, becomes a source of corruption, and then destruction. So Plato formulates his task as to not lose the *topos* of society and to preserve the safety of the Moutain people. His society has to support the emancipation of man. Man's emancipation depends - first and foremost - on his independence from hitherto existing economic values and behaviours, which made commercial achievements a main goal of life. However, Plato does not want to impose restrictions on the economy and to limit it to a minimum. This area of human life has to become not exactly invisible, but it has to be deprived of ambiguity, which is created by commercialism. Man needs the society in which there is the division of labour. At a minimum he needs: rulers, guardians, peasants, and artisans. The people employed in this new economy cannot develop according to the 'World soul'. We know the main rules: autarchy given by the state and the good work of the individual. Plato specifies parts of the new economy and numbers: gathering, the 'noble' agriculture, handicraft, and other occupations which do not breed commercial temptations (*Laws* 743d). He wants the development of agriculture and the crafts, which adjusted to the *topos* resources, which will give support to the values of beauty, courage and wisdom. Building a new niche for people does not mean a negation of the economy; just the opposite, the new economy has to be a contrivance of the transition.

The New Economy: A Contrivance of Transition

In order to achieve the first stage of morality, Plato requires a healthy economy. The new economy should overcome difficulties resulting from the imbalances between the changing population, quantity of needed products and the stable Lowland fertility. In this connection he defines what is an economic success, and describes the transition in order to give a recipe to secure the economic Lowland *topos*.

Plato considers the growth of the economy caused by the division of labour and its specialisation which, in turn, causes a need to employ more people. This process develops spontaneously, and meets with no obstacles. In this way the continuously developing economy pulls up the growth of population. Because of the fact that the resources of land are stable, the growth in population means that the resources per capita diminishes. The state has to seek new resources. All of the Earth lowlands being populated, war remains as the only way to gain more land. War needs the army and the cost of holding the army becomes an additional burden, which increases the exhaustion of resources. Rarer and rarer resources, and competition (congestion) both create economic differences, and the society starts to split into rich and poor states. The transition means firstly - in a pragmatic order - wasteful economy, ruination of the *topos*, and destruction of man, and secondly - in the order of ideas - the unreasonable resistance of both man and society against the perfectibility of the macrocosm. God takes care of the human world during the Mountain period of scarcity and the first period of the true abundance. In the transition he leaves this world to its fate (*Statesman* 268e-274e). So far man and society do not learn to imitate their successful ancestors.

Economic success lies in the prevention of the transition, in other words, of reconstructing the previous state of the economy and environment. This is a closed economy limited by natural fertility. On the supply side nature (land and water) gives us the means of consumption, and on the demand side nature needs to have its natural fertility respected. The lack maintaining this balance brings on the transition, with all its problems.

In developing an anti-transition social programme, Plato draws a conclusion from the history of Athens and Atlantis. The population must be prudent, even in the easy period of the Mountain. Plato is leery of the favourable initial conditions of the fertility of the land (good configuration of the ground, plenty of water) and sees it as a mixed blessing. If the Lowland has too many advantages: fertile land, an easy access to the sea, plain lowland; the people will not develop good manners and social behaviours. Of the three initial conditions, Plato feels that only fertile land is necessarily good, however, even here he offers the stipulation that some parts of the land should be mountainous and unqualified for cultivation. These hindrances can result in a delay in the onset of the transition as they can give time for the people to reflect on the social goals to wish to achieve. Excesses of crops over needs, and nearness to the sea, created the danger of the development of wholesale trade and all that such trade initiates: the rise of commercial values, which as Athenian states (*Laws* IV 704d-705b) 'nothing is a more serious impediment to the development of noble and righteous character in society'.

Plato pays much more attention to the effect this has on man. In this regard he offers two propositions: it is impossible to establish the true welfare of society without the transformation of the human personality; and limiting the consumption of man is the best mechanism for preventing the transition. Plato's propositions have generated considerable reaction over the years. Is this a naive solution due to its unrealistic and utopian features? In our own time this might seem so. If one considers the vast sums of money spent on diets and weight lose products in the wealthy countries today we might conclude that limiting consumption is a utopian suggestion. However, considering the postulates formulated during other periods of the transition, especially in the Enlightenment period, it does not fall outside of the realm of possibility.

In an agrarian economy man is often seen as a consumer in a privileged position. In fact he has two privileges: first - he does not have to worry about food; and second - he receives this food almost for nothing. And it will be this way always, if only he shows restraint in digestion and in propagation. In addition to preserving this style of life, such a diet gives a promise of a long and healthy life. What more can man ask for? The only possible rational position is to accept this pattern of behaviour. In the cultures where feudal institutions persist longer, patterns of behaviours were dominated by this way of thinking.

Conclusions

After over two thousand years, it is clear that Plato's message still has relevance. From Plato's perspective, we are creating a society of small Tantaluses; we steal the ambrosia and the nectar of Gods and we deceive ourselves into believing that we can avoid punishment. We remain in our virtual world to try and touch the mirage of wealth but never to taste it. His analysis is based on two characters from Greek mythology: Tantalus and Sisyphus. Human history is seen as the history of endless learning and practices. With great effort people came together and helped in the period of scarcity. But, in conquering scarcity they created the bigger burden of insatiability, and eventually are killed by it in the future.

This interpretation of Plato's economic theory unexpectedly shows the importance of his economic thinking: firstly - for his philosophy and psychology; and secondly - for us, Plato appears as an Ancient Malthusian. Historians of economics have relegated Plato to secondary role in the history of economic thought. They have for the most part avoided his descriptions of Atlantis or Old Athens and instead only considered his conception of the ideal state in the *Republic* and the *Laws*. What the majority of commentators have taken for picturesque additions or non-important digressions, are in fact, a coherent entity. Plato takes the economy seriously and says that a lot depends on this sphere of human life. In the economic realm he starts his investigations, here also is situated the main cause of mankind's failures, and finally here he finds the confirmation of his recommendations. At last, in the majority of his statements on economy, especially in the *Republic*, the *Laws*, and the *Critias*, are based on an economic argument and perspective, which we can consider an economic theory. He creates his own economic nomenclature in which such the notions as: *topos*; fertility; abundance; over-abundance; scarcity; density; congestion; and environment; becomes the basic points of reference. Like all relevant economic theory, Plato's is shaped by its close relationship with his contemporary economic life. His economic theory is an economic and demographic warning to Athens.

Plato's economic thinking is sophisticated in its economic methodology as well as in its theory. In his methodology he is not a reductionist. His analysis of society are based on ideal models of the Mountain and Lowland (*Critias, Timaeus, Laws*); and two models of ideal states (*Republic, Laws*); and two models known as the 'City of Pigs' and the 'Luxurious City' (*Republic*). These models cover all the possible economic situations on macro and microeconomic levels. His theoretical arguments are verified or confirmed by means of the historical examples of Atlantis and Old Athens. In writing about the exhaustion of land and water resources, he is describing his contemporary environment. In his analysis of consumption he differentiates between the differing needs of particular social groups and professions.

His economics spread out between two macroeconomic poles: the Mountain, where there conditions of scarcity do not allowed for the establishment of society; and the Lowland, where eventually over-abundance brings about the society's downfall. We can overcome the state of scarcity, yet we are not capable of overcoming the state of surplus, - this is his main conclusion. It is interesting to note that Plato does not touch - by the traditional means - the subject of good crops or bad crops, in particular he refuses to explain the fertility of agriculture via disasters caused by the gods. The social context of the transition, and the resulting patterns of economic behaviours, are the culprit and not ill fortune. Neither nature nor man possesses automatic mechanisms that put limits and control the pursuit of wealth pursuit.

The general opinion that Plato is only interested in consumption is not quite adequate. He is interested in production. He analyses the Earth and land as the basic resources of production. In his economics, the Earth, written with a capital 'E', and land, written with a small 'l', gives space and produce goods. These conditions offered by the Mountain and the Lowlands give the *topos*, the main notion of Plato's economics. To establish the interrelation between space and economic practices is the great economic achievement of Plato. From this point of view we can compare Plato with Adam Smith. Smith showed the relationship between the division of labour and the quantity of production and the size of market. Smith's *topos* was expansive and limited just by the size of market. Plato shows the *topos* as a main aspect of the economy and he emphases its tendencies to bend and to limit the economic space. These tendencies resulted from the relation that connects the expansive *topos* of luxury goods with the limited space offered by agricultural products: the stable production of food. Therefore it is different from Smith's analysis of the division of labour, trade and handcraft. Plato worries that the results of the division of labour will lead to the increased consumption of food. In his opinion, in a developed Lowland civilisation, there is no danger of scarcity of luxury goods, however for this civilisation there is a limit on the production of food. Thus more luxury goods means more people which strains the lands capacity to produce food.

Although Plato is not read now by economists, the importance of Plato's economic ideas are testified by their vitality in the history of economic thought. The most obvious examples are the ideas of Malthus,[7] Veblen and Hirsch, the theory of economic crisis as well as economic ecology. His conclusion concerning the division of labour is Malthusian pessimistic; agriculture cannot cope with the elemental development of society. Apart from Malthus we may draw one more parallel, even closer to our times, between Plato's and both Veblen's and Hirsch's understandings of the economic competition and space - density and congestion.

During and at the turn of the nineteenth Century, Plato was seen as a great economic utopian (Gide and Rist, 1948, p. 213). The rigours of the ideal state, restrictions on propagation and consumption and experiences of fascism, Nazism, Stalinism, caused many in the 20th century to interpret Plato's ideas as an approval of totalitarism. Popper detected fascism and communism, Schumpeter wrote about fascism (Schumpeter, 1982, p.55), and Galbraith mentioned Plato's 'partially inclination to communism' (Galbraith, 1987, p.17), even a very influential philosophical commentator, Voeglin, was fascinated by Plato's vision of order. For all of them the starting point was Plato's thinking about the ideal state and the ideal social order. Popper was of the opinion that Plato has formulated a law of 'general degeneration' and therefore he considered that only a totalitarian state in which the main rule will be no change could be a good state. The economic analysis of the transition shows, according to Plato, only the state which can use its economic space intelligently can prevent the transition and to manage without corruption.

Looking for the rules of Plato's social order, a political philosopher, Eric Voeglin, finds the 'poleogonic construction', 'closely resembling the Hesiodan theogony' however its subject is the *polis*, not the gods (Voeglin, 1957, p. 96). This construction consisted of four different orders: 'the primitive *polis*, the luxurious *polis*, the purified *polis*, and the philosopher *polis*' (Ibid., pp. 97-8). According to him 'the transition from primitive to the luxurious *polis* was motivated by the human type in the person of Glaukon, whose endowments are to rich to find fulfilment in the simple life' (Ibid., p.100). So he concluded that: 'The criteria of right order of human existence can be found nowhere but in the soul of the philosopher' (Ibid., p. 102). We can find the rules only in a philosopher soul, so we will not come across any other connection among these orders, for example between the *topos* and economic activities. Therefore, he explains, the meaning of the deluges in Plato's theory as a construction like 'deus ex machina'. He stated that Plato, in his examples of old Athens and Atlantis, was trying to put together the real political order and the mythical order: 'The myth of prehistoric aeon of Athens and Atlantis has the same relation to the problem of political order in history as the myth of the precosmic struggle between Nous and Ananke' (Ibid., p. 206). In my interpretation Plato thinks that human history works according to the cosmological rules described by him in the *Timaeus*. The peaceful coexistence between people and their *topos* results in the Lowlands welfare and a lack of poverty of the Mountain. The wars and the violation of balance of nature result in the deluge or other kind of catastrophe, which is the *topos* reaction on 'blows' (*Timaeus* 53a). Such is the nature of the *topos* that it 'returns the blows with the same intensity' (*Timaeus* 53a, Siwek's trans. Timajos, Kritias, 1986). We cannot improve our welfare by violating our environment because it is a violation of the cosmic rules. Thus Plato connects both the mythical and human order. Watching our environment we can find the instructions sent by the macrocosm. Our historical and empirical investigations can teach us to practice the economic virtue. Plato's virtue is not only inside the philosopher soul, it is also outside.

Historians of economic thought James Bonar, Henry William Spiegel and Eric Roll have defended Plato against these labels. Eric Roll has seen, in the *Laws* and the *Republic*, 'spiritual and romantic revolt' against commercialisation (Roll, 1987, p. 27), and he emphasised Plato's discovery of the connection between, on the one hand, the division of labour, and on the other - the city, commercialisation, and corruption (Roll, 1987, p. 27-31). I think Roll was right, it was a revolt against commercialisation, though it is legitimate to add to these adjectives another one: 'economic'. From the perspective of Plato's economics we can say that he gives a careful report of two different cultures: agrarian and commercial. His goal was to defend the values of the agrarian culture. However he did it not only by means of spiritual and romantic inspection but also used economic arguments. It is characteristic of Plato's writings that during his discussion about the ideal models or historical examples of Atlantis and Old Athens that he never relied on arguments based on high values. On the contrary his argumentation is very simple and strongly connected with everyday economic practice. He showed that the new commercial patterns of behaviour were doomed to unsatiated consumption, and this consumption became an economic and psychological source of individual, social, as well as environmental, disasters.

Was Plato's theory a true one? Did some of the Ancient civilisation decline because of the economic-ecological catastrophe? J. Donald Hughes states that the abuse of the environment was an important factor of the decline of Ancient civilisations (Hughes, 1975). In fact, there is much evidence to support this theory. The last archaeological investigations of Maya's culture provide evidence that an ecological catastrophe (namely the lack of land) was the causes of Maya's decline.[8]

When we considers Plato's theory of the agrarian economy, his description of the Lowland civilisation as a sinusoidal curve, in which short periods of order are interlaced with long periods of disorder, his proto-theory of crises, the first lecture on economic ecology as well as his pre-Malthusian relationship to man and nature, it seems we have to revise his place in the history of economics.

Notes

1. See L. Baeck's two articles: 'Plato's Political Economy. Initiator of a Mediterranean tradition' (1992) and 'The Mediterranean tradition in economic thought' (1993).
2. These deluges are often sent by the gods as punishment for living contrary to the dictates of the gods.
3. There is some possibility of a cosmic disaster even in the Mountains. Plato in the *Timaeus* describes it. *Critias* relates a story told by Solon: 'Now this has the form of myth, but really signifies a declination of the bodies moving in the heavens around the earth, and a great conflagration of things upon the earth, which recurs after long intervals; at such times those who live upon the mountains and in dry and lofty places are more liable to destruction than those who dwell by rivers or on the seashore' (Timaeus 22c). However this is only once when Plato mentions a possibility of such a disaster. In *Republic, Critias, Timaeus,* and *Laws* he writes - as Socrates - about the deluges, and these deluges becomes his object of interest, for two reasons: Athens was an example of the Lowland civilisations; and deluges - contrary to this cosmic-mountain disaster - happen more often.
4. See Skladankowa, M., Mitologia Iranu [Mythology of Iran], Warszawa 1989, pp. 73-109.
5. Bracketed terms are from *Plato The Collected Dialogues*.
6. In this way Alasdair MacIntyre has shown that 'measure' or its later equivalent 'restraint', as a manager of virtue, see his book *After Virtue. A Study in Moral Theory* (1981).
7. In Samuel Hollander's extensive book *The Economics of Thomas Robert Malthus* (University of Toronto Press 1997) there is no mention concerning Plato's inspiration. Contrary to the present, in Malthus' times Plato was widely read, and there is a possibility of such connection.
8. See Wolanski, N., Zabijcza dieta - Majowie [The killer diet - Mayas], 'Wprost' 15.08.1999.

References

Baeck, L. (1992), 'Plato's Political Economy: Initiator of a Mediterranean Tradition', Research Papers in Economic Development, Katholiekie Universiteit Leuven.

Baeck, L. (1993), 'Greek Economic Thought: Initiators of a Mediterranean Tradition' in: Price, B., B., (ed.), *Ancient Economic Thought*, Routledge, London and New York, pp.146-171.

Bonar, James (1967), *Philosophy and Political Economy*. George Allen-Unwin, London-New York.

Galbraith, John Kenneth (1987), *Economics in Perspective. A Critical History*, Houghton Mifflin Company, Boston.

Gide, Charles and Rist, Charles (1948), *A History of Economic Doctrines from the time of the physiocrats to the present day*, George G. Harap Company, London.

Guriewicz, A. (1976), *Kategorie kultury sredniowiecznej*, trans. by Dancygier, J., Panstwowy Instytut Wydawniczy: Warszawa.

Herskovits, Melville Jean (1955), *Cultural Anthropology*, Knoph, New York.

Hirsch, Fred (1995), *Social Limits to Growth*, rev.ed. Routledge, London.

Hollander, S.amuel (1995), *The Economics of Thomas Robert Malthus*, University of Toronto Press, Toronto.

Hughes, Johnson D. (1975), *Ecology in Ancient Civilizations*, Albuquerque, N., M., University of New Mexico Press.

MacIntyre, Alastair (1996), *Dziedzictwo cnoty. Studium z teorii moralnosci [After Virtue. A Study in Moral Theory]*, Wydawnictwo Naukowe PWN, Warszawa.

Malthus, Thomas Robert (1960), *On Population*, ed. and introduction Himmelfarb, G., Random House, Inc., Modern Library, New York.

Landreth, Harry and Colander, David C. (1998), *Historia mysli ekonomicznej* [History of Economic Thought], Wydawnictwo Naukowe PWN, Warszawa.

Plato (1997), *Republic*, trans. by Davies, J. L., Vaughan, D. J., Wordsworth Classics of World Literature.

Plato (1992), *Republic*, translated by G.M.A. Grube, Hackett Publishing Company, Indianapolis.

Plato (1989), *The Collected Dialogues of Plato*, edited by Edith Hamilton and Huntington Cairns, Princeton University Press, Princeton.

Platon (1987), *Listy* [Letters], trans. by Maykowska, M., revis. by Pekcinska, M., Panstwowe Wydawnictwo Naukowe, Warszawa.

Platon (1986), *Timajos, Kritias*, trans. by Siwek, P., Panstwowe Wydawnictwo Naukowe, Warszawa.

Platon (1982), *Uczta* [Symposium]. Eutyfron. Obrona Sokratesa. Kriton. Fedon., trans. by Witwicki, W., Panstwowe Wydawnictwo Naukowe Warszawa.

Platon (1960), *Prawa* [Laws], trans. by Maykowska, M., Panstwowe Wydawnictwo Naukowe Warszawa.

Platon (1958), *Gorgiasz* [Gorgias], trans. by Witwicki, W., Panstwowe Wydawnictwo Naukowe Warszawa.

Platon (1958), *Panstwo* [Republic], trans. by Witwicki, W., Panstwowe Wydawnictwo Naukowe Warszawa.

Popper, Karl R. (1993), *Spoleczenstwo otwarte i jego wrogowie* [The Open Society and Its Enemies. vol. i, Urok Platona [The Spell of Plato], Wydawnictwo Naukowe PWN, Warszawa.
Roll, Eric (1987), *A History of Economic Thought*, Faber and Faber, London-Boston.
Schefold, B. (1997), 'Aristotle and Pre-Aristotelian Greek economic thought,, in: B., B., Price (ed.), *Ancient Economic Thought*, Routledge, London - New York.
Schumpeter, Joseph A. (1982), *History of Economic Analysis*, Allen-Unwin, London.
Skladankowa, M. (1989), *Mitologia Iranu* [Mythology of Iran], Wiedza Powszechna, Warszawa.
Smith, Adam (1899), *An Inquiry into the Nature and Causes of the Wealth of Nations*, George Bell and Sons, London.
Spiegel, Henry W. (1991), *The Growth of Economic Thought*, Duke University Press, Durham-London.
Veblen, Thorstein (1971), *Teoria klasy prozniaczej* [Theory of Leisure Class], Panstwowe Wydawnictwo Naukowe, Warszawa.
Voegelin, E. (1957), *Plato and Aristotle*, vol. viii of his *Order and History*, Louisiana State University Press, Baton Rouge.
Wolanski, N. (1999), *Zabijcza dieta - Majowie* [The killer diet - Majas, 'Wprost' August 15].

Chapter Two

Karl Polanyi's *Great Transformation* and the Current Transformations in Central Europe

Eric R. Hake and Walter C. Neale

Karl Polanyi and Great Transformations

Karl Polanyi's The Great Transformation[1] analyses two transformations: the first, in Britain in the five decades following the instituting of the Speenhamland system of outdoor relief in 1795; the second, in Europe and its European offspring during the two decades between the 1st and 2nd World Wars.[2] To these we propose to add a third transformation. For the world it may date from the origins of current IMF/World Bank policies in the 1970s; but the most important parts of it are the transformations in central and eastern Europe since the demise of the former Soviet Union--the focus of the chapters by Hake and Neale, Champlin, and Schaniel. All are based on the analyses in *The Great Transformation* and Polanyi's 'Our Outmoded Market Mentality'.[3]

In the first transformation the newly constructed institutions for a self-regulating market were products of circumstances quite specific to the time and to an emergingly dominant ideology. A self-regulating market system required that markets be instituted for land, labour, and money capital: '... an economic system consisting of markets and under the sole control of market prices'.[4] Because these elements in the productive processes are not themselves produced-they are here as results of geologic history, reproduction by our species, and legislation governing the monetary system-Polanyi called them 'fictitious commodities'. These ideas are the core of Polanyi's analysis.

The second transformation was a response-a massive *counter-movement*, in Polanyi's phrase-to the problems that had arisen under the market system and to the failure to re-establish the 19th century system after World War One. Some nations adopted new ideologies ('socialism in one country', Fascism, Nazism); in other nations the changes appear to have been much less ideological (the New Deal in the United States, the national government in Britain).

In the third transformation there appears to be a general ideology of the self-regulating market and 'globalization'. However, the current central and eastern European transformation differs from the first transformation in Britain in that the circumstances underlying the changes are radically different from those in Britain two centuries ago and in that the ideology has been borrowed wholesale from abroad.

Creating and Reforming Institutions

An important element in Polanyi's argument is the role of institutions. Institutions are the social structures-economic, social, political-that effectively organize the working of a social system. All change requires the creation or reformation of institutions. Social transformation requires a major rebuilding of the institutional structure. A declaration of principles or intent can never be more than the first step toward reform. As Polanyi said, 'No mere declaration of rights can suffice: institutions are required to make the rights effective'.[5]

To greater and lesser degrees institutions are consciously created or changed, and to greater or lesser degrees they emerge as consequences of social processes. More may be conscious when the changes are purposeful efforts to reform a society, but the changes made as consequences of less conscious social processes are always *vitally important* to the success or failure of attempted reforms.

The establishment of free markets and the privatization of firms begin with legislation that sets *only part* of the framework of a new economy. Equally necessary are the emergence of informal rules smoothing and regulating the flows of goods and services. They might be likened to 'customs of the trade' that govern who has what powers to do what, under what constraints, and with what expectations of actions by others. This is as true of the privatization of publicly-owned firms, the activities of banks, and the interpretation of contracts as it once long ago was of the relations between masters and journeymen or buyers and sellers in cattle markets. These rules cannot all be legislated; a few can, but mostly they evolve from the beliefs, attitudes, and experiences of the participants. (There will also be gaps in the legislation that become apparent only with experience of their workings.)

An example in point is the history of British central banking. The Bank Charter Act of 1844 was explicit in restricting the Bank of England to issuance of money and credit only in proportion to the amount of gold in its possession. With experience of financial crises there arose an informal agreement between the Bank and the government that the explicit requirement could be ignored when the liquidity of the London money markets (and of the nation's businesses) was threatened. Thus was the role of the Bank as 'lender of last resort' recognized.

These processes take time. They may occur fairly swiftly, but are never instantaneous, and the absence of informal rules opens the possibility to all sorts of actions, many of which can be badly damaging to the success of the reforms.

We cannot say with anything like certainty, but it has occurred to us that the success of Solidarity in the 1980s may have owed much to 'customs of the trade' deeply rooted in the experiences of shipyard workers, perhaps dating back to before World War II. If so, the informal rules, and associated attitudes, did not need to be articulated by the leadership: everyone knew them, almost subconsciously.

Further brief illustration is provided by the term 'The Market'. There is no such thing as The Market. There are many, many markets, each with its own rules, which are different for dealings between potato merchants, between coal suppliers and users, between lawyers and clients, between employers and workers in mines, between employers and workers in textile factories, between employer and worker in MacDonalds' fast-food restaurants.

Our Obsolete Market Mentality

In his article of this title Polanyi restates the themes in *The Great Transformation* and comments on their moral implications. Starvation of an individual member of society only became a constant threat in the modern market society. Prior to the creation of the self-regulating market system, individuals only risked starvation if their entire society risked starvation.[6] This striking difference, the apparent absence of compassion in modern civilization, provides us with a key to understanding the role of values in organizing human activity. Unlike earlier societies, the ideology of the modern, capitalist era is based on the liberal fallacy that man and land are commodities created for purchase. The prices of land or labour, their worth, are determined by supply and demand. This has allowed the values of the market to become the sole ideology driving all human activity. In our obsolete market mentality, hunger and gain are considered the only motivators of mankind. These assumptions created a new economic sphere that was distinct from all other social activities. Honour, civic duty, self respect-all are deemed irrelevant to production in the modern market society. Here lies the danger of our obsolete market mentality. The assumed primacy of market values strips away those beliefs which bind society together and provide individuals with a sense of purpose. Devoid of civil values, the impetus to private gain threatens the fabric of society and thus the welfare of the individual.

Great Transformations: Then and Now

The First Transformation

In 1795 Britain five conditions were precedent to a great transformation. First, Britain had become a thoroughly commercialized society: a market system as described by Adam Smith. Second, private property had become, not only the existing norm, but a primary social value. Third, the employment of steam to power the large engines of the incipient industrial revolution was beginning. Steam began to power the looms of the cotton textile industry, steam-driven pumps to pump out mines had spread as part of the development of the coal-to-coke and iron industries. Fourth, the agricultural revolution, with its new systems of drainage, marling of soils, and hedging of fields was adding large fixed costs to farming. Fifth, the enclosures of the 1790s were creating an army of unemployed. To feed the unemployed the justices of the peace who managed the system of poor law relief began to provide outdoor relief by subsidizing wages.

Over the next three decades, the subsidization of wages became increasingly burdensome for the farmers and landlords in the parishes. During the same period the costly machines of the industrial revolution threatened the solvency of businesses if they could not acquire inputs when wanted and could not reduce expenditures on inputs when they were not needed. The solution in a market economy was to make land (including natural resources) and labour both freely available and easily disposable on markets. The enclosures created a market for land. The market for labour, however, was circumscribed by the increasingly burdensome Speenhamland system of subsidizing rural wages. By abolishing the Speenhamland system and making the poor houses for the unemployed extremely unpleasant places in which to live, the Poor Law Reform of 1834 created a freely functioning market for labour. The dominant ideology held that there should be no interference with the workings of the markets: that the systems of markets should be self-regulating, supply (and therefore employment) responding to demand where all purchasing power was derived from sales on markets. Enclosures and Poor Law Reform had assured such markets for natural resources and labour. Businesses needed markets in which to acquire funds to buy the new machines and to finance the associated inventories. To assure that the whole system be internally self-regulating and independent of discretionary action by government, the Bank Charter Act of 1844, following the arguments of David Ricardo and the Banking School, attempted to create a monetary system that tied the supply of money exclusively to the availability of the commodity gold.

The consequences were several, and mostly bad. Labour is people, and people's incomes, places of residence, means of livelihood-in short, their lives and welfare-were left entirely to market demand. Charles Dickens and Friedrich Engels have described some of the results.[7] Land is the environment and, in many respects, the future. The state of the countryside and the cities, the streams and water supplies-and, we now know, much else--were left without protection against whatever uses to which the highest bidder wanted to put them. Availability of money for business depended on the flows of gold into and out of the Bank of England. This affected not only the rate of investment in capital structures and equipment; more importantly, at least in the short run, it affected the liquidity of business firms and hence current output and employment as well as the survival of firms whose longer-run prospects were favourable.

One should add here what was only implicit in Polanyi's argument. The sanctity of property and contract played an important role in shaping the consequences of the self-regulating market. Whereas workers were left without incomes when they were not needed, borrowers still had to pay interest even if they could honestly say that the money/machines/inventories were not being used. Similarly, tenant farmers continued to have to pay rents even when the land was producing far less value (as happened after the repeal of the Corn Laws). The ideology of the self-regulating market not only forbade discretionary action by public authorities, it was strongly biassed in favour of the propertied and against labourers.

Almost from the start of the movement to establish the self-regulating market there emerged a counter-movement (the second half of what Polanyi called the double-movement). The counter-movement consisted of a large number of specific movements to protect various sectors of the economy. It had no unifying ideology, although there were a number of different ideologies for different groups (e.g., the Owenite movement, the Chartists). Mostly the movements had quite specific aims: to protect liquidity for businesses and banks; to remove women and children from the mines and to protect them against excessive hours of work; to provide clean water and garbage and sewage disposal to the towns; to allow trade unions. These movements tended to limit the power of the self-regulating market. These were the beginnings of what later became known as the welfare state, but as late as 1914 the ideology of the self-regulating market dominated.

The Second Transformation

By 1914 the peaceful balance of power necessary to the functioning of an international, self-regulating market system had disappeared in the European alliances, and peace disappeared. The breakdown of international trade during World War One, the realization that nations needed to protect their agriculture in case of further wars, the conditions imposed by the Treaty of Versailles, and inflation destroyed the international self-regulating market system. The dominant ideology held that the objective of policies should be the restoration of the international system as it had existed before 1914. It was thought that the first thing to do was to restore the pre-war gold standard, and this aim dominated British policies in the 1920s, and was important in all other countries. The efforts to achieve this aim were an important element in precipitating and extending the crisis of 1929-33. The failure to restore the gold-standard, the depression, the rise of authoritarian governments, and the development of many elements of the welfare state was the second transformation. There were many ideologies-Communist, Fascist, Nazi, socialist-but there was no shared ideology. In some cases pragmatism (the New Deal in the United States, the National government in Britain) may have outweighed ideology. But all used discretionary public policies to control market forces.

And Now, the Third Transformation

In recent years what Polanyi called 'our obsolete market mentality' has taken on new, even global strength. As was the case in the first transformation, there is a strong ideological element in the third transformation, an ideology very close to that of the first. We are tempted to date this transformation from December, 1976, when British

Prime Minister James Callaghan accepted the lending terms of the IMF. Since then the view that there is one economic (market) model and one medicine for all ills has become common; and it shares with the early 19th century ideology the strong tendencies to favour property and contract and to put disproportionate burdens upon workers. This increasing application of the market logic can be seen in the collapse of Bretton Woods and the growing use of specific targets such as deficit/GDP ratios and inflation rates by aid agencies such as the IMF.

This transformation began to embrace an additional large portion of the human race when the Soviet Union and Central European countries began economic reforms, and became even more forceful with the demise of the Soviet Union. While recent events in east and southeast Asia reflect the ideology and practices of the third transformation, the changes in central and eastern Europe have been both more thorough and wide-ranging, probably as a result of the political revolutions of the late 1980s and early 1990s. In contrast to the cases in east Asia, the path of reform took on a democratic shape that required a distinctive break from previous ideology, a responsiveness to popular opinion, and an acquiescence to the pressures of international agencies. In its attempts to integrate into the global market economy, Central Europe adopted the rhetoric and program of our obsolete market mentality.

The political reality can be seen in the collapse of the Comecon trade network and the 'shock' thesis that anything less than rapid conversion to the market mechanism would merely prolong the inefficiencies, distortions, and privileges of the old regime. The adoption of the obsolete market mentality allowed individuals and political groups to distance themselves from the previous political system and to gain increased support from abroad, while it simultaneously required that they commit themselves to the swift creation of a self-regulating market system. Pronouncements expressing the ideology of the market mentality may be just as important, perhaps even more important, than the processes actually used in the formation of economic policy. The economies of Western Europe and America do not mirror textbook liberal capitalism, but vocal support of anything less in Central Europe has threatened a collapse of foreign investors' confidence and increasing political challenges from within. As a result, discussions about privatizing the railways or the post office, or about the wholesale scrapping of agricultural policies, are more common today in Central than in Western Europe.

By adopting the obsolete market mentality, the political leadership of the transforming countries may fail to recognize the dangers of social upheaval and in spontaneous, undirected economic change. The consequences of the third transformation will be greatly affected by those agencies that can temper the influence of the market mentality and respond to political pressures while, at same time, coordinating economic development. Democratic government must play a role in creating the institutional framework of Central Europe and the Soviet Union, balancing economic growth with social adjustment, addressing corruption, and promoting common values. To ignore the role of democratic institutions in these matters and to accept whole cloth the logic of liberal capitalism is to risk grave social disruption. In this respect, the third transformation in Central Europe differs from the first in Britain: in Britain the limitation of the suffrage to propertied people meant that the governments of the time did not need to be so sensitive to the opinions of the generality of the population. British governments then could not do anything they wanted to do, but they could do a lot of things that many people did not want them to do.

Here we address three distinct but connected aspects of Polanyi's thesis. First, social backlash-what Polanyi called the counter-movement-is an unavoidable consequence of the expansion of the market mechanism in coordinating the provisioning of society. Individuals previously protected from the commodification of land, labour, and capital will resist reforms because they perceive them as attacks on their ways of life and their beliefs. Ignoring the social costs of transformation, or assuming they will vanish through the growth of the market-based economy, will intensify the conflict and ultimately threaten the process of reform. The politics of the Polish Peasant Party will be discussed in this light. Secondly, for economic change to be perceived as progress, government must recognize its role as a *regulator* of the pace of economic change. Government, by responding to social conflicts and adopting measures to cushion the influence of the market, can minimize social backlash and ensure that economic change is seen as progress. Developments in Polish retirement programs provide an example of a government cushion. Thirdly, the implementation of institutional reform must be coordinated with indigenous beliefs. Poorly coordinated institutional reform provides an opportunity for corrupt behaviour--rational but undesirable behaviour on the part of individual actors. Czech privatization, the subsequent development of financial markets, and political soul-searching provide a case in point.

Social Backlash: Counter-Movements in Central Europe

As the result of the rapid political revolutions of 1989 and 1990, an attitude of optimism prevailed during the early stages of the current economic transformation-a period Leszek Balcerowicz refers to as extraordinary politics during post-liberalization euphoria.[8] The rosy predictions for rapid economic growth and recovery coupled with the need to satisfy the concerns of foreign governments and international business interests produced an environment where pro-market political forces rose to power. The implementation of pro-market policies resulted in an initial decline in the economic position of several previously protected groups, such as state employees in key industrial sectors, and in a general concern over issues of unemployment and declining standards of living. While governments did force through economic reform packages, the differential impact of these reforms divided the ranks of pro-reform governments and created a divisive political atmosphere.

Polish Agriculture and the Polish Peasantry

In Poland, the farmers and their political groups provide a clear example of a group who will continue to resist the process of commercialization, and to use political power to ensure continuing state support of subsidies. While concerns over Polish agriculture and the Polish Peasant Party are responsible for only a fraction of the political turmoil from 1990-93, the economic impact of the Balcerowicz plan on the farming community was dramatic and therefore resulted in a dramatic response. While agricultural incomes had increased in real terms in 1988 and 1989, they fell by 51 percent in 1990 and by another 7 percent in 1991.[9] This was the logical consequence of the abandonment of agricultural policies that attempted to bring urban and rural incomes into parity, the rapid liberalization of farm input prices, high inflation, and high interest rates. The policies of early 1990 were ultimately aimed at the rational concentration of Polish agriculture-to promote larger farms and use of mechanical equipment-but little change in the structure of Polish agriculture actually occurred. The percentage of the population involved in agriculture declined only slightly, to 24 percent in 1995, and the average size of farms has remained virtually the same (approximately 7.4 hectares).

This relative lack of change is a consequence of the large numbers involved in family/subsistence agriculture. More than one-third of all farms fall into the 1-3 hectare size. Collective or state farms would benefit from commercialization, but Polish farm politics are dominated by a population that still exists outside the commercial system. In this sector, the primary sources of cash are social payments and the sale of surplus. It is this segment of Polish agriculture which dominates the Polish Peasant Party (PSL). While the state farm sector would benefit from liberal reform programs to promote rationalization, this sector does not represent the major faction in the PSL, as evidenced by the departure of former deputy prime minister Roman Jagielinski from the PSL.[10] Polish farmers will continue to resist attempts to rationalize the sector because these programs will destroy subsistence production. Indeed, reductions in social benefits and the continued privatization of state enterprises will increase Polish dependence on small-scale agriculture.

The end of the post-liberalization euphoria can be dated to mid-1990, when a three month train strike was followed by an acceleration of wildcat strikes and rising criticism of privatization programs. The Polish Peasant Party (PSL), which represented the interests of a large, subsistence agricultural segment of the population, became increasingly vocal about the Mazowiecki government's continuation of rapid economic reform.[11] The ensuing political storm culminated in divisive presidential elections in which a weakened Solidarity movement coalesced around Lech Walesa and the Mazowiecki government was disbanded. As the political environment continued to fragment, a series of reform-minded governments under Bielecki, Olszewski, and Suchocka moved quickly into and out of power, while the increasing power of opposition parties such as the Democratic Left Alliance (SLD) and the PSL (Polish Peasant Party) ended in their control over parliament in 1993. Although the PSL was not yet in power during 1991-92, various programs were enacted to support farm prices, such as the Agricultural Marketing Agency in 1990 and minimum price floors. In power from 1993 to 1997, the PSL did little to initiate further reform of agriculture, despite factions within its own party that would have benefited from commercialization of the sector.

Institutional Reform and Corruption

Polany's thesis about the nature of social transformation illuminates the often discussed problem of corruption and lack of transparency in the economies of Central Europe and the Former Soviet Union. Organized behaviour is the result of institutions, a system of rules and associated folkviews about proper behaviour. To promote market behaviour, the government must necessarily be involved in shaping and enforcing institutional arrangements that will result in the desired behaviour. The institutional structure of each market requires a clear, operational definition of property rights, rules governing contracts, and a system for resolving conflicts. This framework must be applied and modified to address the activities of production, trade, and finance.[12]

The formation of instituted process is the most difficult aspect of a transformation because it requires that rules be formulated that respect local beliefs and attitudes. General ideological statements will not suffice. A transformation will be easier and more humane if it is a democratic, pragmatic process that allows government the latitude to reformulate policy initiatives in response to unintended consequences.

Unfortunately, by adopting the ideology of the self-regulating market, it has been assumed that the government has only a slight role in establishing institutional structures that produce acceptable behaviour among market participants. However, many profitable activities are not socially acceptable, and some individuals may continue to behave in non-market ways. While many of the transforming economies have adopted new commercial codes and business regulations, the centrality of these developments--and the importance of enforcement--has been diminished due to the excessive focus on stabilization, liberalization, and privatization.

The resulting paucity of organized exchange, new regulations, and enforcement practices produces a 'cowboy capitalism' where unscrupulous individuals are the most successful. Skirting poorly defined legislation and exploiting loopholes becomes standard practice in business. From this perspective, we can view Russia's mafia as businessmen operating in an environment lacking an external system for enforcing contracts. Under these conditions, Russia's mafia is behaving rationally and has adopted the threat of violence as the most efficacious method of enforcing contractual obligations. In Poland, the scandals of the early 90s (known as Art-B and FOZZ) represent a similar profiteering attitude under conditions of ineffective legislation.

Those unwilling to adopt these standards of behaviour view the entire process with disdain. The issue of corruption clearly has a moral component, an aspect that has been stressed by many writers. In his Parliamentary address of December 7, 1997, Vaclav Havel noted that the missing ingredient in the Czech transformation was something that went beyond macro-economic data:

Things like rules of the game; the rule of law; the moral order behind that system of rules that is essential for making the rules work; a climate of co-existence. The declared ideal of success and profit was turned to ridicule because we allowed a situation in which the biggest success could be achieved by the most immoral ones, and the biggest profits could go to unpunishable thieves.

Other writers have echoed this theme, alternately suggesting that the problems of transformation are the result of 50 years of moral corruption under communism or the lack of morality in capitalism.[13] This should come as no surprise. The expansion of the self-regulating market mechanism and its value system does conflict with other value systems. The goal should be to develop an institutional framework that organizes market behaviour in consonance with enough existing folkviews and beliefs to make it acceptable.

Privatization Without Suitable Institutions

The Czech Republic received its greatest attention for the vigour with which it pursued the privatization of state enterprises. Unlike Hungary and Poland, Czechoslovakia had experienced only limited economic reform prior to 1989; the state continued to exercise direct control over the majority of its assets. This centralization of assets allowed Czechoslovakia to undertake a privatization scheme that was rapid, inexpensive, and politically feasible. The centrality of state ownership allowed the application of a grand experiment in voucher privatization-i.e., the mass distribution of state ownership to the public in the form of company stock. In part, this technique only appeared plausible in the Czech case due to the government's ability to limit the influence of existing management and employees. The initial results were stunning. In three years, government ownership of industry fell from 86 percent into the range of 10-35 percent.[14] The medium term results are much less than stunning. The Czech economy has suffered from a collapse of foreign support, the stock exchange of 2,000 listings is largely stagnant, and privatized industry is unable to attract the funds to support reorganization.

Voucher privatization was supposed to produce a vibrant stock exchange where profit-minded shareholders effectively governed the behaviour of professional management teams. The flow of company information and share trading would both be facilitated by private investment companies and funds. However, this did not happen. (1) Because the state's assets were privatized before a new system was set up, the new owners had to become *actively* involved-unlike the largely passive stockholders in the west-in financing and coordinating the process of reorganization. (2) In voucher privatization the state gave away the shares, with the consequence that the share market was so flooded that it was impossible to raise new equity finance.

Several shortcomings in the legal framework, however, have become increasingly obvious, and are widely considered responsible for the continuing stagnation of the Prague Stock Exchange. The problems include, but are not limited to, a series of financial scandals, the emergence of close-knit industrial/financial ownership structures, and abuse of minority shareholders. The current state of industrial ownership has stifled the reorganization of Czech industry. This is the uncoordinated aspect of Czech privatization-the successful reorganization of industry required foreign support and investment, while the regulatory structure of privatization stifled foreign interest. The primary flaw was not in the letter of the law, but rather in its interpretation and subsequent enforcement. As written, Czech privatization law should have limited insider trading, majority ownership rights, and the emergence of bank-dominated ownership structures. As practised, it did not, most probably because there was little effort to develop an institutional structure of rules with their evolving, associated values.

While Czech law attempted to limit cross-ownership between banks and the investment companies that were created during voucher privatization, limits on cross ownership were not applied to the funds created by the new investment companies. In the language of Matthew,[15] founding companies (such as banks) begat investment companies and investment companies begat investment funds. We refer to these affiliated parent-child-grandchild financial companies as 'Investment Groups'. Webs of ownership rapidly emerged between parent banks and granddaughter investment funds created by investment companies. So common did this practice become that Investicni a Postovna banka was only the first of the big four Czech banks to self-privatize. It did so by allowing affiliated granddaughters to accumulate shareholdings larger than those held by the National Assets Fund.[16] Because laws governing industry ownership did not address the possibility of cross-shareholdings in the financial community and the subsequent development of Investment Groups, financial intermediaries were able to consolidate control over individual firms. Coupled with the lack of minority shareholding protections, it became possible for domestic financial groups to gain control over operating companies and squeeze out foreign or minority shareholders by cancelling outstanding shares, halting dividend payments, or changing their own company charters to limit the voting rights of minority shareholders.

The development of Czech financial markets suffers because such rules as exist are not enforced. Even the much anticipated stock market watchdog, the Czech Securities Commission established in 1998, does not have an independent budget, has limited ability to levy fines, and has had several of its decisions challenged in the courts.[17] Czech privatization has suffered from a lack of institutional coordination. While the Czech program for industrial development was designed to attract foreign owners and financiers (not necessarily a good idea), the lax regulatory conditions have produced an opaque ownership structure dominated by financial interests that are at best poorly prepared for the task of reorganizing industry.

The lack of institutional coordination in Czech financial developments-a dependence on foreign investment and expertise coupled with a regulatory environment that fails to attract foreigners-could be compared to Slovakia's attempts to resolve the financial/managerial shortcomings of their industries through the promotion of domestic ownership and tax laws favourable to domestic investors.[18] While Slovakia has apparently shunned foreign ownership interests, they have simultaneously attempted to produce a legal environment capable of dealing with their need for finance-including laws on bond privatization, direct sales of state assets, and allowing new owners to write off the acquisition cost if the new owners invest in more physical capital.[19]

The carelessness with which Czech financial institutions were developed allowed corruption to prosper in an environment of lax regulation and enforcement, and dramatizes the importance of coordinating institutional processes. Failure to recognize the role of 'nation-building' in the transformation process and excessive willingness to depend on the unrestrained rational behaviour of individuals will result in outcomes that are unacceptable to the society at large.

Moderating the Impact of Economic Transformation

As Polanyi argued in *The Great Transformation*, the conspicuous failure of liberal philosophy was its misunderstanding of the issue of progress. Progress is not solely a rapid rate of economic growth; greater growth must be accompanied by social adaptation to new circumstances. The rate of economic growth will only be perceived as progress if it is in rough equality with the rate of social adaptation.[20] Assuming that undirected economic change is inherently beneficial forfeits the traditional role of the state as regulator of economic change and protector of social welfare. Government programs that delay or dampen the impact of unregulated market forces can therefore provide the time necessary to adapt to new conditions. Conversely, in programs of employee retraining or job placement programs governments can actively attempt to increase the rate of social adjustment.

If this role of government is ignored, we risk social disruption and disaffection as various sectors of society seek ways to protect themselves from the new economic circumstances for which they are entirely unprepared. So long as the ways they seek are peaceful and remain within the rules of a democratic, constitutional system, such counter-movements should be considered all to the good. But it is possible that some will turn to authoritarian and ultra-nationalist ways of protecting themselves and this, we may agree, would be bad. Government programs that retard the rate of economic change should not be considered a failure because they ultimately become obsolete as society adapts to the new conditions. The role of government as a regulator of progress is not to stop economic change; it is to make it more acceptable.

Several examples of this interventionist role for government immediately spring to mind. Let us take, for instance, the initial plans for economic reform in those countries typically deemed shock therapists, Poland and Czechoslovakia. In both countries, initial optimism provided support for liberal reform programs created by domestic leaders and supported by western advisors. Early political disagreements over the pace of reform were resolved in favour of a liberal or neo-liberal policy. In Poland, the shock elements were stabilization and liberalization, which sought a tight monetary policy and a fiscally conservative budget to control the inflationary effect of the rapid price liberalization. In Czechoslovakia, the shock components were tight monetary policy and privatization of state enterprises.

In both countries, however, certain government policies were designed to limit the impact of these programs. In Czechoslovakia, these were known as the 'pillows' of reform. Fixing the koruna at a low value made Czech exports cheaper and also dampened domestic demand for foreign goods. It became easier to maintain a positive trade balance. Additionally, price liberalization was not as rapid as in Poland.[21] Key prices, such as fuel, housing, and wages, were not liberalized in the early stages of reform.

The Case of Polish Pensions

While Poland's shock therapy is generally considered to be the most far-reaching, there have been attempts to moderate the impact of this economic transformation. The use of the pension system as a social buffer provides one clear example. During the 1990s, pensioners represented one of the fastest growing segments of society, such that by 1996 there were 9.2 million pensioners-greater than the total employment of Poland and representing approximately 1/4 of the population. The rapid growth of pensioners--the number of retirees grew 37.3 percent from 1990 to 1995-has been possible due to a liberal disability certification system and the opportunity for retirement in the case of firm bankruptcy. The liberal use of exceptions to the general retirement guidelines has also inflated the number of people drawing pensions who are below the general retirement age. By May 1996, some 42.5 percent of retired men and 30.7 percent of retired women were below the required retirement age. These decisions helped, to a large extent, to reduce the scale of unemployment in Poland.[22]

The cost of benefits has also increased rapidly, due both to the increasing number of pensioners and to the increase in the size of pension benefits. As of 1995, pension benefits constituted some 16 percent of GNP.[23] Poland will ultimately have to raise the retirement age to comply with European Union standards and has discussed converting the pension system from a pay-as-you-go system to a fund in an attempt to lower costs (which it will not do, but the belief that it will is an article of faith among those with an outmoded market mentality). However, the current use of the pension system to cushion the blow of market transformation should be deemed a success, coordinating the paces of economic change and social adjustment.

A Private Case

In *The Great Transformation* Polanyi insisted strongly that Robert Owen stood out as the person who recognized 'the reality of society'-that there was much more to worry about than efficiency of markets-and pointed to New Lanark as the exceptional example of a private effort to mitigate the effects of the market.[24] A Polish company provides an excellent example of how non-market behaviour can cushion the blows that would be associated with a sudden, complete-and therefore impossible -reconstruction of social beliefs.[25] This company was privatized in 1989, closed down many of its facilities, but expanded some to satisfy demands of other industries in the region. The net effect was a reduction in its work force.

As was common in socialized production, the company had provided housing for its employees and built schools for the children, supplying heat and other services to this community. Now, despite privatization and complete reorientation of production, the company continues to provide services both to other companies and to tenants of the now privately-held housing estates. Indeed, it has been estimated that 80 percent of the company's energy costs are associated with the maintenance of disused facilities to benefit other companies in the region and to heat the school and housing estate--all of which is done without contract and with only nominal payment. This behaviour on the part of company management is clearly not dominated by a desire for gain. When questioned about these activities, management was hard pressed to provide an explanation other than continuity with past behaviour. Although these activities certainly constitute a burden on the operations and profitability of the company, they constitute a continuation of non-market oriented behaviour. If the company were unwilling to continue these services, these costs would most likely be added to the fiscal burden of the municipal or national government.

Conclusion

Polanyi's interpretation of the nature of market transformations is clearly applicable to late 20th century developments in central Europe and the Former Soviet Union. An appreciation of the significance of an outmoded market mentality combined with democratic government allows a greater understanding of the complex linkages between social unrest, political conciliation, and corruption.

Due to the general acceptance of the obsolete market mentality, the countries of Central Europe and the Former Soviet Union are experiencing a transformation in important ways that are not unlike the transformation in early 19th century Britain-that is, the creation of a self-regulating market system that elevates the importance of 'economic motives' while denigrating or ignoring the social functions of other systems of value. In Polish agriculture this fundamental shift has produced a counter-movement as segments of society resist the conversion of their life and the abolition of their folkviews. In the Czech Republic disillusion with privatization may be the root of a counter-movement. The primary hope for the transforming countries lies in the political revolutions of the late 1980s that allow political pressures to dampen the impact of market forces, as has happened in the management of the Polish retirement system (but not yet in Czech privatization and finance). These political pressures express an appreciation for the continuing role of governments in moderating the rate of economic change and ensuring the coordination of institutional reform. The continuing risk, as can be seen in Russia, is that the emergent democratic institutions will not be strong enough to combat the application of pure market logic. Under such circumstances, the continued human privation and absence of common values could result in social disruption, or worse.

Notes

1. Rinehart & Co., New York, 1944.
2. Polanyi said (oral communication to Neale, years ago) that the transformation that he had in mind was the one between the wars. Many (including Neale) thought that it was the transformation to capitalism in the 19th century. Both were certainly great transformations.
3. In George Dalton, ed., *Primitive, Archaic and Modern Economies: Essays of Karl Polanyi*, Beacon Paperbacks, Boston, 1968, pp. 59-77; reprinted from *Commentary* (February 1947) 3:109-17.
4. *Great Transformation*, p. 249.
5. *Great Transformation*, p. 256.
6. Karl Polanyi, 'Our Obsolete Market Mentality', in *Primitive, Archaic and Modern Economies: Essays of Karl Polanyi,* ed. George Dalton. Beacon Press, Boston, 1968, pp. 65-66.
7. Charles Dickens, *Oliver Twist* or *Hard Times*; Friedrich Engels, *The Condition of the Working Class in 1844.*
8. Leszek Balcerowicz, 'The Interplay Between Economic and Political Transition' in *Lessons from the Economic Transition,* ed. Salvatore Zecchini, Kluwer Academic Publishers, Boston, 1997, p. 160.
9. Ben Slay, *The Polish Economy: Crisis Reform and Transformation,* Princeton University Press, Princeton, 1994, p. 147.
10. *Donosy: Liberal Digest,* no. 2206, 2 December, 1997.
11. Ben Slay, *The Polish Economy: Crisis Reform and Transformation,* Princeton University Press, Princeton, 1994, p. 126.
12. Michael D. Intriligator, 'Reform of the Russian Economy: The Role of Institutions', *International Journal of Social Economics*, vol. 23, no. 10/11, 1996, pp.58-72.
13. Tomas J.F. Riha, 'Missing: Morality in the Transformation of Former Socialist Countries', *International Journal of Social Economics,* vol. 21, no. 10/11/12, 1994, pp. 10-31.
14. John C. Coffee, Jr., 'Institutional Investors in Transitional Economies: Lessons From the Czech Experience', pp. 111-86 in Roman Frydman, Cheryl W. Gray, and Andrzej Rapaczynski, eds., *Corporate Governance in Central Europe and Russia. Volume 1. Banks, Funds, and Foreign Investors.* CEU Press, Budapest, London, and New York, 1996. 10-35 percent is the range of estimates.
15. *Holy Bible* (King James version), Matthew:1:1-5.
16. Dean Calbreath, 'Good Luck in Following the IPB-Ownership Shell Game', *Prague Post,* February 19-25, 1997, pp. 5, 9.
17. Hana Lesenarova, '"Things Fall Apart" at SEC; Jana to the Rescue' *Prague Business Journal* April 20, 1998. p. 22. 'CS Infrastrukturni Sues Securities Commission' *Hospodarske Noviny* June 5, 1998, p. 10.

18. Adrian Smith, *Reconstructing the Regional Economy*, Edward Elgar, Cheltenham, UK, 1998, p. 249.
19. Recognition of the logical consistency of Slovak privatization does not constitute support of former Prime Minister Meciar's anti-democratic policies.
20. Karl Polanyi, *The Great Transformation*, Rinehart & Co., New York, 1944. p. 38.
21. Ben Slay, *The Polish Economy: Crisis Reform and Transformation*. Princeton University Press, Princeton, 1994, p. 89.
22. 'Delayed Reforms of the Social Policy', Centrum Analiz Spoleczno-Ekonomicznych [Center for Social and Economic Research]. From *Economic Scenarios for Poland*, Conference Papers, 1997.
23. Bozena Leven, 'Distributional Effects of Poland's Transition: The Status of Pensioners', *Comparative Economic Studies*, Winter, 1996, pp. 121-135.
24. *Great Transformation*, pp. 166-72 especially, and a dozen other places *passim*.
25. The company's name and information that might allow its identification is withheld pending approval. Observations based on Eric Hake's interview (4 June 1998) with David Hake (University of Tennessee-Knoxville) and a participant in a meeting with the management of company.

Chapter Three

On Building up a Market Society: Lessons from the Wealth of Nations and The Great Transformation

António Almodovar and Maria de Fátima Brandão

Introduction

Both Adam Smith and Karl Polanyi wrote extensively on the workings of a society where the market played an important economic role. Adam Smith's *Wealth of Nations* is the most famous blueprint for such a society, and is considered nowadays as the gospel for each and every supporter of an efficient capitalist social order. As for Polanyi, writing some one hundred and fifty years after Smith, his *The Great Transformation* attempts to ascertain the almost unnatural character of the livelihood of men under a market society, where for the first time in the history of mankind, both land and labour are perceived as mere commodities, with Polanyi highlighting the dreadful social consequences of such an assessment. At a time when many Eastern European countries are making a deliberate effort to switch from an inherited planned economy to a market oriented one, the wisdom and the doubts of the aforementioned authors may prove to be of some help, namely in the identification of some of the major difficulties to be expected from this current great transformation.

We will start by looking at Adam Smith's renowned advocacy of the system of natural liberty, in accordance to which economic activities could be organized to the best social effect on the basis of individual interests and initiatives, under the discipline of market transactions and without government direct intervention. Then we will summarize the main arguments used by Karl Polanyi, for whom the freedom to dispose of the productive powers of labour, land and money in the context of the market exchange, seriously endangered the chances of survival of the civilized society. Finally, we will return to Adam Smith's concerns and doubts about the conceivable damaging consequences to be expected from the evolvement of the central features of a market based society, comparing them with those put forward by Karl Polanyi.

Smith's Society of Perfect Liberty

When dealing with the progress of opulence in different ages and nations, Adam

Smith mentions two specific systems of political economy, one to be called the modern system of commerce, the other the system of agriculture. In spite of their own peculiarities, Adam Smith considers that they are related to by the fact that 'all systems either of preference or of restraint' ascribe to the sovereign 'a duty, in the attempting to perform which he must always be exposed to innumerable delusions, and for the proper performance of which no human wisdom or knowledge could ever be sufficient'(Smith, 1976b, p. 687). The very impossibility to perform such an unreasonable duty – that of 'superintending the industry of private people, and of directing it towards the employment most suitable to the interest of society' (Ibid.) – is in fact the major argument already put forward by Adam Smith in *The Theory of Moral Sentiments*, against the foolishness of those who believe in the feasibility of any kind of a rational, deliberate societal scheme.

There he opposes 'the man whose public spirit is prompted altogether by humanity and benevolence' (Smith, 1976a, p. 233), one which is always willing to identify and take into account the established prejudices and confirmed habits of both individuals and classes, to 'the man of system ... often so enamoured with the supposed beauty of his own ideal plan of government, that he cannot suffer the smallest deviation from any part of it' (Ibid., pp. 233-34). Such a man of system 'seems to imagine that he can arrange the different members of a great society with as much ease as the hand arranges the different pieces upon a chessboard' (Ibid.). As far as 'he does not consider that the pieces upon the chessboard have no other principle of motion besides that which the hand impresses upon them', the man of system is absolutely unable even to conceive that 'every single piece has a principle of motion of its own, altogether different from that which the legislature might choose to impress upon it' (Ibid.).

This is not to say that a good statesman is an unconditional supporter of the *status quo*, for he is clearly entitled to have his own projects and ideals for social and political betterment. The point is that he must escape from the evils of arrogance and make a serious effort to understand and consider his fellow-countrymen, departing from their idiosyncrasies to the conception of any feasible plans of political reform. Otherwise, only the worst may be expected, when abstract ideas and plans are allowed to hold sway regardless of circumstances. As Adam Smith remarks:

> [S]ome general, and even systematical, idea of the perfection of policy and law, may no doubt be necessary for directing the views of the statesman. But to insist upon establishing, and upon establishing all at once, and in spite of all opposition, every thing which that idea may seem to require, must often be the highest degree of arrogance. It is to erect his own judgement into the supreme standard of right and wrong. It is to fancy himself the only wise and worthy man in the commonwealth, and that his fellow-citizens should accommodate themselves to him and not he to them. It is upon this account, that all political speculators, sovereign princes are by far the most dangerous (Ibid.).

Being so, it is obviously of the utmost importance for any public man to have a fair understanding of the workings of the 'pieces' performing in the social arena; and that is precisely what Adam Smith was willing to provide him with, by means of a comprehensive inquiry into the major working principles of individual and social motion – as revealed in the *Theory of Moral Sentiments* (1759, 1976a), *the Lectures on Jurisprudence* (1766, 1978) and the *Wealth of Nations* (1776, 1976b).

There one may learn that as a rule, people act in accordance with their own interests and sentiments, always trying to better their livelihood. But even more important than that, one may discover that provided certain important environmental conditions are met, there is a providential outcome to be expected from the overall interactions among those not so perfect individuals. In political terms, this means that, to a certain extent, one can rely on a set of basic instincts to attain the regular progress of mankind, for each and every human being has a set of built-in propensities which spur him towards an everlasting effort for self-improvement. These individual propensities, as selfish as they may be, are socially advantageous provided that some type of general controlling institutions are set in place. This is why overall justice and security are of the utmost importance to Adam Smith, since they provide for the kind of institutional arrangements which preclude the inevitable clash of interests (be it on an individual or even a class basis) from becoming socially harmful.

According to Adam Smith, 'the obvious and simple system of perfect liberty' (1976b, p. 687), was then the most feasible system for achieving prosperity and progress. In this natural and perfunctory system, 'every man, as long as he does not violate the laws of justice, is left perfectly free to pursue his own interests his own way, and to bring both his industry and capital into competition with those of any other man, or order of men' (Ibid.), thus accomplishing the material copiousness of society and systematically fostering its progress as well.

Now what about the market? In fact, everything we have seen so far describes a global system of political economy, a comprehensive view of the ideal transactions of any society, without any specific mention to the role to be performed by the market.[1] Of course, Adam Smith mentions the existence and functioning of the market, namely when he makes the distinction between the natural and the market price of a commodity:

> When the price of any commodity is neither more nor less than that what is sufficient to pay the rent of the land, the wages of the labour, and the profits of the stock employed in raising, preparing, and bringing it to the market, according to their natural rates, the commodity is then sold for what may be called its natural price. The commodity is then sold precisely for what it is worth, or what it really costs the person who brings it to the market (Ibid., p. 72).

As for the other type of price, Adam Smith says that 'the actual price at which any commodity is commonly sold is called its market price. It may either be above, or below, or exactly the same with its natural price' (Ibid., p. 73).

Thus one may assert that any concrete price is a market price, although not always a natural one, since for a price to be 'natural' it has to be the natural outcome of what Adam Smith calls the 'ordinary or average rate' of wages, profit and rent (Ibid., p. 72). In their turn, the ordinary or average rates of wages, profit and rent are 'naturally regulated' (Ibid.) by the ordinary conditions prevailing in 'every society or neighbourhood' (Ibid.). In the case of both wages and profits, 'partly by the general circumstances of the society, their riches or poverty, their advancing, stationary, or declining condition; and partly by the particular nature of each employment' (Ibid.). In the case of rent, 'partly by the general circumstances of the society or neighbourhood in which the land is situated, and partly by the natural or improved fertility of the land' (Ibid.).

Although Adam Smith does lay emphasis on the general circumstances of every society, it becomes fairly obvious that the natural rates of wages, profit, and rent are in fact more likely to be determined by the conditions prevailing on the neighbourhood rather than on the nation as a whole, and as such are in fact more likely to be determined by custom and power rather than by competition in the market place. A closer reading of the *Wealth of Nations* allows us to understand that the natural rate of wages in any 'modern' society is in fact established by 'the contract usually made between ... two parties, whose interests are by no means the same. The workmen desire to get as much, the masters as little as possible. The former are disposed to combine in order to raise, the latter in order to lower the wages of labour' (Ibid., p. 83). It also allows us to understand the reasons why masters usually 'have the advantage in the dispute, and force the other into a compliance with their terms' (Ibid.). On the one hand, 'being fewer in number, [masters] can combine more easily; and the law, besides, authorises or at least does not prohibit their combinations, while it prohibits those of workmen' (Ibid., pp. 83-84). On the other hand, 'masters can hold out much longer' in case of a dispute, because they 'could generally live a year or two upon the stocks which they have already acquired', whereas 'many workmen could not subsist a week, few could subsist a month, and scarce any a year without employment' for lack of means (Ibid.).

Much the same happens with rent, because the landlord naturally tends to ask for the highest 'price paid for the use of land', a price 'which is evidently the highest the tenant can afford to pay in the actual circumstances of the land', or rather, a price which 'is evidently the smallest share with which the tenant can content himself without being a loser, and the landlord seldom means to leave him any more' (Ibid., p. 160).

As for the profits of stock, the natural rate is harder to determine, because '[p]rofit is so very fluctuating, that the person who carries on a particular trade cannot always tell you himself what is the average of his annual profit. It is affected, not only by every variation of price in the commodities which he deals in, but by the good or bad fortune both of his rivals and of his customers, and by a thousand other accidents to which goods ... are liable. It varies, therefore, not only from year to year, but from day to day, and almost from hour to hour' (Ibid., p. 105).

These meaningful remarks amount to say that a natural price is nothing else than an established and commonly accepted one, a price that although being loosely defined nevertheless allows all the individuals concerned to reach a consensus regarding the size of the composing parts of the value of a specific commodity – that is, the price to be paid for the indispensable use of labour, land and stock, the price 'that will induce a man to apply all his art and industry to some particular branch of business' (Smith, 1978, p. 353). Whether or not that very price is actually paid and received is made dependent upon another set of circumstances, precisely those behind the free formation of the market price. As a matter of fact:

> when a buyer comes to the market, he never asks of the seller what expences he has been at in producing them. The regulation of the market price of goods depends on the ... demand or need for the commodity ... the abundance or scarcity of the commodity in proportion to the need of it ... the riches or poverty of those who demand (Ibid., p. 496).

However, no matter how different the circumstances behind their formation, the natural price and the market price were closely related, on account of the interplay among the people interested in buying the goods they can afford, the people interested in selling the goods under their command, and the people interested in buying and selling the elements indispensable to the production of those goods. For Adam Smith there were good reasons to regard the outcome of this interplay with favourable eyes, because it naturally worked favourably to the interests of both the individuals involved in market transactions and the society as a whole.

Although the outcome of market transactions was nothing but uncertain, in the form of market prices which varied in accordance with individual decisions and evaluations, the fact remains that these prices varied in accordance with a well-defined pattern which induced individual buyers and sellers to adequate their respective behaviours to the overall needs of society. In fact, market prices were constantly evolving around natural prices, because:

> if the market price be so high as to be more than sufficient to make up the natural price, and answers all those things for which every tradesman has a demand ... this will appear to be a vastly profitable trade and all will crowd into it with expectations of making a fortune. As the number of hands increases so will the quantity of the work done, and consequently it will become the purchase of a lower rank of men and fall down to its natural price .... If the trade ... becomes overstocked, and instead of the great price for this work they do not get even the price ordinary in other trades, then no one will enter into it, and many who have engaged in it will learn some other ... rather than continue at so unprofitable a business in which the labourers do not even get their due reward (Ibid., pp. 359-60).

The allocation adjustments which follow individual decisions of demand and offer naturally tended to bring the market price of goods as close as possible to their natural price, that is, to the lowest level 'at which a dealer ... is likely to sell them for any considerable time; at least where there is perfect liberty, or where he may change his trade as often as he pleases' (1976b, p. 73). Given the perfect liberty of every one involved in market transactions, the factors pushing and pulling the market prices of goods, labour, land and capital towards their natural prices, contributed to ensure that the owners of labour, land and capital would be paid what was socially due to their own productive efforts, and that the society as a whole got the goods it demanded at the best possible price.

Without government direct intervention, economic activities could thus be organized to the best social effect on the basis of individual initiatives, since 'it is the interest of all those who employ their land, labour, or stock, in bringing any commodity to market, that the quantity never should exceed the effectual demand; and it is the interest of all other people that it never should fall short of that demand' (Ibid., p. 74). Constrained by the existence of people whose main interest lay in acquiring goods at the lowest possible market price, the individual efforts of the owners of the factors of production had to be directed towards their best productive use at the least possible cost, towards taking advantage of the benefits of the division of labour and the dimension of the market whenever necessary. However, being free to choose the best employment for the productive powers of labour, land, and capital, individual economic agents also had to take on to themselves the responsibility of securing the natural reward of their employment in any branch of economic activity. The problem was, that in the context of an economy increasingly orientated towards the market, and increasingly governed by the market, as was the case of the commercial society Adam Smith had before his eyes, no institution or law could guarantee that all productive efforts would always meet their natural recompense and enable the owners of productive powers, particularly labourers, to make a decent living out of their use. Adam Smith had good reasons to assume that the situations where the market prices of goods fell below their natural prices, thereby pushing the market prices of labour, land and capital below their natural prices, would naturally clear themselves away. He also had good reasons to assume that since the workings of a system in which the natural prices of goods tended to the lowest possible level, they actually did not put in jeopardy the prospects of individual and social betterment, owing to the ensuing pressure to bring costs down to the lowest possible level, which in turn paved the only secure way to the easier access to the goods and services demanded by society.

A different stand was taken on these matters by Karl Polanyi, for whom the freedom to organize the productive powers of labour, land and capital in the context of the market exchange, seriously endangered the chances of survival of the civilized society. To 'Smith's own view ... that universal plenty could not help percolate down to the people [because] it was impossible that society should get wealthier and wealthier and the people poorer and poorer' (Polanyi, 1957, p. 124), Karl Polanyi opposed the view that society needed to protect itself against the evils of the market, and, by so doing, seriously undermined the very chances of the market economy.

Karl Polanyi and the Great Transformation

Apparently what really annoyed Karl Polanyi was the fact that land, labour and money were viewed as mere commodities: 'to separate labor from other activities of life and to subject it to the laws of the market was to annihilate all organic forms of existence and to replace them by a different type of organisation, an atomistic and individualistic one' (1957, p. 163); 'what we call land is an element of nature inextricably interwoven with man's institutions. To isolate it and form a market out of it was perhaps the weirdest of all undertakings of our ancestors' (Ibid., p. 178); 'actual money ... is merely a token of purchasing power which, as a rule, is not produced at all, but comes into being through the mechanism of banking and state finance' (Ibid., p. 72). These vehement remarks are of course to be understood in the context of the serious crisis that Western Civilisation was experiencing after World War I, a time when almost every traditionally reliable institution seemed to be on the verge of collapse. Therefore, Karl Polanyi may be seen as one amongst several others intellectuals (to mention but a few, one may recall Keynes, Hayek and Schumpeter[2]) who were seriously concerned with the survival of a world that seemed to have been severely damaged in its very foundations. However, *The Great Transformation* actually started a new and thought provoking research path on the ways of organising a decent society displayed by past and present societies.[3]

Departing from the identification of the four institutions which lay at the very foundations of nineteenth-century civilization – namely the balance-of-power system, the international gold standard, the self-regulating market and the liberal state – Polanyi goes on arguing that the key to the disastrous situation experienced by Western economies and societies after the World War I, was in fact the widespread acceptance of a 'stark utopia' (Ibid., p. 3), that of the supposed feasibility of a society built around a self-adjusting market system. His main thesis was that such a peculiar society could not possibly survive for 'the commodity fiction handed over the fate of man and nature to the play of an automaton that ran in its own grooves and was governed by its own laws' (1977, pp. 10-11), eclipsing political thinking, and generating an 'unsubstantial concept of justice, law, and freedom' (Ibid., p. 16). This amounts to saying two different things. Firstly that a market society was perfectly unique in the sense that it had developed a relationship between the economic processes and the political and cultural spheres absolutely unlike any other known historical pattern. Secondly that a market society was doomed to collapse on account of its socially disruptive economic principles, which jeopardised the social cohesiveness traditionally inherent in the livelihood of men.

According to Polanyi, this inevitable collapse was actually under way in the aftermath of World War I. Even worse, from his point of view, was the fact that 'the market cannot be superseded as a general frame of reference unless the social sciences succeed in developing a wider frame of reference to which the market itself is referable' (1965b, p. 270). That is the reason why he embraced a research program designed to make known all the historical and anthropological evidence that could warrant his advocacy for a 'new thought pattern', away from the 'obsolete market mentality' characteristic of 'liberal capitalism' (1947, p. 109), that would make possible the re-embedding of the economy into the social relations that constitute the fabric of society, without destroying individual freedom, justice and law, that is, those 'institutionalized values [which] first make their appearance in the economic sphere as a result of state action' (1977, p. 16). It is precisely in this context that his studies on reciprocity, redistribution and householding took place, particularly conspicuous was his concern with the presentation of evidence that in archaic empires 'the absence, or at least the very subordinate role, of markets did not imply ponderous administrative methods tightly held in the hands of a central bureaucracy. On the contrary, gainless transactions and regulated dispositions, as legitimised by law, opened up ... a sphere of personal freedom formerly unknown in the economic life of man' (1977, p. 74).

Being a keen adversary of the market society 'stark utopia', it was only natural that Karl Polanyi would criticize its purported authors. As he viewed it, the intellectual history of the market society had begun with the Physiocrats, who first noticed 'an interdependence of fluctuating prices which directly affected multitudes of men' (Ibid., p. 6). The discovery of 'the economy' was, in his own words, 'one of the emotional and intellectual experiences that formed our modern world', being so powerful an experience that it 'came to the physiocrats as an illumination and constituted them a philosophical sect' (Ibid., p. 7).[4] Then followed Adam Smith, who 'was able to include wages and rent in the group of "prices" and thus, for the first time, glimpse a vision of the wealth of nations as an integration of the varied manifestations of an underlying system of markets' (Ibid., pp. 7-8), thereby becoming 'the founder of political economy because he recognised, however dimly, the tendency towards interdependence of these different kinds of prices insofar as they resulted from competitive markets' (Ibid., p. 8).

These two authors contributed to launch the perception of what Karl Polanyi calls 'the economistic transformation', which 'represented a violent break with the conditions that preceded it. What was before merely a thin spread of isolated markets was now transmuted into a self-regulating system of markets' (Ibid., p. 10). However, their contributions also laid the ground for the emergence of the 'economic solipsism' developed throughout the nineteenth century by 'the utopians of the market', and which came to be characterised by the complete blindness 'to the sphere of state, nation, and power, to the point of doubting their existence' (Ibid., p. 14). As a result of the 'eclipse of political thinking' from the analysis of economic activities, 'economics stepped into the vacuum, and a hypercritical attitude towards the moral vindication of political actions set in' (Ibid., p. 15). However, as Polanyi forcefully argues, this last attitude had the damaging consequence of preventing people to realise that 'each of [the] steps towards man's introduction into a realm of justice, law, and freedom originally resulted from the organising action the state in the economic field ... such recognitions of the early role of the state were barred by economic solipsism' (Ibid., p. 17). This critical assessment of the alleged social and political blindness of nineteenth-century economists and fellow social thinkers contrasts sharply with the favourable assessment of the social and political awareness of their eighteenth-century predecessors.

Smith and the State

According to Karl Polanyi, 'neither Quesnay nor Smith aimed at the establishment of the economy as a sphere of social existence that transcends market, money, or price', because 'the traditional unity of all human affairs that still informed their thinking made them averse to the notion of a separate economic sphere in society, although it did not prevent them from investing the economy with the characteristics of the market' (1977, p. 8). As regards Adam Smith, Polanyi (1957, pp. 111; 112) observed that:

> it was true [that he] treated material wealth as a separate field of study; [but] to have done so with a great sense of realism made him the founder of a new science, economics. For all that, wealth was to him merely an aspect of the life of the community, to the purposes of which it remained subordinate; it was an appurtenance of the nations struggling for survival in history and could not be dissociated from them .... The economic sphere, with him, is not yet subjected to laws of its own that provide us with a standard of good and evil.

This assessment of Adam Smith's approach to the material wealth of nations is particularly accurate. In fact, the 'system of natural liberty' advocated either in the *Lectures on Jurisprudence* or in the *Wealth of Nations*, although relying heavily on the workings of the market, does nevertheless take into great account its social and political environment. To begin with, the convergence of market prices towards natural prices is made dependent upon not only the 'perfect liberty' of all those involved in market transactions, as has been referred to earlier on, but also upon the security they 'shall enjoy the fruits of [their] own labour', both of which solely the laws of the government could provide for (Smith, 1976b, p. 540).

When assessing the impact of bounties upon exportations, Adam Smith compared Great Britain -'certainly one of the richest countries in Europe'-with Spain and Portugal - ranking 'perhaps among the most beggarly' (Ibid., p. 541)- and explained the contrast by the circumstance that 'in Great Britain industry is perfectly secure; and though is far from being perfectly free, it is as free or freer than in any other part of Europe' (Ibid., p. 540). On the contrary, in Spain and Portugal 'industry is ... neither free nor secure, and [their] civil and ecclesiastical governments ... are such as would alone be sufficient to perpetuate their present state of poverty, even though their regulations of commerce were as wise as the greater part of them are absurd and foolish' (Ibid., p. 541). In addition, it has also been stated earlier that market prices are not actually freely formed in a kind of social and political vacuum, but rather evolve around the trend set by the natural rates of wages, rents and profits, that is, by the rates deemed as socially acceptable by the more or less extended community where workers, landowners and capitalists are bound together in their efforts to improve the material conditions of their own lives. Finally, Adam Smith's strong arguments in favour of freer and more secure market transactions did not preclude the pre-eminence of the interests of the nation as a whole, and, consequently, the need of government interference with the workings of the market to preserve them whenever necessary. As a matter of fact, the economic advantages of free and secure market transactions extending to all sectors of economic activities should never be allowed to prevail against the security and defence of the nation itself. The acknowledgement of the advantages of the unlimited, unrestrained freedom of trade, did not prevent Adam Smith from praising the 'act of navigation' as 'perhaps the wisest of all the commercial regulations of England' (Ibid., p. 465). It certainly was not 'favourable to foreign commerce, or to the growth of opulence which can arise from it' (Ibid., p. 464), but it certainly contributed to 'the defence of the country', which, 'depends very much upon the number of its sailors and shipping', by means of dispositions that aimed at giving 'the sailors and shipping of Great Britain the monopoly of trade of their own country' (Ibid., p. 463). Similarly, he praised the caution taken by governments when they made a law that fell short of the ideal of the unlimited, unrestrained freedom of trade, when he considered that 'though not the best in itself, it is the best which the interests, prejudices, and temper of times would admit of', further adding that 'it may perhaps in due time prepare the way for a better [law]' (Ibid., p. 543). In terms of political agenda, the question centred upon a better law to solve part of the present problems under the prevailing circumstances, rather than upon the best law to bring about outrightly the system of natural liberty. Adam Smith duly called the attention to the fact that 'to expect indeed that the freedom of trade should ever be entirely restored in Great Britain, is as absurd as to expect that an Oceana or Utopia should ever be established in it. Not only the prejudices of the publick, but what is much more unconquerable, the private interests of many individuals, irresistibly oppose it' (Ibid., p. 471). The successful overcoming of the opposition raised against the measures designed to change things for the better, in the light of the principles of the system of natural liberty, required time and effort to deal with the resulting dislocation of ideas and interests, and, above all, the willingness to give preference to second-best solutions more in tune with the sentiments of the people.

Having 'worked out the "system of natural liberty and perfect justice" in economic affairs in greater practical detail than any predecessor' (Winch, 1983, p. 505), left nonetheless Adam Smith well aware of the dangers facing societies willing to undergo the necessary changes and, if need be, of the corresponding duty on the part of the state to intervene in order to avert them.[5] For example, and as regards the dangers inherent in the progress of the division of labour, he was of the opinion that they might be averted mainly through the 'education of the common people [which] requires, perhaps, in a civilized and commercial society, the attention of the public more than that of people of some rank and fortune' (Smith, 1976b, p. 784). Another serious cause of concern came from the assessment made as regards the interests of the order composed of those men who live by profit, particularly of those men who live on the profits made on capitals invested in trading and manufacturing activities. As merchants and master manufacturers, they figured prominently in a civilized, commercial society because they were 'the two classes of people who commonly employ the largest capitals, and who by their wealth draw to themselves the greatest share of publick consideration' (Ibid., p. 266). Notwithstanding, he was of the opinion that:

> the proposal of any new law or regulation of commerce which comes from this order, ought always to be listened to with great precaution, and ought never to be adopted till after having been long and carefully examined, not only with the most scrupulous, but with the most suspicious attention. It comes from an order of men, whose interest is never exactly the same with that of the publick, who have generally an interest to deceive and even to oppress, and who accordingly have, upon many occasions, both deceived and oppressed it (Ibid., p. 267).

Deceit and oppression brought about by their congenital interest in widening the market, while at the same time narrowing competition, in order to raise 'their profits above what they naturally would be', and thus 'levy, for their own benefit, an absurd tax upon the rest of their fellow-citizens' (Ibid.). To avert this danger, governments had to favour instead the congenital interest of the nation as a whole in having markets as wide and competitive as its social and political circumstances permitted.

And yet, no matter how important the action of the state might become in the process of averting the dangers facing a developing commercial society, or in the process of making room for freer, more secure and extensive market transactions, the fact remains that Adam Smith's arguments in favour of the pre-eminence of the system of natural liberty, consistently helped to show that 'the unassisted development and "natural progress" towards wealth was not only feasible but also most advantageous' (Brown, 1994, p. 158). In his turn, Karl Polanyi made the best effort to show that such development and progress was neither socially feasible nor socially most advantageous.

Polanyi and the State

Karl Polanyi did so, because he was of the opinion that in the wake of Quesnay and Smith, who had invested the economy with the characteristics of the market, nineteenth-century classical economists and fellow-liberal-social thinkers further invested the society with the characteristics of the market, and this he regarded as a move against the nature of human societies. In his opinion, the awareness and perception of the growing importance of market phenomena in the context of the eighteenth-century commercial society, had paved the way for the emergence of the nineteenth-century industrial society as a market society, i.e., a society ruled by the workings of the market.

Under the pressure exerted by the forces of the Industrial Revolution and the guidance provided for by economic and social liberalism, governments were led to intervene in such a way as to promote the extension of market transactions to realms which had so far remained deeply embedded in other human institutions, namely kinship or neighbourhood. As Karl Polanyi explained:

> The use of specialized machines in an agrarian and commercial society must produce typical effects. Such a society consists of agriculturalists and of merchants who buy and sell the produce of the land. Production with the help of specialized, elaborate, expensive tools and plants can be fitted into such a society only by making it incidental to buying and selling ... all factors involved must be on sale, that is, they must be available in the needed quantities to anybody who is prepared to pay for them. Unless this condition is fulfilled, production with the help of specialized machines is too risky to be undertaken both from the point of view of the merchant who stakes his money and of the community as a whole which comes to depend upon continuous production for incomes, employment, and provisions. Now, in an agricultural society such conditions would not naturally be given; they would have to be created (Polanyi, 1957, pp. 40-1).

In his perception of the emergence of industrial capitalism, such conditions had been created gradually by state intervention, by means of reforms which brought about the separation of labour, land and money from all aspects of social life other than the economic aspect, as it could be viewed in the context provided by market transactions. Accordingly, governments made arrangements in order to enforce by law the fictitious nature of labour, land and money as mere commodities, thereby making room for the organization of markets where labour, land and money could be exchanged as if they had been produced for sale, like any other commodity. With the help of this 'commodity fiction', governments aimed at the liquidation of 'the noncontractual organizations of kinship, neighbourhood, profession, and creed' as regards labour and land, and at the establishment of a 'system of commodity money' (Ibid., pp. 163;178;193). As a result, there emerged a 'market economy', or, in other words, 'an economic system controlled, regulated and directed by markets alone' (Ibid., p. 68), where economic activities were allowed to proceed on the basis of the prices freely formed in the markets by means of the interplay among individuals who demanded and offered goods, services, and factors of production; where nations were led to trade among themselves on the basis of the workings of 'a system of international commodity money' which 'required the lowering of domestic prices whenever the exchange was threatened by depreciation' (Ibid., pp. 193; 194).

The problem for Karl Polanyi was that the attempt to form a market economy had far reaching and dangerous effects, because 'the control of the economic system by the market is of overwhelming consequence to the whole organization of society: it means no less than the running of society as an adjunct of the market. Instead of the economy being embedded in social relations, social relations are embedded in the economic system' (Ibid., p. 57). In response to the challenge of the machine, the atomistic and individualistic forms characteristic of market transactions gradually replaced the traditional organic forms of social life which had governed the activities of production and distribution until the advent of the Industrial Revolution. In this way, man, nature and the capitalist productive organization were all made dependent upon the workings of the markets established for commodities, services, and factors of production. When the order in both production and distribution was thus placed under the rule of an international system of interrelated markets, the positive effects derived from the extensive use of the machine and the worldwide expansion of trade, had to be set against the negative effects derived from the commercialization of the elements that were the constituent parts of human society. According to Karl Polanyi (Ibid., p. 162):

> the competitive labor market hit the bearer of labor power, namely man. International free trade was primarily a threat to the largest industry dependent upon nature, namely agriculture. The gold standard imperiled productive organizations depending for their functioning on the relative movement of prices. In each of these fields markets were developed, which implied a latent threat to society in some vital aspects of its existence.

Quite naturally, society responded to this latent threat by means of a protective countermovement aiming at the removal of man, nature and productive organizations from the orbit of the market. Since the middle of the nineteenth century, the protection of society was in fact gradually entrusted to politics, in as many ways as were needed to mitigate the harmful effects of the establishment of markets for the factors of production, namely, 'factory legislation and social laws ... land laws and agrarian tariffs ... central banking and the management of the monetary system' (Ibid., p. 132).

On the eve of the First World War, when the development of the market world system reached its peak, the intervention of the state had already contributed to the emergence of 'a more closely knit type of society' in western countries (Ibid., pp. 130; 162). Notwithstanding, this society was then standing 'in danger of total disruption' (Ibid.), and bearing witness in the process to the impending disruption of the nineteenth-century civilization. As Karl Polanyi explained, 'In the half century 1879-1929, Western societies developed into closely knit units, in which powerful disruptive strains were latent. The more immediate source of this development was the impaired self-regulation of market economy.... Impaired self-regulation was an effect of protectionism' (Ibid., p. 201). When protectionism was further extended to the international order, in consequence of the failure to restore the gold standard and the disruption of the world trade brought about by the Great Depression, the market society and economy finally collapsed, under the strain of policies which persisted in restoring to politics the control over labour, land and money.[6]

And yet, the challenge of the machine still remained to be properly answered. Writing soon after the end of the Second World War, Karl Polanyi raised the question of 'how to organize human life in a machine society' without subordinating 'man to the needs of the machine' (1947, p. 109), as had been the case with the market society and economy where freedom had been secured at the expense of justice and security. The task lying ahead involved the promotion of justice and security, without sacrificing freedom.[7] However he was keen to observe that 'the breakdown of market-economy imperils two kinds of freedoms: some good, some bad' (Ibid., p. 116), and of course he was particularly concerned with the preservation of the good kind of freedoms. He held as a good thing the disappearance of 'the freedom to exploit one's fellows, or the freedom to make inordinate gains without commensurable service to the community, the freedom to keep technological inventions from being used for the public benefit, or the freedom to profit from public calamities secretly engineered for private advantage ... together with the free market' (Ibid.). But he thought otherwise about the prospect of the concomitant disappearance of the good freedoms that 'to a large extent ... were by-products of the same economy that was also responsible for the evil freedoms', although he remained convinced that the 'freedom of conscience, freedom of speech, freedom of meeting, freedom of association, freedom to choose one's job', that were cherished 'for their own sake', were to survive the collapse of the market economy and society (Ibid., p. 117).

As a matter of fact, he did not share Hayek's view 'that since free institutions were a product of market-economy, they must give place to serfdom once that economy disappears', arguing instead that the 'institutional guarantees of personal freedom are compatible with any economic system' (1947, p. 117). On the one hand, he called attention to the fact that the management of a war economy, by American and British governments during the Second World War, had not impaired the respect for public liberties. On the other hand, he regarded the socialist experiment brought about by the Russian Revolution, as 'part of a simultaneous universal transformation' away from the market society and economy (1957, p. 247),[8] and he felt apprehensive with 'the Communist's expectation of the "withering away of the State" [because it] seems ... to combine elements of liberal utopianism with practical indifference to institutional freedoms' (1947, p.116). The solution to the problems raised by the complexity of the industrial civilization would actually lie in the preservation of the newly-found unity between economy and politics, and in the attempt to look at economic phenomena as embedded in relationships that were not in themselves necessarily of an economic nature.[9] Whatever the difficulties of such an enterprise, Karl Polanyi held an optimistic view over the future of industrial societies. As he explained:

> the passing of market-economy can become the beginning of an era of unprecedented freedom. Juridical and actual freedom can be made wider and more general than ever before; regulation and control can achieve freedom not only for the few, but for all .... old freedoms and civic rights [will] be added to the fund of new freedom generated by the leisure and security that industrial society offers to all. Such a society can afford to be both just and free' (1957, p. 256).

And it could actually afford to be both just and free, because 'the end of market society means in no way the absence of markets. These continue, in various fashions, to ensure the freedom of the consumer, to indicate the shifting of demand, to influence producer's income, and to serve as an instrument of accountancy, while ceasing altogether to be an organ of economic self-regulation' (Ibid., p. 252). That is, while ceasing altogether to be the constituent parts of a self-regulating market system 'the only purpose of which was the automatic increase of material welfare' (Ibid., p. 219), regardless of the ill-effects that might befall over man, nature and productive organizations. Despite the collapse of the market economy, Polanyi remained optimistic about the possibility of securing the 'stupendous industrial achievements' it had engendered in the past (Ibid., p.186), by means of markets embedded in social relations geared to bring about both increased individual freedom and protection against the dislocation of interests entailed by economic and social change. He argued that 'the rate of change is often of no less importance than the direction of the change itself; but while the latter frequently does not depend upon our volition, it is the rate we allow change to take place which well may depend upon us' (Ibid., pp. 36-7). Consequently, he regarded the role of government in economic life of the utmost importance, consisting 'often in altering the rate of change, speeding it up or slowing it down as the case may be' (Ibid.), in order to attenuate the unintended ill-effects of unerring change.

Conclusion

The views of Adam Smith and Karl Polanyi, on the difficulties to be expected from the dislocation of interests inherent in the emergence of the system of natural liberty and of the market economy, may prove to be of some help, at a time when many Eastern European countries are making a deliberate effort to switch from an inherited planned economy to a market oriented one. Both provide arguments which underline the beneficial character of individual freedom in the context of extended market transactions, in the form of greater and better production. Both provide arguments which show that market and state go together in the process of building up and sustaining an economy where the market plays a prominent role. However, they provide different insights into the articulation between market and state, as regards the aim to organize economic activities to the best social effect.

In Adam Smith, the natural character of the system of natural liberty precludes any attempt on the part of the state to control and direct the outcome of socially embedded markets. Emerging and evolving in accordance with the prejudices, habits and interests of the different members of society, different classes or groups of people, the system of natural liberty will naturally tend to bring about the regular material progress of society without endangering its fabric. The fact that the system of natural liberty is not enforced from upside down by the state ensures that society will undergo the inherent changes, at the pace allowed by the successful overcoming of the opposition raised against the expansion of individual freedom, in the context of market transactions extending from production to distribution. Time and effort have to be devoted to deal with the peaceful dislocation of ideas and interests entailed by the acceptance of growing individual freedom, and quite a lot of effort is required from the state. Firstly, the state is required to confine individual freedom to the limits imposed by justice and security, providing for the institutional arrangements which preclude the inevitable clash of interests from becoming socially harmful. If need be, the state must not hesitate to take measures which encroach upon individual freedom, but as a rule no measures should be taken which diminish the security of individual initiative. Secondly, the state is required to avert the dangers facing a society undergoing changes directed towards freer, more secure and extensive market transactions. Measures have always to be taken to fight against the unintended ill-effects of economic changes, and against the congenital interest of individual members of society, classes or groups of people to avoid competition with a view to socially unfair advantages.

In Karl Polanyi, the unnatural character of the self-regulating market system requires the systematic intervention of the state in order to protect society from the outcome of socially disembedded markets. Emerging and evolving in accordance with the idea of the supposed feasibility of an economy organized on the basis of uncontrolled individual freedom, the self-regulating market system will naturally tend to bring about the regular disruption of society, on account of the systematic sacrifice of justice and security. In consequence, and under the pressure of the disruption of economic activities inherent in the blind workings of the market, the state is naturally pushed to counter the evils of the system it has helped to enforce from upside down. By so doing, the state ends up taking protective measures, which gradually impair the self-regulation of the market and pave the way for the re-embedding of markets in social relations geared to promote a freer, more just and more secure world to live on.

The recent collapse of the socialist experiment in Eastern European countries undoubtedly sheds new light on Adam Smith's cautious attitude as regards the designs of well-intended governments, and his acute awareness as regards the unintended effects of the designs of human nature. In its turn, the growing interventionism experienced by Western economies, after World War Two, undoubtedly sheds new light on Karl Polanyi's views on the prospects of a system of uncontrolled markets.

Notes

1. See Brown (1994, chaps. 6,7) on the secondary role of the market analysis in Adam Smith's system of natural liberty. See Rashid (1998) for a discussion on Adam Smith's contribution to the understanding of the market mechanism.

2. See, for example, Keynes' 'Concluding Notes on the Social Philosophy Towards which the General Theory Might Lead', appearing at the end of *The General Theory* (1978, pp. 372-84), Hayek's *The Road to Serfdom*, and Schumpeter's *Capitalism, Socialism and Democracy*.
3. See the results of the collective research in *Trade and Market in the Early Empires*, edited by Karl Polanyi, Conrad M. Arensberg and Harry W. Pearson. See also Karl Polanyi's essays in *Primitive, Archaic and Modern Economies*. On the relevance of Karl Polanyi's contribution to the field of comparative economic systems, see Dalton (1971), Bohannan & Dalton (1965, pp. 1508-9) and North (1977). A critical assessment of Karl Polanyi's views, on the changing place of the economy in society and their influence on the field of economic anthropology, may be found in Cook (1966) and Godelier (1975); Kindleberger (1973) provides a critical assessment of his historical interpretation of the transformation underwent by traditional societies in the wake of the Industrial Revolution; Hechter (1981) prresents a critique of his social theory, in the context of te debate between the utilitarian and sociological approaches in social science. Neale (1976) and Eichengreen (1996) bear witness to Karl Polanyi's influence on the study of the emergence and workings of modern western monetary systems, whereas Stanfield (1980) underlies the importance of his contribution to institutional economics. Several other works bear witness to the wide-ranging influence of Karl Polanyi's on science and society, namely, Szecsi (1979), Block & Somers (1984), Mendell and Salée (1991), McRobbie (1994), or Baum (1996).
4. On the subject of the perception and conception of an independent economic sphere in society, see also the essay 'Aristotle Discovers the Economy' (Polanyi 1965a). Making use of this contribution, Robert Heilbroner has kept the suggestive title of *The Making of Economic Society* in the various editions of his historical perspective of capitalism.
5. See Winch (1979, pp. 70-102), on the advantages and disadavantages of commercial societies in Adam Smith. See Skinner (1996), on the economic role of the state in Adam Smith.
6. For a critical assessment of Polanyi's diagnosis of the collapse of the market economy, see: Sievers (1951, pp. 343-68); Szecsi (1979, p. 44); Hecher (1981, pp. 409-21); Levitt & Mendell (1987, p. 36); and Bienefeld (1991, pp. 6-28).
7. The goal of preserving and expanding the individual freedoms brought about by the action of the state, in the process of making legal room for the formation of a market society, is of the utmost importance for Karl Polanyi (see, 1957, pp. 249-58; 1947, pp. 116-17; 1977, pp. 73-4). On this subject see also Szecsi (1979, pp. 43-33).
8. On the sympathy shown by Karl Polanyi towards the socialist experiment under the Soviet regime see other passages in *The Great Transformation* (1957, pp. 234; 246; 256-7), Sievers (1951, pp. 276-79; 347-8; 353), Polanyi-Levitt and Mendell (1987, pp. 31-2), and Nagy (1994, pp. 98-102).
9. On the question of the further development of the good kinds of freedom that had evolved together with the market economy, in the context of the changes experienced by Western societies throughout the 1930s, and in the context of Karl Polanyi's attempt to bring together again economics and politics, see also the chapters on 'Popular Government and Market Economy' and 'Freedom in a Complex Society' in *The Great Transformation*, and the essays on 'The Place of Economies in Societies'

and on 'The Economy as Instituted Process'. On the relevance of the socialist approach and solution to Karl Polanyi's attempt to re-embed economic phenomena into a wider social environment traditionally ignored by formal economics, see Sievers' views on 'Polanyi's Positive Program' (1951, pp. 284-312), Baum's on 'The Ethical Foundations of Polanyi's Social Theory' (1996, pp. 20-38), Polanyi-Levitt's on 'Karl Polanyi as Socialist' (1994), Bishop's on 'Karl Polanyi and Christian Socialism' (1994), Litvan's on the 'Democratic and Socialist Values in Karl Polanyi's Thought' (1991), Szelenyi's on 'Karl Polanyi and the Theory of a Socialist Mixed Economy' (1991), and Schroyer's on 'Karl Polanyi's Post-Marxist Critical Theory' (1991).

References

Baum, Gregory (1996), *Karl Polanyi on Ethics and Economics,*, McGill-Queen's University Press, Montreal.

Bienefeld, Manfred (1991), 'Karl Polanyi and the Contradictions of the 1980s', *The Legacy of Karl Polanyi: Market, State and Society at the End of the Twentieth Century*, ed. M. Mendell & D. Salée, St. Martin's Press, New York, pp. 3-28.

Bishop, Jordan (1994), 'Karl Polanyi and Christian Socialism: Unlikely Identities', *Humanity, Society and Commitment: On Karl Polanyi*, ed. K. McRobbie, Black Rose Books, Montreal, pp. 162-78.

Block, Fred & Somers, Margaret R. (1984), 'Beyond the Economistic Fallacy - the Hollistic Social Science of Karl Polanyi', *Vision and Method of Historical Sociology*, ed. T. Skocpol, Cambridge University Press, Cambridge and New York, pp. 47-84.

Bohannan, Paul and Dalton, George (1965), 'Karl Polanyi', *American Anthropologist*, (New Series) vol. 67, pp. 1508-11.

Brown, Vivienne (1994), *Adam Smith's Discourse. Canonicity, Commerce and Conscience*, Routledge, London.

Cook, Scott (1966), 'The Obsolete "Anti-Market" Mentality: A Critique of the Substantive Approach to Economic Anthropology', *American Anthropologist*, vo. 68, pp. 323-45.

Dalton, George. (1971) [1968], 'Introduction', *Primitive Archaic and Modern Economies. Essays of Karl Polanyi*, ed. G. Dalton, Beacon Press, Boston, pp. ix-liv.

Godelier, Maurice (1975), 'Présentation', *Les Systèmes Économiques dans L'histoire et dans la Théorie*, ed. K. Polanyi, C.M. Arensberg & H.W. Pearson, Librairie Larousse, Paris, pp. 9-32.

Hayek, F.A. (1944), *The Road to Freedom*, George Routledge & Sons Ltd., London.

Heilbroner, Robert & Milberg, William (1998) [1962], *The Making of Economic Society*, 10th ed., Prentice Hall, New Jersey,.

Keynes, John Maynard (1978) [1936], *The General Theory of Employment, Interest and Money, The Collected Writings of John Maynard Keynes*, vol. VII, The MacMillan Press Ltd., London.

Litvan, Gyorgy (1991), 'Democratic and Socialist Values in Karl Polanyi's Thought', *The Legacy of Karl Polanyi: Market, State and Society at the End of the Twentieth Century*, ed. M. Mendell & D. Salée, St. Martin's Press, New York, pp. 251-71.

McRobbie, K. ed. (1994), *Humanity, Society and Commitment: On Karl Polanyi*, Black Rose

Books, Montreal.
Mendell, M. and Salée, D. ed. (1994), *The Legacy of Karl Polanyi: Market, State and Society at the End of the Twentieth Century*, St. Martin's Press, New York.
Nagy, Endre J. (1994), 'After Brotherhood's Golden Age: Karl and Michael Polanyi', *Humanity, Society and Commitment: On Karl Polanyi*, ed. K. McRobbie, Black Rose Books, Montreal, pp. 81-111.
North, Douglass C. (1977), 'Markets and other Allocation Systems in History: The Challenge of Karl Polanyi', *Journal of European Economic History*, vol. 3, no. 3, pp. 703-16.
Polanyi, Karl (1977), *The Livelihood of Man*, ed. H.W. Pearson, Academic Press, New York.
Polanyi, Karl (1971) [1968], *Primitive Archaic and Modern Economies. Essays of Karl Polanyi*, ed. G. Dalton, Beacon Press, Boston.
Polanyi, Karl (1965-a) [1957], 'Aristotle Discovers the Economy', *Trade and Market in the Early Empires*, ed. K. Polanyi, C.M. Arensberg & H.W. Pearson, The Free Press, New York, pp. 64-94.
Polanyi, Karl. (1965-b) [1957], 'The Economy as Instituted Process', *Trade and Market in the Early Empires*, ed. K. Polanyi, C.M. Arensberg & H.W. Pearson, The Free Press, New York, pp. 243-70.
Polanyi, Karl Arensberg, Conrad and Pearson, Harry W. (1965-c) [1957], 'The Place of Economies in Societies', *Trade and Market in the Early Empires*, ed. K. Polanyi, C.M. Arensberg & H.W. Pearson, The Free Press, New York, pp. 239-42.
Polanyi, Karl (1957) [1944], *The Great Transformation. The Political and Economic Origins of our Time*, The Beacon Press, Boston.
Polanyi, Karl (1947), 'Our Obsolete Market Mentality. Civilization Must Find a New Thought Pattern', *Commentary*, no. 3, pp. 107-117.
Polanyi-Levitt, Kari (1994), 'Karl Polanyi as Socialist', *Humanity, Society and Commitment: On Karl Polanyi*, ed. K. McRobbie, Black Rose Books, Montreal, pp. 115-40.
Polanyi-Levitt, Kari & Mendell, Marguerite (1987), 'Karl Polanyi: His Life and Times', *Studies in Political Economy*, vol. 22, Spring, pp. 7-39.
Rashid, Salim (1998), 'Adam Smith and the Market Mechanism', *The Myth of Adam Smith*, Edward Elgar, Cheltenham/Northampton, pp. 30-51.
Schumpeter, Joseph (1942), *Capitalism, Socialism and Democracy*, George Allen & Unwin Ltd., London.
Schroyer, Trent (1991), 'Karl Polanyi's Post-Marxist Critical Theory', *The Legacy of Karl Polanyi: Market, State and Society at the End of the Twentieth Century*, ed. M. Mendell & D. Salée, St. Martin's Press, New York, pp. 66-85.
Sievers, Allen Morris (1951) [1949], *Has Market Capitalism Collapsed? A Critique of Karl Polanyi's New Economics*, Columbia University Press, New York.
Skinner, Andrew S. (1996), 'The Role of the State', in *A System of Social Science: Papers Relating to Adam Smith*, Clarendon Press, Oxford, pp. 183-208.
Smith, Adam (1978) [1766], *Lectures on Jurisprudence*, ed. R.L. Meek, D.D. Raphael and P.G. Stein, Liberty Classics, Liberty Press, Indianapolis.
Smith, Adam (1976a) [1759], *The Theory of Moral Sentiments*, ed. D.D. Raphael and A.L. Macfie, Liberty Classics, Liberty Press, Indianapolis.
Smith, Adam (1976b) [1776], *An Inquiry into the Nature and Causes of the Wealth of Nations*, ed. R.H. Campbell, A.S. Skinner and W.B. Todd, Liberty Classics, Liberty Press, Indianapolis.
Stanfield, J. Ron (1980), 'The Institutional Economics of Karl Polanyi', *Journal of Economic*

Issues, vol. 24, no. 3, Sept., pp. 593-614.

Szecsi, Maria (1979), 'Looking back on *The Great Transformation*', *Monthly Review*, vol. 30, no. 8, pp. 34-45.

Szelenyi, Ivan (1991), 'Karl Polanyi and the Theory of a Socialist Mixed Economy', *The Legacy of Karl Polanyi: Market, State and Society at the End of the Twentieth Century* ed. M. Mendell & D. Salée, St. Martin's Press, New York, pp. 231-48.

Winch, Donald (1983), 'Science and the Legislator: Adam Smith and after', *The Economic Journal*, vol. 93, pp. 501-20.

Winch, Donald (1979), [1978], *Adam Smith's Politics*, Cambridge University Press, Cambridge.

Chapter Four

Groundwork for an Institutional Economic Approach to 'Transition': Smith and Polanyi Reconsidered

Eyüp Özveren

> *'The house is crazy, says a weary traveller to himself, and will not stand very long; but it is a chance if it falls to-night, and I will venture, therefore, to sleep in it to-night'.*
> --Adam Smith (1776), *Wealth of Nations*.

In response to the recent surge of interest[1] in the ongoing economic transformation of the former Eastern Bloc countries, thanks to its hegemony *vis-a-vis* the all powerful international economic institutions such as the World Bank and the International Monetary Fund, economic orthodoxy has once again come to the foreground. Long-time prescriptions have once more been polished up and fine tuned to the exigencies of the dire circumstances in which former communist countries now find themselves.[2] The ever present problem with international economic institutions was that they were caught in a dilemma. On the one hand, because of their adherence to orthodoxy, they had to defend a liberal, *laissez-faire*, and preferably free-trade doctrine that leaves little room for policy implementation, yet on the other hand, they were created to come up with policies that would help cure the ills of a situation which would not, or could not, resolve itself. Hence, such institutions were always forced to betray their doctrinal commitments by virtue of their *raison d'etre* and learn to live with a permanent contradiction between what they professed and what they actually did.

Over the last decade international economic institutions have proven themselves to be less effective than all parties concerned wished them to be in coming to terms with the phenomenon of the so-called post-communist transformation. It goes without saying that they have gone beyond mainstream economic theory, to which they nevertheless remain fully committed in rhetoric. This has been so because, prey to its own comparative static methodology, mainstream theory could compare a market economy with a non-market one and argue for the superiority of the former over the latter in terms of efficient resource allocation and consumer satisfaction, yet could not prescribe a strategy for moving from the latter to the former over time. It could at best naively recommend the forceful undoing of 'fetters' so as to unleash the natural forces in favour of market mechanism.[3]

What is at issue in the case of the post-communist transformation under way is a far more complex problem of 'transition' that has to be addressed by way of its proper analytical categories and dynamics. Karl Marx had at one time envisaged the analytical problem of the transition from capitalist mode of production to the post-capitalist one in relation with whether or not backward countries like Russia could skip the capitalist stage and transform themselves into a communist society. He had approached the question with his original yet patchy conception of the previous transition from feudalism to capitalism operating as a referential framework at the back of his mind.[4] The kind of transition we now face in front of us is far more complicated as it seems to be a transition in reverse, that is from allegedly more advanced communism to the historically backward capitalism.

But we need to be much more specific on the essential qualifications of this transition. To be able to do this we have to look back first at different conceptualizations of a historically antecedent transition. On the one side, for Karl Marx and Thorstein Veblen, the critical transition witnessed in the course of the 'long nineteenth century' was from an agrarian backward formation to a industrial capitalist, hence production-oriented, society. On the other side, for Adam Smith and Karl Polanyi, the same nineteenth-century could best be understood as a transition from a mercantilist, administered society to a commercial, market society. The difference between the two approaches is one of emphasis as their conclusions overlap in many ways. Nevertheless, because we need to develop tools to explain better the post-communist transition now under way, we need first to characterize the ongoing phenomena. What we have in front of us is a transition from an industrial, allegedly production-oriented highly regulated system to a commercial,[5] market society. This means practically sacrificing at least some production for the sake of market, a phenomenon that reflects itself in sector-specific de-industrialization and unemployment. Once the transition is qualified as such, we see that the further pursuit of this discussion in terms of the Adam Smith-Karl Polanyi line of thought will make more sense. Because of this, we will attempt to develop a groundwork by bringing into close contact Adam Smith's *Wealth of Nations* (1776) with Karl Polanyi's *Great Transformation* (1944). Instead of pursuing a conventional paradigmatic contrast of the two approaches, we choose a hermeneutic engagement by way of which we will explore similarities in order to build up a common ground on which an institutional theory of transition can eventually be erected.

A Smithian Prologue

Time has proven *Wealth of Nations* as a landmark in economic thought irrespectively of whether or not it represents a break with Smith's earlier *Theory of Moral Sentiments* (1759) in particular (Özveren, 1993), or the entire corpus of what came to be re-classified as pre-Classical economic thought in general. Even Schumpeter, who insisted that Smith's text was a compendium of the economic thinking to his day with little originality except for its systematic treatment of its subject-matter, nevertheless, could not help singling it out as the first 'classical situation' in the history of economic analysis (Schumpeter, 1954). Given such a monumental posture, it is no coincidence that economic orthodoxy, though systematically forgetful of its own history, every now and then aspires to be, if anything, Smithian. We shall argue that, contrary to expectations in the light of the above fact, *The Wealth of Nations* lends itself rather easily to a novel interpretation developed along institutional lines.[6] As with any classic text, it would be absurd to speak of a 'correct' interpretation. In fact, what makes a text classic, besides other things, is its openness to a multiplicity of readings. As such, we do not propose that we disclose in the following presentation the ultimate meaning of *The Wealth of Nations*. We insist, however, that our interpretation is at least as loyal as its hitherto formulated alternatives to the message of the Smithian quest and furthermore, can serve productively to the constitution of a new approach to 'transition'.

Among the factors responsible for making *The Wealth of Nations* such a controversial text, the fact that a new science of political economy in-the-making was presented in old clothes, that is to say, a traditional format, comes first. Hence mainstream economists all too readily discover in Smith an antecedent of their neoclassical economics by focussing conveniently on the substance of the First Book-and sometimes the first two books-of *The Wealth of Nations*. It is often forgotten that these two books were followed by three others. Adam Smith conceived his work within the traditional *genre* of advice to the sovereigns, notwithstanding the novelty that it was as much an advice to the monarch as it was to the commonwealth. Written at the time of the revolt of the North American colonies, in its ultimate conclusion by defining the dilemma Great Britain faced, the text reveals what was at the back of its author's mind. Britain should either realize an imperial project by flexibly accommodating the demands for representation of its colonies in return for a fair financial contribution to the maintenance of the Empire, or give up its imaginary empire, become a modest nation-state and adjust her finances 'to the real mediocrity of her circumstances' (Smith, II, 1976, pp. 486). Obviously, Smith's worry was that Britain was caught in a vicious circle of imperial territorial expansion and indebtedness by way of which she was rapidly losing control of her sound finances. While designing a specific policy for Great Britain, Adam Smith wrote a book that referred in its title to the 'nation' in the plural. Remarkably enough, Adam Smith approached this fundamental question of state finances in conjunction with the 'wealth' of nations by way of a comparative historical and institutional perspective:

> In China, besides, in Indostan, and in several other governments of Asia, the revenue of the sovereign arises almost altogether from a land-tax or land-rent, which rises or falls

with the rise and fall of the annual produce of the land. The great interest of the sovereign, therefore, his revenue, is in such countries necessarily and immediately connected with the cultivation of the land, with the greatness of its produce, and with the value of its produce. . . But the revenue of the sovereign does not, in any part of Europe, arise chiefly from a land-tax or land-rent. In all the great kingdoms of Europe, perhaps, the greater part of it may ultimately depend upon the produce of the land: But that dependency is neither so immediate, nor so evident. In Europe, therefore, the sovereign does not feel himself so directly called upon to promote the increase, both in quantity and value, of the produce of the land, or, by maintaining good roads and canals, to provide the most extensive market for that produce (Smith, II, 1976, p. 252).

Hence Smith sees the motive behind his inquiry as the specification of policies that can raise simultaneously both the revenue of the sovereign and the wealth of the nation, and can thus come to terms with the above peculiarity of Europe.

It is one thing to argue that the more obscure and often neglected books of *The Wealth of Nations* develop a historical and institutional comparative approach, it is quite another to demonstrate that this methodology penetrates deep into the First Book noted for its allegedly 'theoretical' substance. As early as in his discussion of the profits of stock in the First Book, Smith (I, 1976, p. 106) underscored the way in which an institutional setup framed economic performance:

China seems to have been long stationary, and had probably long ago acquired the full complement of riches which is consistent with the nature of its laws and institutions. But this complement may be much inferior to what, with other laws and institutions, the nature of its soil, climate, and situation might admit of.

Not only does this statement acknowledge that all optimization takes place within the constraint of an institutional framework,[7] but it also suggests a comparative static analysis of alternative institutional setups. Another case that emphasizes how great a difference an institutional setup can in fact make is where Smith pursues a comparative institutional analysis of the governance structures of the British dominions:[8] 'The difference between the genius of the British constitution which protects and governs North America, and that of the mercantile company which oppresses and domineers in the East Indies, cannot perhaps be better illustrated than by the different state of those countries' (Ibid., p. 82). Therefore, for Adam Smith of *The Wealth of Nations*, institutions mattered. Whereas neoclassical mainstream approaches deny both the existence and the significance of institutions, Adam Smith parted ways with them to demonstrate the usefulness of comparative institutional analysis.

Having noted the status of institutions in Adam Smith's analysis, we should further elaborate the role attributed to them. For Smith, institutions were in general relatively flexible. While they were flexible, they were by no means infinitely elastic. Had they been infinitely elastic, this would amount to assuming them away in the neoclassical manner.[9] It is precisely because institutions are less than fully elastic that they make a difference. Because he noted with certainty that institutions were nowhere fully elastic, the institutional component of Adam Smith's economic analysis is indispensable.

Whereas institutional economists usually emphasize the relative rigidity of institutions that constrain the otherwise dynamic economy, Adam Smith explored the relative flexibility of institutions. This was so because he was interested in the problematic of the so-called 'transition'. In principle, there can be two options, either a gradual transition characterized by an institutional continuity or a discontinuous transition that comes with an institutional rupture. Adam Smith's conception of the 'transition' needs to be problematized *vis-a-vis* these two alternatives. On the whole, because Smith emphasized the flexibility instead of the rigidity of institutions, one tends to think that he opted for the likelihood of a gradual transition.[10] It is only when the institutions display an insurmountable rigidity that one would witness a breaking-point characteristic of discontinuous transition. We know that Adam Smith sought to accommodate a nascent market economy within the existing framework of British institutions. On the whole, he believed that the British institutions were flexible enough to tolerate to a greater degree the 'natural system of perfect liberty'. It would be a mistake to generalize the Smithian emphasis on the flexibility of British institutions of his time to all institutions as some have tended to do so.[11] Adam Smith was well aware that the British institutions he faced were either the products of, or deeply affected by, 'the Revolution', better known as the Glorious Revolution (1688) to us (Smith, II, 1976, pp. 49; 366; 447; 483).[12] As such, an institutional rupture had already taken place prior to the late eighteenth-century quest for the further liberalization of the economic sphere.

The Smithian conception of 'transition' deserves a closer scrutiny. Adam Smith did identify the economic system of his time as a commercial or mercantile system that would hopefully change further in a liberal direction. However, he did not conceive a full transition to the 'natural system of perfect liberty'. In fact, the 'natural system of perfect liberty' in the Smithian discourse is pretty much an ideal construct that can never be attained and yet serves as a point of reference for the evaluation of the actual situation. Smith did provide an image of this ideal construct as early as in the First Book:

> In a country which had acquired its full complement of riches, where in every particular branch of business there was the greatest quantity of stock that could be employed in it, as the ordinary rate of profit would be very small, so the usual market rate of interest which could be afforded out of it, would be so low as to render it impossible for any but the wealthiest people to live upon the interest of their money. All people of small or middling fortunes would be obliged to superintend themselves the employment of their own stocks. It would be necessary that *almost every man should be a man of business*, or engage in some sort of trade. The province of Holland seems to be *approaching* near this state (I, 1976, p. 108, emphases added).

The ideal construct also provides a limit that ought to be approached by way of appropriate economic policies. However, the critical question remains: Can the 'natural system of perfect liberty' ever be attained? It is only if it can be, that we can speak of a proper 'transition'. Otherwise, what is at issue would be, at the most, a process of prolonged adaptation. 'To expect, indeed, that the freedom of trade should ever be entirely restored in Great Britain, is as absurd as to expect that an Oceana or Utopia should ever be established in it. Not only the prejudices of the public, but what is much more unconquerable, the private interests of many individuals, irresistibly oppose it' (Ibid., p. 493). Because Smith qualifies free trade as an irreproachable utopia given the existing forms of instituted power in the hands of the special interests (II, 1976, p. 425), but especially, the 'monopolizing spirit of merchants and manufacturers' (I, 1976, p. 519) what is at issue is not a transition -proper but a gradual adaptation. In fact the impossibility of a full transition is further secured by the self-reinforcing distortions of the mercantile regime. 'Such are the unfortunate effects of all the regulations of the mercantile system! They not only introduce very dangerous disorders into the state of the body politic, but disorders which it is often difficult to remedy, without occasioning, for a time at least, still greater disorders' (II, 1976, pp. 120-21). Once on a mercantilist path, an economic system has a tendency to remain so due to the cumulative vicious effects of being on that very path. As such, the possibility of a full-fledged transition becomes at the best a remote possibility in the course of time. The implicit path-dependency argument we encounter here has, in fact, further important repercussions within the entire *corpus* of the Smithian analysis.

According to Adam Smith, 'the natural course of things' would presuppose a growing surplus in the agricultural sector leading to the deepening of a division of labor and the extension of the market, stimulating specialization in manufactures, the concomitant growth of towns, and eventually foreign trade. Within the Smithian natural order of things, therefore, agriculture would rank first among the sectors of the economy as an engine of growth. Adam Smith developed one of his most original arguments in this context.[13] He insisted that Europe presented a counter-example to this natural course of development and devoted Book III and IV to the explanation of this paradox:

> Agriculture, therefore, is almost every-where capable of absorbing a much greater capital than has ever yet been employed in it. What circumstances in the policy of Europe have given the trades which are carried on in towns so great an advantage over that which is carried on in the country, that private persons frequently find it more for their advantage to employ their capitals in the most distant carrying trades of Asia and America, than in the improvement and cultivation of the most fertile fields in their own neighbourhood...[?] (I, 1976, p. 397).

According to Smith, institutions were responsible for the deviation from 'the natural course of things'. In other words, institutions had been effective enough to subvert the power of the natural tendency: 'Had human institutions therefore, never disturbed the natural course of things, the progressive wealth and increase of the towns would, in every political society, be consequential, and in proportion to the improvement and cultivation of the territory or country' (Ibid, p. 404).[14] The cumulative effect of institutions has been to force Europe onto a path other than that of the natural course of things:

> But though this natural order of things must have taken place in some degree in every such society, it has, in all the modern states of Europe, been, in many respects *entirely inverted*. The foreign commerce of some of their cities has introduced all their finer manufactures, or such as were fit for distant sale; and manufactures and foreign commerce together, have given birth to the principal improvements of agriculture. The manners and customs which the nature of their original government introduced, and which remained after that government was greatly altered, necessarily forced them into this *unnatural* and *retrograde* order (Ibid., pp. 405-06, emphases added).

According to Smith, the fall of the Roman Empire under the impact of the barbarians was a historic turning-point (Ibid., p. 445) that put the institutions of Europe on a track other than that of the natural state of things. Hence, historical and institutional perversity of Europe extended as a chain from this historic date, 'the third great revolution in the history of mankind' (II, 1976, p. 227) all the way down to the mercantile 'policy of Europe' that systematically distorted the allocation of resources in violation of the natural system of perfect liberty. By alluding to the 'natural' alternative to which both the developments in the North American colonies (I, 1976, p. 441)-immune from the inhibiting European institutional brakes-and the historical path taken by China (Ibid., p. 142; II, 1976, p. 201), as well as the heritage of European Antiquity (II, 1976, pp. 204-5) approximated better, Adam Smith made a further case for European exceptionalism starting with the post-Roman period.[15]

At the bottom line, even if all counterproductive policies were given up and legislation repealed (contrary to what common sense suggests in the light of his own arguments enlisted above), Adam Smith believed that his ideal construct would come into effect naturally if only it could: 'All systems either of preference or of restraint, therefore, being thus completely taken away, the obvious and simple system of natural liberty establishes itself of its own accord' (Ibid., p. 208). In other words, for Adam Smith, the cumulative effect of historical and institutional factors was to block this otherwise natural tendency. In the light of this fact, we can speak of a dualist strain in Adam Smith's thought.[16] On the one side, there is the argument that, had things been left to their own, the market economy would have emerged naturally, hence the neoclassical dimension of his legacy. On the other side, the argument that things have not been left, and cannot be ever left, to their own. This is so, thanks to the inevitability of history and institutions by way of which we find ourselves on a path dependency within the parameters of which we can at best strive to approximate to a market economy, hence the institutionalist dimension.

A Polanyi-esque Epilogue

It is precisely at the above point that Karl Polanyi differs sharply from Adam Smith. To put it differently, the most important contrast among Smith and Polanyi was that Smith believed that there existed a natural tendency towards the realization of a market system,-had it not been for the institutional factors that intervened,-whereas Polanyi insisted that the market society was itself artificial and instituted and could never have come about by and of itself: 'There was nothing natural about *laissez-faire*; free markets could never have come into being merely by allowing things to take their course' (Polanyi, 1944, p. 139).

The one single most important contribution Karl Polanyi made to institutional analysis is to argue forcefully that the market itself is as much an institutionalized phenomenon. Other approaches to institutional analysis have also deviated sharply from the neoclassical mainstream by bringing to the foreground the role of various institutions on the economy. For example, the Austrian School in economics has been particularly fecund as far as the institutional dimension of economic processes is concerned partly because of its historic affinity with the German Historical School. However, the litmus test of institutional economics should be conceived as whether or not the market itself is seen as an institution. In this respect, Karl Polanyi occupies one end of the spectrum by arguing that 'the market economy is an institutional structure' (Ibid., p. 37) that should serve as a center of gravity for an institutional economic analysis. The Austrians occupy the opposite end, precisely because they maintain a fundamental difference between the market which they see as a 'spontaneous order' that forms the antithesis of everything else that is categorically institutional.[17]

In juxtaposition to the self-image of the liberal mainstream, for Karl Polanyi matters had run a different course:

> The road to the free market was opened and kept open by an enormous increase in continuous, centrally organized and controlled interventionism. To make Adam Smith's 'simple and natural liberty' compatible with the needs of a human society was a most complicated affair. Witness the complexity of the provisions in the innumerable enclosure laws; the amount of bureaucratic control involved in the administration of the New Poor Laws which for the first time since Queen Elizabeth's reign were effectively supervised by central authority; or the increase in governmental administration entailed in the meritorious task of municipal reform. And yet all these strongholds of governmental interference were erected with a view to the organizing of some simple freedom--such as that of land, labor, or municipal administration. Just as, contrary to expectation, the invention of labor-saving machinery had not diminished but actually increased the uses of human labor, the introduction of free markets, far from doing away with the need for control, regulation, and intervention, enormously increased their range. Administrators had to be constantly on the watch to ensure the free working of the system. Thus even those who wished most ardently to free the state from all unnecessary duties, and whose whole

philosophy demanded the restriction of state activities, could not but entrust the self-same state with the new powers, organs, and instruments required for the establishment of *laissez-faire* (Ibid., pp. 140-41).

At this stage, a closer investigation of the constituents of Karl Polanyi's understanding of the transition is in order. In fact, Polanyi preferred to speak of a 'transformation' in place of 'transition'. He characterized both end-points of the market society as transformations, the latter, he named the 'great transformation' as in the name of his book, and the former he characterized as follows: 'The transformation to this system from the earlier economy is so complete that it resembles more the metamorphosis of the caterpillar than any alteration that can be expressed in terms of continuous growth and development' (Ibid., p. 42).

Polanyi conceived the pre-transition formation as a society where economic activities were inseparably embedded within a social whole (Ibid., p. 57) motivated towards the fulfillment of human livelihood needs. With the coming of the great expansion in productive powers following the Industrial Revolution[18] there occurred a major leap characterized by a structural discontinuity. There emerged a market society where the logic of market transactions dictated the entire reorganization of the economy, politics, and whatever had remained in wounded form of the once all-inclusive society. The essential point to underscore is that a discontinuity in the transition is not only a historic fact but also a logical necessity because we have before us two contradictory logics, namely the logic of subsistence in the former and the logic of gain in the latter (Ibid., p. 41). The market society was distinguished from all other epochs of history, in both the past and the future, in so far as it represented an exception where the economy was disembedded from the social and furthermore assumed a determining influence. For Polanyi, market society as such is 'a distinct stage', 'a singular departure' (Ibid., p. 71), an exception (Ibid., p. 249), in fact, a parenthesis in the history of industrial civilization (Ibid., p. 5).

Polanyi insisted that the exceptionalism of the market society was due to the spread of the logic of market exchange to the domain of three 'fictitious commodities', labour, land, and money. Whereas in reality these were unlike other commodities in so far as their supply was not determined by the demand for them, they were treated as if they were no different from any commodity, hence the fiction:

> The crucial point is this: labor, land, and money are essential elements of industry; they also must be organized in markets; in fact, these markets form an absolutely vital part of the economic system. But labor, land, and money are obviously *not* commodities; the postulate that anything that is bought and sold must have been produced for sale is emphatically untrue in regard to them. In other words, according to the empirical definition of a commodity they are not commodities. Labor is only another name for a human activity which goes with life itself, which in its turn is not produced for sale but for entirely different reasons, nor can the activity be detached from the rest of life, be stored or mobilized; land is only another name for nature, which is not produced by man; actual money, finally, is merely a token of purchasing power which, as a rule, is not produced at

all, but comes into being through the mechanism of banking or state finance. None of them is produced for sale. The commodity description of labor, land, and money is entirely fictitious (Ibid., p. 72).

Because the substance of a fictitious commodity defied characterization as a commodity, a reaction was bound to take place. This was most clearly forthcoming in the case of labour, the live agent among the three. Whereas the emergence of a free labour market had come about in a most prolonged and painful way, once in effect, labour resistance was soon to manifest itself. Hence a market society, by its very process of expansion cultivated the seeds of its own destruction: 'While *laissez-faire* economy was the product of deliberate state action, subsequent restrictions on laissez-faire started in a spontaneous way. *Laissez-faire* was planned; planning was not' (Ibid., p. 141).

As such, there exists an asymmetry between the transition to, and the transition from, a market society even if both are equally 'transformations' of a substance. The first came about by way of political and economic choice as well as determination on the part of its beneficiaries,[19] and a historic rupture whereas the second is inevitable and spontaneous. This raises at first sight the possibility that the transition from a market society can well be gradual and continuous. However, let us not ignore that a full inversion of the causality between the logic of the market and logic of social organization so as to re-embed the economy in society may require more than a mere flexibility of the institutional pattern.

Towards a Theory of Intersections

In attempting to bring together Adam Smith's and Karl Polanyi's approaches to the 'transition' in a constructive engagement, we should remind ourselves that both authors wrote about the 'long nineteenth century'. However, Smith wrote about it in advance whereas Polanyi wrote about it after the close of the period. This was bound to make a difference. Where Adam Smith anticipated a continuity in transition as adaptation, Karl Polanyi discovered *ex post* a discontinuity. For Adam Smith 'the natural system of perfect liberty' was an utopia too good to be realized on earth given the role of history and institutions. For Karl Polanyi, having once come into effect, market system had proven itself to be too poor an utopia to be entertained (Ibid., pp. 102; 150) and could not survive for long under any circumstances. It was an utopia gone sour and one could at best discard it for good (Ibid., p. 258). These two contradictory views on the utopia has, once again, to do with the relative position in time of the authors *vis-a-vis* the market society characteristic of the 'long nineteenth century'.

Both Adam Smith and Karl Polanyi believed that the market system was artificial. Even if Smith referred to it as 'natural', by acknowledging that it had never existed and was most unlikely to exist in its pure form, he inadvertently disclosed its essentially artificial nature. Whereas for Smith, the market system was unlikely to come into existence because of historical and institutional factors, for Polanyi, having once come into existence, the market system was bound to disappear as it could not survive without generating the kind of institutional supports which were detrimental to it in the long term.

The legacy of institutions dictates the parameters within which one could opt for a transitional strategy. They will not only slow down the process of transition, but depending on their flexibility, can dictate the actual course the transition will take, whether by way of a gradual adaptation or radical rupture. It is no coincidence that a leading Hungarian economist enlisted the crucial role of institutions among the prospective determinants of the form of transition:

> The new system inherits the old network of *institutions*: the specific structure and multiple-level hierarchy of the state apparatus, the set of legal regulations, and so on. All these have developed by a decades-long process of evolution in which the old system selected from the possible forms according to its needs. The new regime does not want to employ the Leninist formula of starting to build the new by ruthless destruction of the old; it aims at a peaceful and smooth transition. For that very reason, the old institutions may hamper the development of the new system for a long time. It takes a good while for the new institutions to evolve (Kornai, 1992, p. 578).

Polanyi's discussion of the 'great transformation' (Polanyi, 1944, pp. 3; 227) as the transition under way from the market society in the 1930's, reflects his view that the system had come to an 'institutional deadlock' (Ibid., p. 237) that could only be transcended by radical political and economic departures rather than gradual adjustment.[20] It may well be the case that the East European countries which had undertaken much reform previous to the transition, a flexible gradualist adjustment is a realistic option, whereas for the other countries a chaotic break with the past is inevitable.

In the light of the above discussion, the question of the prolonged 'transition' from a market society takes on a new form and coincides with a much more profound transition of world historic significance (Hopkins & Wallerstein *et. al.*, 1996). It also encompasses the long time ongoing search for establishing a flexible and working balance among market, reciprocity, and redistribution in policy and developing a broader analytical framework in theory:

> A critical survey of the catallactic definitions of trade, money and market should make available a number of concepts which form the raw material of the social sciences in their economic aspect. The bearing of this recognition on questions of theory, policy and outlook should be viewed in the light of the gradual institutional transformation that has been in progress since the First World War. Even in regard to the market system itself, the market as the sole frame of reference is somewhat out of date. Yet, as should be more clearly realized than it sometimes has been in the past, the market cannot be superseded as a general frame of reference unless the social sciences succeed in developing a wider frame

of reference to which the market itself is referable (Polanyi, 1957, pp. 269-70).

Each of the three modes, namely, market, reciprocity, and redistribution entail a different logic. At the same time, each remains less than effective alone in coming to terms with the re-constitution of a society where economic activities would once again be subordinated to social ends. It is no coincidence that the communist experience carries the legacy of replacing market with hierarchical redistribution with little room for horizontal reciprocity. A wholesome transition in reverse could prove equally fatal. It is indeed necessary to shift some economic prerogative from the over-burdened and dysfunctional state to the market. However this agenda should not overshadow the more fundamental problem of how to re-dress the balance between state and civil society while the latter attends to be reconstructed from scratch.[21] In this context, a further warning note resonant with the fundamental institutional lessons of Smith and Polanyi is in order:

> The weak institutional capacities of the state negatively impact prospects for a quick and smooth transition. Establishing market-supporting institutions and stabilizing the economy paradoxically call for a strong state, albeit one using its powers in a different way and to a different purpose than its communist predecessor. Only the state can provide a legal and regulatory infrastructure, assuring the enforcement of contracts and the security of private property rights, which is indispensable to the development of the private sector. Moreover, the lack of a constitutional design outlining the rights and responsibilities of the levels of general government may undermine public finance and the state's ability to supply services. Weak institutional capacity creates an environment conducive to corruption and both organized and unorganized crime (Kaminski, 1996, p. 5).

Neglecting the transformation of the state, and replacing redistribution entirely with the market, without developing at the same time structures of social reciprocity can be tantamount to taking the risk to spend the night in Adam Smith's 'crazy house' that could fall any moment.

Notes

1. The better examples of the response to the intellectual challenge posed by the fall of the Berlin Wall (Blackburn, 1991; Nove, 1991; Kornai, 1992; and Roemer, 1994) have unfortunately been somewhat obscured by the more popular literature.
2. A very interesting example by a leading economist that purports to take note of the lessons of history by comparing the dismemberment of the Soviet Union with the end of the Austro-Hungarian Empire deserves particular attention in this context (Dornbusch, 1994).
3. Lack of a transitional strategy has led to shock therapy prescriptions in Russia with dire implications for political stability (Kotz & Weir, 1997, pp. 161-199).
4. The transition from feudalism to capitalism has since then given rise to a whole body of literature summed up conveniently under the heading of the Dobb-Sweezy debate

(Sweezy et. al., 1978), later continued as a polemic against André Gunder Frank's dependency theory of Latin American underdevelopment (Laclau, 1979). Among the various slightly displaced follow-ups, the so-called Brenner debate occupies a special place (Aston & Philpin, 1987).

5. In this chapter we will maintain a distinction between 'commercial society' as in this context and the 'commercial society' which Smith used interchangeably with 'mercantile society'. Whenever we do not use the term 'mercantile society' it should be clear that we use 'commercial society' not in the Smithian but loose sense. Quite clearly, in the Smithian case, even if mercantilism were to be transcended, we would still remain within the confines of a commercial society as a broader category.

6. Ronald Coase ,who has exerted a major influence on the New Institutional Economics, has already brought to light the transaction-costs dimension of Adam Smith's analysis of the emergence of money (Coase, 1991, p. 231). In a similar way, Smith implied the advantages in the reduction of enforcement costs of contracts (Smith, I, 1976, p. 107). Furthermore, there are many instances where Smith emphasized the role of 'trust' (Ibid., pp. 55; 118), a must for some contemporary institutionalist inquiries that choose to emphasize the-less-than-state structures of regulation from within civil society. Our purpose in this work is not to dwell on such instances at length but move on to the relevance of the broader institutional framework. Half way along this course we meet the entire digression on the Bank of Amsterdam (Ibid., pp. 503-13) that can be interpreted as a study in institutional innovation.

7. Even before in the text, under the discussion of the wages of labour: 'China has been long one of the richest, that is, one of the most fertile, best cultivated, most industrious, and most populous countries in the world. It seems, however, to have been long stationary... It had perhaps, even long before his time, acquired that full complement of riches which *the nature of its laws and institutions permits it to acquire*'. (Smith, I, 1976, p. 80 emphasis added).

8. In a similar way, Adam Smith underscores the comparative superiority of British political institutions over their French, Spanish, and Portuguese counterparts for the improvement and cultivation of the land in the Americas (Smith, II, 1976, p. 83).

9. Douglas North has noted this situation: 'If institutions existed in the zero transaction cost framework, then history would not matter; a change in relative prices or preferences would induce an immediate restructuring of institutions to adjust efficiently...' (North, 1990, p. 93).

10. In fact, one piece of evidence for the gradualist caution of Adam Smith exists in his discussion of the liberalization of trade 'Humanity may in this case require that the freedom of trade should be restored only by slow gradations, and with a good deal of reserve and circumspection. Were those high duties and prohibitions taken away all at once, cheaper foreign goods of the same kind might be poured so fast into the home market, as to deprive all at once many thousands of our people of their ordinary employment and means of subsistence. The disorder which this would occasion might no doubt be very considerable'. (Smith, I, 1976, p. 491).

11. Adam Smith's *Wealth of Nations* was welcomed by a host of absolutist monarchies within the periphery of Europe extending from Portugal and Spain to Russia and the Ottoman Empire. Those who enjoyed political power in these states identified in the Smithian policy prescription a means for accommodating a nascent market economy

within the context of an *ancien regime* by way of which the political establishment could save the day. The point is that in Britain, the *ancien régime* had already been overturned by the Glorious Revolution and succeeded by a more conducive form of government, a shift that Adam Smith took note of.

12. The critical role of the Glorious Revolution in paving the way towards the accelerated growth of the English economy within an efficient institutional setup is also emphasized within the context of New Institutional Economics (North, 1990, pp. 138-39).

13. Ever since Adam Smith, there have been two major approaches to the development of capitalism one stemming from Smith's interpretation of European history and the other more in tune with the characterization of the 'natural' path that was not taken. It is no coincidence that the approach developed by, among others, Henri Pirenne, Paul Sweezy, and Immanuel Wallerstein has a strong affinity with the former formulation of Adam Smith to which they owe much of their originality (Brenner, 1977).

14. To make his point forcefully, Smith repeated his argument within pages: 'If human institutions had never thwarted those natural inclinations, the towns could no-where have increased beyond what the improvement and cultivation of the territory in which they were situated could support...'(Smith, I, 1976, p. 402).

15. This argument ties up nicely with Smith's relatively favourable yet brief discussion of the agricultural system (Physiocracy) as 'the nearest approximation to the truth' (Smith, II, 1976, p. 199) in comparison with his lengthy devastating critique of the mercantile system. Smith noted that the agricultural system existed only in speculation (Ibid., p. 182), much like his ideal construct of a market economy under the rubric of 'natural system of perfect liberty'.

16. *Wealth of Nations* offers fertile ground for arguments of dualism in general (Screpanti and Zamagni, 1995, p. 62-65).

17. Polanyi, while summing up the nineteenth-century orthodoxy concerning the natural tendency towards the emergence and spread of markets, continued to refer to them as 'natural institutions' (Polanyi, 1944, p. 249), and by doing so place them into a subcategory of institutions instead of defining them as the opposite of institutions in the Austrian sense.

18. For Polanyi, the Industrial Revolution represents a watershed in the history of civilization, and the market society its first stage: 'But how shall this Revolution itself be defined? What was its basic characteristic? Was it the rise of the factory towns, the emergence of slums, the long working hours of children, the low wages of certain categories of workers, the rise in the rate of population increase, or the concentration of industries? We submit that all these were merely incidental to one basic change, the establishment of market economy, and that the nature of this institution cannot be fully grasped unless the impact of the machine on a commercial society is realized. We do not intend to assert that the machine caused that which happened, but we insist that once elaborate machines and plant were used for production in a commercial society, the idea of a self-regulating market was bound to take shape' (Polanyi, 1944, p. 40).

19. Once again, Polanyi made his point clear: 'It was not realized that the gearing of markets into a self-regulating system of tremendous power was not the result of any inherent tendency of markets towards excrescence, but rather the effect of highly

artificial stimulants administered to the body social in order to meet a situation which was created by the no less artificial phenomenon of the machine' (Polanyi, 1944, p. 57).
20. It is our contention that whereas Polanyi's identification of the nature and dynamics of market society was in many ways correct, his dating of the process exclusively to 'the long nineteenth century' and mapping of it almost exclusively to England (Polanyi, 1944, p. 30) was erroneous.
21. Fortunately, there exists a profoundly original heritage in Eastern Europe that offers valuable guidelines for the further reconstruction of civil society. The political philosophy of Istvan Bibo is one such exemplary case (Berki, 1992). The general problematic of civil society in the aftermath of the collapse of the Berlin Wall has been expressed in the prolific writings of Ernest Gellner (Gellner, 1994).

References

Aston, T. H. and Philpin, C. H. E., eds. (1987), *The Brenner Debate: Agrarian Class Structure and Economic Development in Pre-Industrial Europe*, Cambridge University Press, Cambridge.
Berki, R. N. (1992), 'The Realism of Moralism: The Political Philosophy of Istvan Bibo', *History of Political Thought*, vol. XIII, no. 3, pp. 513-534.
Blackburn, Robin (1991), *After the Fall: The Failure of Communism and the Future of Socialism*, Verso, London.
Brenner, Robert (1977), 'The Origins of Capitalist Development: A Critique of Neo-Smithian Marxism', *New Left Review*, vol. 104, pp. 25-92.
Coase, Ronald (1991), '1991 Nobel Lecture: The Institutional Structure of Production', in Oliver E. Williamson and Sidney G. Winter, eds., *The Nature of the Firm: Origins, Evolution, and Development*, Oxford University Press, New York.
Dornbusch, Rudiger (1994,) *Post-Communist Monetary Problems: Lessons from the End of the Austro-Hungarian Empire*, Institute for Contemporary Studies Press, San Francisco, California.
Gellner, Ernest (1994), *Conditions of Liberty: Civil society and its Rivals*, Allen Lane, New York.
Hopkins, Terence K. and Wallerstein, Immanuel, et. al. (1996), *The Age of transition: Trajectory of the World-System, 1945-2025*, Zed Books, London.
Kaminski, Bartlomiej (1996), *Economic Transition in Russia and the New States of Eurasia*, M. E. Sharpe, London.
Kornai, Janos (1992), *The Socialist System: The Political Economy of Communism*, Clarendon Press, Oxford.
Kotz, David and Weir, Fred (1997), *Revolution from Above: The Demise of the Soviet System*, Routledge, London.
Laclau, Ernesto (1979), 'Feudalism and Capitalism in Latin America', in his *Politics and Ideology in Marxist Theory*, Verso, London, pp. 15-50.
North, Douglas (1990), *Institutions, Institutional Change and Economic Performance*, Cambridge University Press, Cambridge.
Nove, Alec (1991), *The Economics of Feasible Socialism Revisited*, Academic Press, New York.

Özveren, Eyüp (1993), 'Considerations on the Adam Smith Question', *METU Studies in Development*, vol. 20, (1-2), pp. 151-167.
Polanyi, Karl (1957), 'The Economy as Instituted Process', in Karl Polanyi, Conrad M. Arensberg, and Harry W. Pearson, eds., *Trade and Market in Early Empires: Economies in History and Theory*, Free Press, New York, pp. 243-270.
Polanyi, Karl (1944), *The Great Transformation: the Political and Economic Origins of Our Time*, Beacon Press, Boston.
Roemer, John E. (1994), *A Future for Socialism*, Verso, London.
Schumpeter, Joseph A. (1954), *A History of Economic Analysis*, Oxford University Press, Oxford.
Screpanti, Ernesto and Zamagni, Stefano (1995), *An Outline of the History of Economic Thought*, Oxford University Press, Oxford.
Smith, Adam (1976) [1776], *An Inquiry into the Nature and Causes of the Wealth of Nations*, The University of Chicago Press, Chicago.
Smith, Adam (1976) [1759], *Theory of Moral Sentiments*, Liberty Classics, Indianapolis.
Sweezy, Paul *et. al.* (1978), *The Transition from Feudalism to Capitalism*, Verso, London.

Chapter Five

The Money Fiction and Central Banking

William C. Schaniel*

The current Asian financial crises makes discussions of the commodity fiction of money and of the roles of central banks propitious. The current crises have roots in the same fiction that has fuelled financial crises and worsened depressions since the Napoleonic Wars. This fiction is that money – along with land and labour – is a commodity analogous to commodities produced in factories and mines or on farms. It is not. It is 'produced' by the policies of governments and by social acceptance of the processes used in making payments.

Each fictitious commodity has its own characteristics: land is the product of millennia of geological evolution; labour is human beings doing things; money is the *social process* of engaging in and discharging financially stated obligations. The rules defining how, when, where, and what can be used to incur and/or discharge obligations define what money is, and they are different in different situations.

In the commodification of the factors of production, the commodification of each reinforced the commodification of the other factors and increased the range of obligations that could be incurred and discharged by the use of money. For example, in looking at the commodification of land during the first transformation, one is inclined to focus on the enclosures of common land and the assignment of the rights of alienation. Yet the same events, when analysed from the perspective of money, were the monetization of relationships within the parishes. The enclosure movement and the commercialization of land resulted in new obligations that could be incurred or discharged by the use of money. This increase in the range of obligations that could be transacted, for both expanded the range of markets and the importance of money.

The Money Fiction

Two hundred years ago people thought of gold and silver as money (and of petty coins as money because they were closely attached to coins minted of the precious metals). But already other acceptable means of payment were growing in importance: banknotes, and then payment by checks on demand deposits.[1] These could be accommodated to the view that precious metals were the 'real money' if they could be closely attached to the precious metals. The gold standard was the great attempt to do so.

The gold standard began its career with the British Coinage Act of 1816 and when, in 1821, the Bank of England began buying and selling gold at a fixed price in pounds sterling. It was given ideological expression by the Bank Charter Act of 1844, which required the Bank of England to regulate the credit it advanced in proportion to its holdings of gold.[2] However, nineteenth century financial history is not so much marked by the maintenance of the gold standard as by the responses to a series of financial crises when the convertibility of currency for gold was suspended to save the liquidity of the economy.

In principle, under the gold standard, an export surplus would result in an inflow of gold – and therefore of money – while an import surplus would result in the outflow of gold. The flows of gold raised or lowered the money supply and thus inflated or deflated the domestic price level, which in turn increased imports and decreased exports, or vice-versa. Actually, not much gold flowed internationally. Rising interest rates induced international financiers to keep funds in the country suffering a trade deficit, while higher interest rates also reduced output and thus domestic demand – which is to say, the system worked on output, employment, and income rather than on prices. The spread of financial crises and depressions from country to country showed how deleterious to national economies the efforts to adhere to the gold standard could be.

Central banks were part of the response of society to the vicissitudes of the self-regulating market system. They developed their modern functions to shield society from the effects of the fiction that money could (or should) be treated like any other commodity.[3] Financial panics showed that the sudden withdrawal of gold from even healthy banks required them to call in loans, or suspend specie payment, and that the fall in the value of financial assets used as collateral led to further declines in liquidity. During the mid-nineteenth century the Bank of England developed techniques to assist solvent but illiquid banks to survive financial crises.[4] Thus, in Walter Bagehot's felicitous phrase, the Bank of England became the lender of last resort. After the First World War central banks failed in the attempt to re-establish the gold standard, and by 1933 it had disappeared.[5] (The United States continued to express the value of its dollar in gold and bought gold, but since it would not sell gold on demand, there was no gold standard.) The Bretton Woods system created a new international standard, often called a gold/dollar standard but, in its actual operation, it was a US dollar standard. Central bank policy then evolved to efforts to manage the means of payments so that full employment and price stability were achieved -and, in association with the fiscal policies of governments, these policies worked fairly well.

Today, no money is attached to a precious metal. Instead, national monies are attached to reserves or to discounting facilities at a central bank. Internationally they are attached to reserves of foreign currencies and to drawing rights at the IMF (only at the discretion of the IMF). But the substance of the fiction continues in the belief that these reserves or rights are parts of a system that is, if not quite self-regulating, fundamentally subject to economic laws alone and independent of social and political systems. Whether it is the Chicago School in the United States recommending that the Federal Reserve provide an annual increase of 3 percent in the money supply or the IMF conditioning credit on compliance with terms that are hard to differentiate from an enforcement of the rules of the gold standard, today's doctrine is that money should be treated *as if it were* a commodity (as a century ago banknotes and demand deposits were treated as if they were gold).

In the financial systems of the more highly developed market economies, most money now exists as processes of payment expressed in banks' accounts. In no sense a physical asset, national monies are the debts of the issuing agencies. There is no stuff, no commodity other than accounting notifications of transfers of funds into and out of accounts. Money is a product of lending by private banks. Monetary policy increases or decreases the ability of financial institutions to make loans, affects the rates of interest in the markets, and tries to maintain the credibility and stability of financial institutions.

A strange point has been reached. The monies of the world are no longer commodities, and nations now have in place central banks and other monetary authorities that can engage in discretionary management of their monetary and financial systems in ways to further broad social aims. Yet, at the same time, these nations and international agencies are adopting the same nineteenth century policies as were pursued when it was believed that money was, or should be, a commodity.[6]

There is no natural order for financial markets, and financial institutions can be designed to meet social or cultural objectives. I turn now to discuss some examples of how this has been and may be done.

Monetary Policies Without Fictions

Access to financial institutions depends upon the rules. Different rules either help or hinder different aims and different groups. Consider, for example, markets for mortgages. In the United States, mortgage markets have undergone a series of dramatic changes since the end of World War II. Saving and loan institutions used to be the primary source of mortgage funds. After World War II, mortgage loans made to war veterans were guaranteed by the federal government. A similar guarantee was later extended to any United States citizen who met a set financial standard. These guaranteed loans were initially bought and sold among financial institutions, and later non-financial institutions were included. A large portion of mortgage loans made by financial institutions in the United States are now sold to third parties.[7] *Mortgage loans have been given advantaged access to financial flows.* These guaranteed loans made home ownership much more widespread. They did, indeed, specifically help veterans, and then others, but they also changed the pattern of property ownership in the United States.

In Japan, in 1993, fifty-two percent of Japanese bank assets were held in institutions that specialized in financing forestry, agriculture, fisheries, and small business.[8] Neither are all interventions in financial markets benign. Arrangements for access to finance were quite different in Indonesia under Suharto: friends and family were helped. This example is certainly not to be recommended as a model, but institutions can be designed and modified to improve the living standard and livelihood of a society.

Instruments of monetary policy unavoidably affect the working of other parts of the economy. There are no neutral monetary policies, nor are there neutral financial structures. Critical elements in the development of financial markets make a financial market deep (easy to find buyers and sellers), broad (a large volume of sales), and resilient (sales are sensitive to changes in prices). The choice of tools for monetary intervention can make one market more liquid than another, can directly favour one class of loans over others, and can direct liquidity to a specific economic sector or institutional group. The Federal Reserve Bank of the United States, the Bank of England, and the Bundesbank have *similar* rhetoric for their monetary policy goals, but each employs *different* instruments. Different groups are advantaged in a range ways by the choice of different instruments. The instruments chosen to serve monetary policy can sponsor specific financial markets, business activities, or sectors of a society. The instruments can be short term or long term, public or private, and can be as narrow as loans for specific activities. Central bank policy will always supplement or serve to sponsor specific financial markets or instruments - it can never be neutral.

In the United Sates, the Federal Reserve conducts monetary policy primarily by buying and selling government notes and long-term bonds.[9] The Federal Reserve's daily buying and selling activities make the market for government securities deep, broad, and resilient. It may be ironic that the central bank of the most ideologically free market country has chosen to make the market for government securities market the centerpiece for providing liquidity to the financial system.

The Bank of England conducts monetary policy with short term loans, primarily business loans.[10] On a daily basis the Bank of England conducts monetary policy through the purchase (and, very occasionally, the sale) of qualified market instruments. Banks requiring liquidity discount, or sell, the short term notes to agents of the Bank of England. Banks must maintain an inventory of qualifying paper. The Bank of England, through its choice of what it will purchase to conduct monetary policy, actively supports short term business lending.

Germany's Bundesbank uses both short term and long term instruments. Banks are limited to a 'standard quota' in the amount that they sell to or discount at the Bundesbank. Additional quotas and special refinancing facilities exist also to fund specific purposes: e.g., loans to small and medium businesses, loans for trade and business activity between the former East Germany and West Germany, and loans to promote exports.[11] The banks that make desired types of loans are given special access to Bundesbank funds.

The Polish agricultural problems presented in the paper by Hake and Neale may be used to illustrate possible policy alternatives of either specialized financial institutions and/or differential financial access. Specialized agricultural banks can be established to provide liquidity. Specific classes of loans can be guaranteed. Some loans for demonstration projects can even be forgiven, wholly or in part. The guarantee eliminates risk of default, allowing lower rates to be charged and making agricultural banking attractive for the financial sector. Differential access can be established for small farms: e.g., the creation of specific financial enterprises to assist small farmers. Policies of specialized institutions can also meet other financial problems of an agricultural sector: for example, loan repayments can be reduced during periods of falling agricultural prices. In addition discount facilities can be established to give incentive to banks to finance loans directly to the agricultural sector. The types of loans discounted, the length of the loans, and the authorized parties to the loans can always be changed to meet changing circumstances.

Here let me emphasize that I am not recommending that Poland adopt the specific institutions that have been developed in the United States. In so far as farmers are producing for the consumption of their own families, they do not generate the cash incomes needed to service or repay loans. This means that financial help to small farmers must be limited by the cash flow into their operations. However, as Polish agriculture becomes more commercialized, the central bank can help the agricultural sector as its needs for liquidity increase, not only absolutely but also relative to other sectors.

Similarly, monetary policy instruments could provide an avenue for the Czech National Bank to inhibit undesired activities of the self-privatized banks and investment groups. The discounting of private bank bills can be used to disadvantage those engaging in undesirable financial conduct. The choice of private bank bills puts banks in direct contact with the central bank or, indirectly, through the central bank's agents. Those banks that do not make appropriate, qualifying loans can be denied access, while those following appropriate policies can given additional access to central bank funds. The ability of a private bank to conduct everyday business would require that it keep a large enough inventory of qualifying securities to maintain liquidity.

Again, let me be clear that the suggestions offered about Polish agriculture and Czech banking are *not* recommendations. The point is that financial institutions and instruments can be organized to fulfill the needs and objectives of society. There is no blueprint for the design of a socially responsible financial structure. The architecture of financial institutions should reflect how the transforming societies value different activities and different kinds of organizations.

Conclusions

Central banks now have a wider range of institutional choice than their early twentieth and nineteenth century counterparts. The choices made in the structure of financial institutions and markets can certainly benefit societies, but they can also do much harm as well. One challenge of the third transformation is to avoid the chaos of the second transformation and to move towards improving the livelihood and lives of the members of each society. One must hope that release from the commodity fiction of money, and from the fiction that economic laws should bind central banks, will allow nations to follow policies that make their financial systems reflect their social objectives.

Notes

* The author is indebted to Walter C. Neale (University of Tennessee) for help on this paper. Also, the analysis in this paper draws upon Walter C. Neale, *Monies in Societies* (San Francisco: Chandler & Sharp Publishers, Inc., 1976). The argument in that book derives in part from discussions among members of the Polanyi group at Columbia University in the late 1950's.

1. Walter C. Neale, *Monies in Societies*, Chandler & Sharp Publishers, Inc., San Francisco, 1976; pp. 49-75.
2. Charles P. Kindleberger, *A Financial History of Western Europe*, 2nd ed., Oxford University Press, Oxford, 1993; pp. 60-63.
3. Karl Polanyi, *The Great Transformation*, Beacon Press, Boston, 1957 (1944), p. 194.
4. Neale, *Monies in Societies*, p. 75.
5. Kindleberger, *A Financial History of Western Europe*, pp. 368-374.
6. There are various central bank publications where this policy argument is made. Paul Volker wrote an autobiographical history of the Bretton Woods System with this theme as the standard for successful policy (Paul Volker and Toyoo Gyohten, *Changing Fortunes*, Times Books, New York, 1992). Two other publications of interest are *Central Banking Issues in Emerging Market-Oriented Economies*, Federal Reserve Bank of Kansas City, Kansas City, KS., 1990) and *Maintaining Financial Stability in a Global Economy*, Federal Reserve Bank of Kansas City, Kansas City, KS, 1997.
7. Lawrence S. Ritter, William L. Silber, and Gregory F. Udell, *Principles of Money, Banking and Financial Markets*, 9th ed., Addison-Wesley, Reading, M.A.,1997, pp. 2-28; 125-126.
8. *Japan Today*. Japanese Information Service, 1997; p. 65.
9. Ann-Marie Meulendyke, *U.S. Monetary Policy and Financial Markets*, Federal Reserve Bank of New York, New York, 1989, p. 153.
10. Mike Buckle, and John Thompson: *The UK financial system: Theory and practice*, 2nd ed., Manchester University Press, Manchester, UK, 1995, pp. 202-208.
11. *The Monetary Policy of the Bundesbank*. Deutsche Bundesbank, Frankfurt, 1995, p. 100.

Chapter Six

Labour: A Fictitious Commodity Needs Instituted Power

Dell Champlin and Ann Jennings

Introduction

Most of the Central and Eastern European transition countries including Poland have been faced with high rates of unemployment, falling wages, increasing inequality and job insecurity. A commonly held view is that these problems in the labour market are the unfortunate but necessary steps in the transition to a market economy (Timar, 1995; Godfrey, 1995). Others argue that the adjustments could be eased by a better choice of economic policies (Murrell, 1995). In both cases, however, the underlying assumption is that these problems are *transitional* or *temporary*, and that ultimately the labour market will operate smoothly and become self-adjusting. This is a familiar notion to labour economists in the United States and Western Europe as well. The existence and desirability of a free labour is taken for granted. The only dispute is over 'how to achieve it'. In other words, all roads lead to Rome, the question is which road to take.

The goal of establishing a 'free market for labour' is so widely accepted that few transition economists have found it necessary to spend much time on it. Even in Poland where trade unions have a long and eventful history, the goal of the free labour market was, at least until recently, embraced as the appropriate, ultimate goal (Blejer, 1995). The purpose of this essay is to take a closer look at the 'free market for labour'. In the first part of the paper, we discuss the key premises of the 'free labour market' concept. We begin with Karl Polanyi's significant observation that labour is not a commodity even though in a market system it is treated 'as if' it were. We then explore James Galbraith's assertion that the free labour market, itself, is fictitious. Indeed, it is not a market at all but what he calls 'a dangerous metaphor' that shapes institutions and guides or misguides economic policy (Galbraith, 1996).

Finally, we address the 'free labour market' as a policy goal. Whether or not such a thing exists or has ever existed, the 'free labour market' nonetheless figures prominently in policy recommendations by neoclassical economists in the US and Western Europe.[1] Essentially the same labour market policies are recommended for *all* economies, whether the country is 'in transition to a market economy' or already there (OECD, 1998). We note that while the phrase, 'free labour market', implies self-regulating, free exchange between buyers and sellers unhindered by coercion or interference from any outside force, the reality is that extensive and continuous state involvement is required to establish and maintain this 'free' market -an insight that we can also trace to Polanyi (1957).

The Free Labour Market

In this section we review briefly what is meant and implied by a 'free market for labour'. To many economists, the meaning of a 'free market for labour' is all too obvious. A market exists whenever a commodity is bought and sold. A 'free' market exists when the price of this commodity is determined by the equilibrium of supply and demand. In addition, the market for labour, like any competitive market, is atomistic. It is the result of individuals making rational and uncoerced decisions to exchange their labour for wages. It is, by definition, 'free'. There are other aspects to the microeconomic theory of labour markets, but the core, ideological elements are found in these two ideas: 1) the notion that labour markets operate as outcomes of free and rational choices; and 2) the notion that the wage is a market price. Microeconomic theory presents this simple story as an explanation not only of how labour markets do function but how they *should* function. A 'free labour market' represents economic efficiency, because a market wage sends the proper signals to the rest of the economy. Any deviation from 'correct' wage levels results in a misallocation of resources. In addition to economic efficiency, the self-regulating labour market is a triumph of individual freedom. It is a hallmark of a liberal, market society.

Economic efficiency and freedom of choice are not found in all markets. They are guaranteed only in the 'free' market which has the virtue of being self-regulating. Self-regulation is the core belief of liberal economic theory and neoliberal doctrine as well. Polanyi recognized the importance of self-regulation to the establishment of a market society. Indeed, when Polanyi refers to a market economy he is referring to a system in which 'order in the production and distribution of goods is entrusted to this self-regulating mechanism' (1957, p. 68). The loss of faith in the idea of self-regulation brought about the Great Transformation in 1933 that Polanyi describes (Sievers, 1991, p.66). It is the revival of the idea of self-regulation that marks the neoliberal transformation that began in the 1970s.

According to liberal theory, self-regulation is crucial, because it means that no outside force is necessary to make the market work. The absence of outside force means absence of coercion or complete economic freedom. Would that it were that simple. Polanyi makes three points that undermine the so-called freedom of the labour market. First, the individual is free to make only one kind of choice: the decision to work for gain or not. Since the alternative 'not to work for gain' means poverty and privation, there is really no choice at all. Polanyi (1957) dates the formation of the free market for labour to 1834, the year that Poor Law Reform in

England brought the Speenham land system to an end. This system of poor relief, enacted in 1795, provided a guaranteed income whether or not an individual was working. The Poor Law Reform Act of 1834 ended wage subsidies and outdoor relief. The truly destitute were provided with the doubtful choice of going into a workhouse, which, according to Polanyi, was 'deliberately made into a place of horror' (1957, p. 102). In short, the free market for labour was created in 1834, because from that moment on workers had no alternative except to work for gain. While the workhouses have gone, the lesson of the Poor Law Reform Act of 1834 remains. As we discuss later in the paper, the very same rhetoric that individuals should have 'no choice' but to work for a wage guides neoliberal policy today.

The second, and perhaps more profound, critique that Polanyi makes of the so-called free labour market is the elevation of gain to the sole motivation for working. A commodity is, by definition, something that is produced for the sole purpose of selling it for gain in a market. Labour is a 'fictitious' commodity, because work is a human endeavour with a variety of motivations and meanings. Market society disregards these other motives and substitutes gain as the only motive. The creation of 'fictitious' commodities is part of what Polanyi referred to as the 'economistic fallacy' (1977). In the self-regulating market, working for gain is synonymous with rationality. All other motivations for working are irrelevant. Any individual who makes choices on any grounds other than gain is behaving irrationally. To Polanyi, the reduction of all human existence to the single motive of material gain was 'as radical as it was fantastic' (1977, p. 14).

> To atomize society and make every individual atom behave according to the principles of economic rationalism would, in a sense, place the whole of human existence, with all its depth and wealth, in the frame of reference of the market. This, of course, would not really do--individuals have personalities and society has a history. Personality thrives on experience and education; action implies passion and risk; life demands faith and belief; history is struggle and defeat, victory and redemption (Polanyi, 1977, p. 14).

The notion that the primary reason for working is material gain has become so ingrained in western society that it is difficult to appreciate or understand other motives. A short example will illustrate. A recent news story reported that a hospital in a poverty stricken, rural area had arranged for indigent patients to 'work off' their hospital bill.[2] Individuals did a variety of things including refurbishing hospital furnishings, arranging flowers, donating hand crafted items, landscaping, and so on. In an interview with the hospital administrator, the news reporter asked how the hospital decided 'how much an hour of knitting blankets or visiting sick children was worth'. The administrator responded that they did not attempt to put a dollar value on an hour's worth of time. This was not a 'barter' system, but a program that 'suited the needs of the community'. The reporter then asked what the hospital did with individuals who 'had no skill'. The hospital administrator responded that 'everyone had a skill'. The entire report was an exercise in miscommunication due to the reporter's difficulty in understanding such a 'non-economistic' system. The reporter finally seemed to conclude that the work the patients did had no value at all, and the hospital was just 'writing off' the losses. In other words, a work arrangement centred around reciprocity rather than market motives was incomprehensible. The reporter's inability to make sense of the hospital's scheme illustrates the extent to which motives other than material gain have been eclipsed from market society.

The choice of self-interest as the sole motive of economic life is not arbitrary, of course. It is the key to the principle of self-regulation. One need only recall the much quoted passage from *The Wealth of Nations* regarding the irrelevance of the 'benevolence of the butcher, the brewer, and the baker' (Smith, 1909, p. 20).[3] Given our alleged natural 'propensity to truck, barter, and exchange one thing for another' (Ibid., p. 19), the whole system is quite automatic. This brings us to Polanyi's third point regarding the free market for labour. Its automaticity ultimately absolves us all of any social responsibility for poverty and privation. Earnings in the labour market are the result of the individual's own, free choices and natural laws. If an individual is poor, he or she has simply made the wrong choices given the current trend of impersonal market forces. Poverty, then, is somewhat like being caught out in the rain. If one is wet, one has only oneself and the weather to blame.[4]

Polanyi spends considerable time in *The Great Transformation* with the problem of poverty. The classical economists after Adam Smith went so far as to make poverty entirely the result of natural law. The iron law of wages alleged that the natural level of wages for the mass of workers was subsistence. According to David Ricardo, any attempt to raise wages above this level was doomed. 'The principle of gravitation is not more certain than the tendency of such laws to change wealth and vigour into misery and weakness... until at last all classes should be infected with the plague of universal poverty' (quoted in Polanyi, 1957, p. 127). The poor could look forward only to a gradual improvement in the socially determined subsistence level. Today economists no longer advance the idea that the poor are doomed to subsistence, but we can still see the influence of natural law in the view that a nation's prosperity can be measured with little regard to income distribution. The 20th century version of Ricardo is that the persistence of poverty in a country as wealthy as the US is due to well-meaning but misguided interference with the market. It is not poverty that is the problem but rather the effort to alleviate it by providing public assistance and distorting incentives (Murray, 1984).

Smith had a different view of poverty and inequality. 'Servants, labourers and workmen of different kinds, make up the far greater part of every great political society.... No society can surely be flourishing and happy, of which the far greater part of the members are poor and miserable' (1909, p. 83). Smith also opposed laws regulating the 'free circulation of labour', but not because the poor were doomed by nature to misery, but rather because he recognized that mercantilist laws benefited employers not workers. Finally, Smith believed that economic growth would ultimately benefit even the poor (Ibid.). Unfortunately, the only one of these ideas to survive intact in neoliberalism is the faith that all individuals will ultimately benefit from economic growth. While at one time this 'rising tide lifts all boats' hypothesis referred to job creation and rising wages, in the 1990s it is more likely to refer to worker participation in stock options and mutual funds (Cramer, 1996). Smith's criticism of government policy has been distorted in neoliberalism from opposition to mercantilist policies that favoured business to a selective opposition to policies that might protect the poor. As we describe later in the paper, policies that 'promote competitiveness' are increasingly common.

Smith's point that no society can be said to be prosperous when the majority of the population is poor has been conveniently removed from liberal ideology. Poverty is now purely an individual failure. The elimination of social responsibility from the problem of poverty is directly traceable to the 'free market for labour' concept. Polanyi argued that the free labour market came into existence when workers were given no choice except to sell their labour for material gain. Poverty results when the individual does not manage to sell his or her labour for a high enough price. In the classical economic theory of Smith or Ricardo, wages are not determined in a market. Only the free labour market places earnings directly on the shoulders of the individual worker. If an individual's earnings are low, he or she is free to choose a higher paying job. If no higher paying job is currently available to the individual, then he or she is free to make the necessary investments in human capital. If an individual has no earnings at all, he or she has evidently chosen not to work for the prevailing market wage. The difficulty, of course, is that such ample economic opportunity exists only in the 'theoretical' free labour market of neoclassical theory.

The responsibilities of the employer toward the worker's welfare are also eliminated by the creation of the free market for labour. The employment relationship is nothing more than a simple transaction. The worker is merely another commodity that has been purchased and whose cost must be minimized in the determination of profit. The employer has no inherent obligation to pay the worker a living wage, to provide opportunity for advancement, to provide education and training, to provide safe working conditions, to provide health insurance or to make financial provisions for the worker's retirement. Employers who do provide some or all of these benefits, do so either because they are obligated to by law or contract or because they freely choose to. In either case, any provision made for the worker beyond the payment of the minimum market wage represents a deviation from the ideal of the self-regulating labour market.

In conclusion, the effect of the self-regulating labour market is to make gain the sole organizing principle of social and economic life. Employers have no responsibility for the welfare of their workers. Society bears no responsibility for poverty and inequality. We are linked only by the single-minded, pursuit of personal gain. In Polanyi's view, anonymous market relationships cannot become the only mode of social integration without eventually stripping individuals of everything that sustains them as human beings. What is bought and sold in labour markets is inseparable from life itself.[5] The effort to establish a self-regulating labour market in the 19th century was an attempt to subordinate all social and economic life to the market. Ultimately the attempt failed, because no society can sustain the distortion of values and social relations required in a self-regulating market system.

The Fictitous Labour Market

Polanyi argued that the establishment of free labour markets in 19th century England provoked a spontaneous, counter movement to protect society from its effects (1957). Thus, for Polanyi, 'interference' in the self-regulating market is not only advisable, it is inescapable. For liberals, of course, this 'outside interference' is neither necessary nor welcome. The extent to which real world labour markets are not, in fact, self-regulating is blamed on incorrect government policies, excessive influence by trade unions, misguided social reformers, and institutional rigidities (Ibid., p. 144-145). Galbraith has a different view regarding this so-called 'outside interference' in the free market for labour. He questions whether the competitive model is even applicable to labour markets. Despite the recognition that most product markets in late 20th century capitalism are dominated by corporations with considerable monopoly power, liberal economists persist in using a simple competitive model to analyse employment and wages. Even in the case of a monopolist in the product market, the firm is assumed to purchase labour in a competitive market. One of the best-selling labour economics textbooks in the US asserts '...we assume that the labour market is perfectly competitive but that one particular firm hiring this type of labour is a monopolist in the sale of its product' (McConnell and Brue, 1995, p. 165). A model of monopsony in the labour market is presented but then dismissed, '... monopsony outcomes are not widespread in the US economy' (Ibid., p. 170). Oligopoly is not even considered.

It is doubtful, however, whether a more serious consideration of monopoly power in labour markets would make much difference in the partial equilibrium world of microeconomic theory. Even a model of labour market monopsony assumes that the firm is facing an independent supply curve of labour. The labour must be assumed to possess a unique skill needed only by the monopsonist, otherwise there would be more than one buyer for the labour. Now the question arises: how did the labour acquire this unique skill that is required only by the monopsonist? It seems reasonable to assume that the worker acquired the skill through on-the job training, internal training or work experience *after* being hired. In addition, the monopsonist might have arranged for the establishment of external training centres. For example, the firm might work with schools and colleges to offer specialized training courses. In either case, it seems clear that the firm was instrumental in *creating its own labour supply*. Without independent supply and demand schedules, the wage cannot be assumed to be determined by market forces. Galbraith's point is that monopoly power is complex and pervasive. It does more than distort wages, it makes the entire partial equilibrium market framework inappropriate. Removing rigidities will not produce a 'free market for labour', nor will assuming that monopoly power is either rare or influences markets only through a downward sloping marginal revenue curve.

> Must we see everything through the delusory prism of the competitive model? Are we really so satisfied with the efficiency of markets? ... Are we prepared to rule the issues of power, monopoly and financial control off the table when we discuss the way incomes are apportioned.... We impoverish the analysis when we do so. We weaken the credibility of the case. And we undermine the correspondence between theory and fact (Galbraith, 1998, p. 37).

Galbraith's second criticism of the free labour market framework is that 'the competitive story is necessarily based on individuals rather than groups' (Ibid., p. 316). Liberal theory treats labour as discrete units of input that are combined in the black box of production with other inputs, and the result is an output. Each individual worker's contribution to the value of this output is the basis for the wage. But, workers are not discrete units of input. Employing more than one worker means that the production process is a group effort. Workers are interdependent. Each individual's contribution to the output is a function of every one else's. Moreover, wage workers are hired into a firm with a particular organizational structure, hierarchy, and customary 'working rules'. These are not attributes of individuals but of the culturally and geographically specific setting in which they work.

The self-evident notion that virtually all wage work is joint production is complicated only inside the limited framework of liberal economic theory. For example, a production worker at an Opel factory in Germany is paid DM 48 per hour, while a worker at the Opel factory in Hungary is paid the equivalent of DM 8 per hour.[6] Since the cars from both factories are being sold in the same European markets, how is this difference in wages explained? An industrial relations analyst would no doubt attribute the difference to the organization of work, the production technology, and the institutional differences between Hungary and Germany. In contrast, the liberal economist would be unable to analyse any of these within the framework of the supply and demand model, because the organization of work, the production technology, and the institutional setting cannot be satisfactorily atomized. The usual approach is to attribute wage differences to differences in individual skill or to barriers to mobility, but this merely begs the question. It is a case of what Galbraith calls reasoning backward from an 'effect to a cause that would rationalize and justify it' or (Ibid., p. 264).[7]

In conclusion, the differences between Polanyi, Galbraith, and liberal economic theory can be summed up in the phrase: economic freedom. The liberal ideology is that freedom is found in self-regulation. Power in labour markets, the ultimate threat to freedom, comes from the intervention of the state. Traditionally, liberals in Western Europe and the US have also expressed concern about the power of trade unions.[8] However, the power possessed by unions depends ultimately on the extent to which they are supported by the state. Thus, for liberals, economic freedom is inherent in market society and is threatened only by government interference in the natural order.

To Polanyi and institutionalist economists, the liberal doctrine is not only naive but represents a serious miscalculation. Freedom cannot be *guaranteed* by an economic system.

> Today, freedom in the sense of personal liberty is possible, but only if it is instituted.... Unfortunately, we are still governed by nineteenth century ideology, and, ... economic liberalism does not understand the reality of power.... Only by accepting... the inevitability of power and regulation can freedom be institutionalized. This is to recognize the reality of society, for the reality of power is one component of society (Sievers, 1991, p. 60).

The liberal believes that power can be removed from society by constructing a self-regulating system. For Polanyi, this is a dangerous delusion, because 'no society is possible in which power and compulsion are absent, nor a world in which force has no function' (1957, p. 257). Given the reality of power in society, the question is how to protect freedom and other values. In Polanyi's view, the agenda of liberalism is to try to eliminate or, at least, diminish the very institutions that would provide the greatest protection.

Free Labour Market Policy

The phrase, 'free labour market policy', might at first appear to be an oxymoron. The ideology of liberalism is that self-regulating labour markets do not require government policy. Indeed, the main obstacle to the free operation of markets, according to liberalism, is the state. It would seem, then, that 'free labour market policy' would be a matter of 'undoing' existing policy, of *de*regulating, privatizing, and otherwise 'unleashing' market forces to allow the system to operate on its own. This version of how market economies operate has influenced government policy in some transition economies notably Poland and Hungary. However, events in Russia over the past several years should put this particular interpretation to rest. Free market economic policy does not mean *no* economic policy.[9]

In the first place, as noted earlier in the paper, Polanyi makes a persuasive argument in *The Great Transformation* that without protective government policies it is doubtful that market systems would be able to survive. Second, as we discuss in this section, the goal of government policy in the late 20th (or early 21st) century, is less one of 'allowing the market to operate' than one of actively and aggressively promoting it.

Neoliberal policies are exemplified by the policy recommendations offered by international organizations such as the IMF, the World Bank, and the OECD as well as the views expressed by neoclassical economists and conservative policy makers in the US and Great Britain. The basic framework is the competitive labour market. That is, there are potentially two categories of labour policy: those aimed at influencing labour supply; and those aimed at influencing labour demand. In practice, however, there is only one category: supply side policy. Theoretically, liberal policies are aimed at improving market performance. However, consistently the 'problem' is assumed to be on the supply side of the labour market. For example, the two dominant hypotheses of labour markets in the US and Western Europe throughout the 1980s and 1990s have been the 'skills mismatch' hypothesis and the notion of 'flexibility'. The 'skills mismatch' idea attributes low wages and job insecurity in the US to an excess supply of poorly educated, unskilled workers (Galbraith, 1998). The solution is a supply side policy of increased education and job training. The term, 'flexibility', dominated analyses of unemployment in European labour markets during the 1980s. The lack of 'flexibility' refers to managerial flexibility in hiring, firing, and deploying workers. The problem is deemed to be excessive state regulation and institutional rigidities (Brodsky, 1994). In other words, the policy recommendation is to dismantle policies directed toward labour demand. In sum, free labour market policy - euphemistically called 'labour market reform'[10] -consists of eliminating labour demand policies and implementing only labour supply policies that would enable workers to adjust to whatever jobs are offered.

The notion that labour market reform consists primarily of supply side policy is not surprising. As Polanyi observed, a free labour market requires that workers have no choice except to work for a wage. Thus, one of the most fundamental tasks of the 'free market' policy maker is to eliminate or, restrict as much as possible, any sources of income for workers not linked to work. The most obvious target is government assistance in the form of unemployment benefits or income maintenance. Policy recommendations of this type are all too common in the US. Income maintenance programs were severely curtailed by the Welfare Reform Act of 1996. The next target for reform is the unemployment compensation system, even though the US ranks second lowest on the OECD's Overall Index of Benefit Generosity (OECD, 1998, p. 95).[11]

Tightening the rules for receiving benefits lowers unemployment in two ways. Those who no longer qualify for benefits are forced to look for a job. If they are successful, their status changes from unemployed to employed. If they are unsuccessful, they may leave the labour force. In both cases, the numbers of the unemployed decline. That is, high benefits attract both those who would otherwise be working and those who would otherwise be out of the labour force altogether. The question is, however, whether those who leave the labour force are leaving voluntarily because they do not want to work or whether they have simply given up trying to find a job. This is a major concern in the US. Large numbers of individuals are 'jobless' even though they are not counted in official government statistics as unemployed. In some poor neighbourhoods in American central cities, the jobless rate among working age adults is over 40% (Jaworsky, 1997).

One can observe similar labour market phenomena in Poland. The overall unemployment rate disguises significant regional differences ranging from 2.8% in Warsaw to over 20% in some rural areas (OECD, 1998). Unemployment in Poland declined from 17% in 1994 to 10.5% in 1997, and in Hungary unemployment has also stabilized around 10% (Ibid.). The decline in rates does not, however, reflect increased employment. In the early 1990s high unemployment rates were interpreted as 'artificially inflated' due to overly generous unemployment benefits (Kramer, 1995; OECD, 1998). Governments were urged to restrict benefits, and in 1994 changing eligibility rules resulted in the removal of large numbers of people from the benefit rolls. Approximately one third of these individuals found employment, while two thirds simply lost their status of being unemployed (Hardy and Rainnie, 1996). In Hungary, eligibility for unemployment benefits was tightened in 1991 with no increase in employment at all (Gere, 1998). Of those who remain in the category of 'unemployed', substantial numbers in most transition countries -over half in Bulgaria and over 38% in Poland -are long-term unemployed (OECD, 1998). They have been looking for work for more than a year. How long will these individuals remain in the labour force? It seems likely that the problem of hidden unemployment -already substantial in many regions -will persist, or even exacerbate, into the foreseeable future.

The relevant point for purposes of this paper is how unemployment and other problems in labour markets are consistently depicted as supply side problems. Even in the East European transition countries where it is evident that a major problem has been insufficient labour demand due to declining production in the wake of the dissolution of the Soviet Union in 1992, the policy target in the labour market is still described as the 'labour surplus'. For example, Kaser (1997) asserts that the basic problem is 'over-employment' and untenable expectations of job security that 'bar the way to economic efficiency'. Kramer (1995) criticizes laws in Poland that require benefits be paid to workers involved in mass layoffs but not to workers laid off individually. His criticism is not that workers laid off individually deserve severance pay as well, but that these laws have reduced the number of mass layoffs. In other words, what Poland and other Central and East European countries must do is to increase labour market flexibility. Cultural and institutional obstacles to market mobility must be reduced. Job security must be transformed from a social good into an 'obstacle'. While, in theory, market disequilibrium situations are eliminated by both supply and demand adjustments, in the labour market it is always the task of labour supply to adapt and accommodate itself to the market. In contrast, labour market demand is, by definition, the outcome of profit maximization and cannot be altered without reducing economic efficiency.

While free market labour policy dictates that labour demand be unrestricted, this should not be interpreted as *laissez-faire* policy. The promotion of labour market flexibility is a key ingredient in the neoliberal promotion of 'competitiveness'. In the 1980s and 1990s in the US, corporations have sought and been granted extensive government assistance in the name of 'market competitiveness'. In some cases, these programs are characterized as 'labour market' policies. For example, during the 1980s, virtually the only policy offered in response to high rates of joblessness in central cities was the establishment of state 'enterprise zones'. In the 1990s, they were enacted at the federal level and renamed 'empowerment zones'. These zones give new or existing businesses tax exemptions or subsidies, provide loans and loan guarantees, and, in some cases, underwrite the construction of new roads or other infrastructure. An estimated 79% of all businesses in the US now participate in some kind of program that reduces or eliminates taxes (Greenwald, 1996). Unfortunately, studies indicate that many of these programs have been very costly to local governments in the form of lost tax revenues or increased spending.[12] Moreover, the evidence that such inducements actually result in local job growth is mixed.

A similar experience occurs in developing countries that hope to attract foreign capital and, it is hoped, increased job opportunities and technology transfer. Transnational corporations (TNCs) request tax breaks and other concessions such as tariff protection for domestic sales as a condition for investing. Tax incentives for foreign investment are so commonplace that negotiation with host governments is a routine step in the foreign direct investment (FDI) process. Often the higher the risk or the need of a country for capital, the more generous the tax incentives must be to attract investors. Poland has managed to impose some restrictions on foreign investment particularly regarding job security and mass layoffs. Whether Poland or other Central and Eastern European countries will be able to maintain these restrictions is unclear. As they enter more fully into the global economy, they will be competing in an arena where concessions are common. Despite the rhetoric of the 'free market', the global marketplace is *not* free of government involvement. Hardy and Rainnie (1996) argue that '... the nation-state is not simply a passive conduit for the policies and actions of TNCs, but that the state both influences and is influenced by FDI and large companies in an elaborate bargaining process' (1996, p. 99).

Conclusion

In *The Great Transformation*, Karl Polanyi noted that the transition to a market economy requires the commodification of labour. Relations between employer and employee are to be reduced to a simple market transaction. A commodity is bought and sold, its price is determined by the impersonal forces of supply and demand, and the goal of both buyer and seller is to maximize individual gain. Central and Eastern European countries are urged to implement labour market reform in order to hasten their transition to a market economy. Western European countries are urged to reduce labour market rigidities and emulate the greater flexibility of the US. However, even in the US the buying and selling of labour is not a simple market transaction. The terms of employment including what workers do, how long they work, when and under what conditions they are promoted or allowed to go on leave, and how much they are paid are the outcomes of a negotiated contract. Even workers hired without a formal contract or covered under a collective bargaining arrangement, have successfully argued in court that they were covered by an 'implied' contract. The fact is that the true commodification of labour has not been accomplished in any country. That is, we are *all* apparently 'in transition' to a market economy. One can only hope, for the sake of individual welfare and the cohesion of society that none of us ever actually get there.

Notes

1. An indication of the ideological character of the 'third transformation' is how little attention is given to the specific labour market traditions and institutions of individual countries. Institutions are important only insofar as they interfere with or delay the implementation of policies. See Kaser 1997.
2. The hospital is Franklin Memorial Hospital in Farmington, Maine. The story, 'Trading for Health Care', was reported by Daniel Zwerdling on 'Weekend All Things Considered', August 16, 1998, a program on public radio in the United States. Interested readers may listen to this program by accessing the *All Things Considered Weekend* archives at www.npr.org/programs/watc/archives/1998/.
3. The passage is found in Book I, Chapter 2. 'It is not from the benevolence of the butcher, the brewer, or the baker, that we expect our dinner, but from their regard to their own interest'. (Smith 1909, 21).
4. A colleague, Janet Knoedler, recounts a related use of the rain metaphor in Bellamy (1982) following a discussion of the narrator's discovery of the fact that he and his hosts could walk out into a rainstorm without either boots or umbrellas, because a 'continuous waterproof covering had been let down so as to enclose the sidewalk and turn it into a well-lighted and perfectly dry corridor'. When he explains his surprise at this invention that allows escape from bad weather, his host, Dr. Leete, 'turned to say that the difference between the age of individualism and that of concert was well characterized by the fact that, in the nineteenth century, when it rained, the people of Boston put up three hundred thousand umbrellas over their heads, and in the twentieth century, they put up one umbrella over all their heads. As we walked on, Edith said, 'The private umbrella is Father's favourite figure to illustrate the old way when everyone lived for himself and his family. There is a nineteenth century painting at the art gallery representing a crowd of people in the rain, each one holding his umbrella over himself and his wife, and giving his neighbours the drippings, which he [Father] claims must have been meant by the artist as a satire on the times' (122-123).
5. Although not discussed in this paper, Polanyi made similar arguments regarding the creation of free markets for land via the new system of land tenure that accompanied enclosures in England. Free markets for land meant that the human environment and all natural resources were to be disposed of according to selfish interest in profit opportunities.
6. Information based on personal communication with an employee of Opel in Hungary.
7. Galbraith's description of neoclassical labour market analysis could also be termed a case of the fallacy of *post hoc ergo propter hoc*.
8. In neoclassical analysis the role of the state vis-à-vis the economy is viewed dualistically. That is, the framework is a dichotomy between public and private.

    public / private
    the state / the economy
    the collective / the individual

    In the United States, trade unions are on the same side as the state. Unions are portrayed as interfering with individual rights. For example, state laws placing significant restrictions on unions are termed, 'right-to-work' laws. In Poland, the situation is more complex. In the early 1980s, Solidarity was an opposing force to the power of the state. Thus, in the dualistic framework above, Solidarity would appear to be solidly on the side of the freedom of the individual against the collective power of the state. When Solidarity came to power, the finance minister, Balcerowicz, was in the forefront of 'neoliberal' approaches to the transition. To observers in the west, who are used to unions residing on the 'collective' or 'public' side of the dichotomy, Balcerowicz's position seemed unexpected. On the other hand, the ZPGG union was, in effect, the official state union and was always on the 'public' side of the dichotomy.

9. Even mainstream economists who make up the rapidly growing field of 'transition economics' recognize that active government policy is required to establish a market system (Murrell 1995). For example, the appropriate political, social and legal infrastructure is required to protect private property, one of the key institutions of capitalism. However, the term, 'transition', used to describe both countries and policies, implies that active government intervention in the economy is required for only a finite period of time and that ultimately the system will be truly self-regulating.

10. This is common usage in reports prepared by the IBRD and the IMF. See (International Monetary Fund, 1996, p. 55).

11. Japan ranks the lowest on this scale which is based on both level and duration of unemployment benefits.

12. The incentives are not restricted to subsidies and tax breaks but can involve major capital expenditures. For example, South Carolina promised to spend $40 million to improve a local airport in order to induce BMW to invest (Rinehart, 1995).

References

Barber, Bernard (1995), 'All Economies are Embedded: the career of a concept and beyond'. *Social Research* 62, no. 2, Summer, pp. 387-414.

Blank, Rebecca M. (1997), 'Is There a Trade-off between Unemployment and Inequality? No Easy Answers: Labour Market Problems in the United States versus Europe?' Jerome Levy Economics Institute of Bard College, Annandale-on-Hudson, NY, Public Policy Brief No. 33.

Blejer, Mario (1995), *The Making of Economic Reform in Eastern Europe*, Elgar, Aldershot.

Bonamo, Mark J. (1997), 'Poland's Privatization Process: A View from the Inside'. *Journal of International Affairs* 50, no. 2, Winter, pp. 573-81.

Brodsky, Melvin M. (1994), 'Labour Market flexibility: A Changing International Perspective'. *Monthly Labour Review* 117, no. 11, November, pp. 53-61.

Cramer, James 1996, 'Let them Eat Stocks: A Solution to Downsizing'. *The New Republic*, 214, no. 18, April 29, pp. 24-26.

Domanski, Henryk (1997), 'Distribution of Incomes in Eastern Europe'. *International Journal of Comparative Sociology* 38, no. 3-4, December, pp. 249-271.

Donnorummo, Robert (1994), 'Poland's political and economic transition'. *East European Quarterly* 28, no. 2, Summer, pp. 259-281.

Elsey, Ena (1996), 'Monitoring Economic Transition: The Polish Case'. *Europe-Asia Studies*, 48, no. 5, July, pp. 849-51.

Evensky, Jerry (1998), 'Adam Smith's Moral Philosophy: the Role of Religion and its Relationship to Philosophy and Ethics in the Evolution of Society'. *History of Political Economy* 30, no. 1, Spring, pp. 17-43.
Fields, Gary (1991), 'The Road from Gdansk: How Solidarity found haven in the Marketplace'. *Monthly Review* 43, no. 3, July-August, pp. 95-122.
Galbraith, James (1998), *Created Unequal*, The Free Press, New York.
Galbraith, James (1996), 'Unemployment, Inflation and the Job Structure', Jerome Levy Economics Institute of Bard College, Annandale-on-Hudson, NY, Working Paper No. 154.
Gere, I. (1998), 'Country Study: Hungary'. International Labour Organization, Geneva, Switzerland, Labour Administration Branch.
Giffin, Phillip E. and Lucien Ellington (1995), 'The Origins of Capitalist Markets: Transition in Poland with Comparisons to East Asian Capitalism'. *Journal of Economic Issues* 29, no. 2, June, pp. 585-91.
Godfrey, Martin (1995), 'The Struggle Against Unemployment: Medium term Policy Options for Transitional Economies'. *International Labour Review* 134, no. 1, Jan.-Feb., pp. 3-16.
Greenwald, John (1996), 'A No-win War Between the States: Politicians are Handing Out Fatter Tax Breaks than Ever to Lure Jobs to their Areas. They May be Devastating Cities in the Process', *Time* 15, pp. 44-46.
Hardy, Jane and Al Rainnie (1996), *Restructuring Krakow: Desperately Seeking Capitalism*. Mansell Publishing, Ltd., London.
Holmes, Stephen (1997), 'What Russia Teaches us Now: How Weak States Threaten Freedom'. *The American Prospect* no. 33, July-August, pp. 30-39.
Howell, David R. (1997), 'Institutional Failure and the American Worker', Jerome Levy Economics Institute of Bard College, Annandale-on-Hudson, NY Public Policy Brief No. 29.
International Monetary Fund (1996), 'Strengthening the Functioning of Labour Markets', *World Economic Outlook*, October, pp. 52-57.
Jaworsky, Paul (1997), *Poverty and Place: Ghettos, Barrios and the American City*, Russell Sage Foundation, New York.
Kaser, Michael (1997), 'Securing the Market System after Transition', *Europe-Asia Studies* 49, no. 3, May, pp. 463-468.
Kramer, Mark (1995), 'Polish Workers and the Post-Communist Transition, 1989-93', *Europe-Asia Studies* 47, no 4, June, pp. 669-713.
Leven, Bozena (1993), 'Short-Term Effects of Economic Transition on Inequality and Poverty: The Polish Case', *Journal of Economic Issues* 27, no. 1, March, pp. 237-244.
Levitt, Kari Polanyi (1995), 'Toward Alternatives: re-reading the Great Transformation', *Monthly Review* 47, no. 2, June, pp. 1-17.
Lie, John (1993), 'Visualizing the Invisible Hand: The Social Origins of Market Society in England, 1550-1750'. *Politics and Society* 21, no 3, September, pp. 275-305.
Lie, John (1992), 'The Concept of Mode of Exchange', *American Sociological Review*, vol. 57, August, pp. 508-23.
Locke, Richard M. and Wade Jacoby (1997), 'The Dilemmas of Diffusion: Social Embeddedness and the problems of institutional change in Eastern Germany', *Politics and Society* 25, no. 1, March, pp. 34-66.
Martin, Roderick (1998), 'Central and Eastern Europe and the International Economy: the Limits to Globalization', *Europe-Asia Studies* 50, no. 1, January, pp. 7-27.
McConnell, Campbell R. and Stanley L. Brue (1995), *Contemporary Labour Economics*, 4th

ed. , McGraw Hill, Inc., New York.
Murray, Charles (1984), *Losing Ground,* Basic Books, New York.
Murrell, Peter (1996), 'How Far has the Transition Progressed?' *Journal of Economic Perspectives* 10, no. 2, Spring, pp. 25-44.
Murrell, Peter (1995), 'The transition according to Cambridge, Mass', *Journal of Economic Literature* 33, no. 1, March, pp. 64-79.
Murrell, Peter (1993), 'Privatization's Harms: Economics in Eastern Europe', *Current,* no. 349, January, pp. 34-40.
Organization for Economic Cooperation and Development (1998), *OECD Economic Surveys 1997-1998: Poland,* OECD Publications, Paris, France.
Pejovich, Svetozar (1994), 'The Market for institutions vs. capitalism by fiat: the case of Eastern Europe', *KYKLOS* , vol. 47, no. 4, Winter, pp. 519-30.
Polanyi, Karl (1977), 'The Economistic Fallacy', in *The Livelihood of Man,* edited by Harry W. Pearson, Academic Press, New York.
Polanyi, Karl (1968), 'Our Obsolete Market Mentality', *In Primitive, Archaic and Modern Economies: Essays of Karl Polanyi,* Beacon Press, Boston.
Polanyi, Karl (1957), *The Great Transformation,* Beacon Press, Boston.
Pujol, Thierry (1996), 'The Role of Labour Market Rigidities During the Transition: Lessons from Poland', International Monetary Fund.
Rondinelli, Dennis A. and Jay Yurkiewicz (1996), 'Privatization and Economic Restructuring in Poland: An Assessment of Transition Policies', *The American Journal of Economics an d Sociology* vol. 55, no. 2, April, pp. 145-161.
Sievers, Allen M. (1991), 'Reconsidering Karl Polanyi's Neo-Heterodoxy with Special Reference to the Marx Connection', In *Explorations in Political Economy: Essays in Criticisms,* Edited by Rajani K. Kanth and E.K. Hunt, Rowman and Littlefield Publishers, Savage, MD.
Smith, Adam (1909), *An Inquiry into the Nature and Causes of the Wealth of Nations,* P.F. Collier & Son, Co., New York.
Sorrentino, Constance (1992), 'Analyzing Labour Markets in Central and Eastern Europe', *Monthly Labour Review,* vol. 115, no. 11, November, pp. 43-47.
Supiot, Alain (1996), 'Perspectives on Work: Introduction', *International Labour Review,* vol. 135, no. 6, Nov. -Dec., pp. 603-615.
Thirkell, J., Scase, R. and Vickerstaff, S. (1994), 'Labour Relations in Transition in Eastern Europe', *Industrial Relations Journal,* 25 no. 2 (June), pp. 84-96.
Timar, Janos (1995), 'Particular Features of Employment and Unemployment in the Present Stage of Transformation of the post-socialist Countries', *Europe-Asia Studies* vol. 47, no. 4 (June), pp. 633-650.
Young, Jeffrey T. and Barry Gordon (1996), 'Distributive Justice as a Normative Criterion in Adam Smith's Political Economy', *History of Political Economy, vol.* 28, no. 1, Spring, pp. 1-25.

Chapter Seven

Three Paths to Capitalism: An Agenda for Research

Ana Bela Nunes and Nuno Valério

Introduction

Market capitalist economies developed historically in three different contexts: i) gradual transformation of traditional economies; ii) dismantling of war economy schemes; and iii) failure of attempts to consolidate socialist centrally planned economies. The first path to capitalism has been the topic of extensive discussion by the founding fathers of economic science and by economic historians. In the second section of this chapter we survey the main theoretical approaches to this issue. The other two paths to capitalism remained hitherto, for the most part, unexplored theoretically. In the third section of this chapter we survey the main factual analysis and theoretical insights already presented about these processes. As a conclusion, we argue that a comparison of the three paths to capitalism must become the main agenda for research of those interested in studying the emergence of market capitalist economies, providing a sound basis to deepen theoretical frames for those transition processes.

Gradual transformation of traditional economies

According to Brenner (1987), classical analyses of the transformation of traditional economies into market capitalist economies may be divided into two main types, which may be labelled, according to two of the founding fathers of economic science, the Smithian and Marxian approaches.

The Smithian Approach

The Smithian approach corresponds to the views that predominated during the 18th century Enlightenment. A good summary may be found in Adam Smith's *Wealth of Nations*, namely in Book III, chapter IV. He argues that, when subject to the appropriate proper exogenous stimuli, i.e., the growth of commerce (and manufacture), landlords, acting as rational self-interested individuals, performed actions conductive to the development of capitalist property relations. The growth of urban centres and of its artisan-produced manufactures created a social division of labour that was decisive to improve the rural economic performance and, which also changed the rural property relations that characterized pre-capitalist structures. Eager to raise their consumption of manufactures, landowners reduced their unproductive expenses, namely relinquishing their military retinue and their peasant serfs, who became market dependent tenant farmers and wage labourers. As a consequence, landlords raised their incomes to meet their consumption needs and lost their means of coercion and jurisdictional legitimacy while transforming the social and political structures.

The main weakness of this Smithian approach is obvious: the transformation of the traditional economy is propelled by exogenous stimuli, and this implies that a market capitalist economy, or at least an embryo of its structures, must exist before the transition process starts. Of course, this leads to the unending quest of the origins of these embryonic structures. The usual way out, fully developed in the mainstream neo-classical vision, is to assume that the market capitalist system is the natural state of human economies, and that departures from it are artificial consequences of particular historical situations (as an example of such argument, from an Austrian perspective, Friedrich Hayek's Nobel lecture may be mentioned).

The Marxian Approach

The Marxian approach corresponds to the much more historicist and evolutionist intellectual scenery of the 19th century. A good summary may be found in Karl Marx's *Das Kapital*, namely in Volume I, section VIII. According to the historical materialism theory, market capitalism is a new institutional framework needed to overcome the inadequacy of the pre-capitalist institutional framework, namely feudal property relations, to the degree of development of productive forces. The separation of the workers from the means of production, specially in the rural world by means of the enclosure movement in Great Britain, and the primitive (an inadequate name according to Marx) accumulation of capital are the key elements of the birth process of this new institutional framework.

This approach avoids the difficulty of introducing trade and manufacturing as exogenous elements to the process, but does not avoid introducing the tendency to the improvement of productive forces as a kind of *deus ex machina* that ensures an endogenous factor of transformation of traditional economies.

Classical Approaches Until the Mid-20th Century

It may be said that the Smithian and Marxian approaches dominated the study of the transition to market capitalist economies until the mid-20th century, the Smithian approach prevailing in the non-Marxian field, specially in the mainstream schools, and the Marxian approach prevailing in the Marxian field and in some historicist and institutionalist schools. Pirenne (1933) and Dobb (1946) are good examples of this situation.

Institutionalism

Many new insights about the endogenous factors that may propel the transformation of traditional economies were presented by those emphasizing an historical approach. Sombart (1902-1928) and Weber (1904-1905) argued that cultural factors played a role as important as the one assigned by Marxists to the improvement of productive forces. Werner Sombart underlined the 'spirit of capitalism', which sacrifices immediate reward to obtain long-term gain. Max Weber evoked the development of a 'capitalist ethic', linked to particular religious experiences (Calvinism), which succeeded in influencing the values of a much larger number of people than their adherents. Both stressed, however, the need for an exceptional combination of technological opportunities, political situation (the formation of national states) and cultural elements to produce the unique transformation of traditional economies into capitalist economies. On the other hand, Polanyi (1944) identified the role of the institutional changes promoted by the state as the decisive factor in what he called the 'Great Transformation', that is to say, the quite unnatural submission of all social life to market mechanisms.

Although one cannot classify him as an institutionalist, Schumpeter (1942) introduced another interesting perspective, which stressed the role of exceptional individuals the entrepreneurs who introduced the technological, organizational and geographical innovations needed to trigger the transition process.

Exogenous Suggestions in the Marxian Camp

Paul Sweezy's critique of Maurice Dobb from an assumed Marxian perspective would introduce the first significant breach in the uniformity of the Marxist camp. Sweezy's interpretation of Karl Marx's *Das Kapital*, namely of volume II, section V, chapter XXIII, on this matter led him to emphasize the rise of long-distance trade, an element outside the feudal society, as the cause of the decline of feudalism. Long-distance trade and the development of towns gave rise to a system of production for exchange that showed the economic inefficiencies of the old system of production for subsistence and the inability of the feudal ruling class to go on controlling and over-exploiting the labour force. These outside factors gave feudal lords the opportunity for obtaining commodities and gave the serfs either the possibility of fleeing, or of getting concessions in terms of both looser extra-economic coercion and transforming feudal obligations into money rents. According to Sweezy, the period between the end of feudalism and the beginning of capitalism is a different, specific system, which he defines as the system of precapitalist production of commodities. The work of Maurice Dobb and Paul Sweezy led to a protracted Marxian debate over the transition from feudalism to capitalism. Its main texts may be found in Sweezy et al (1976).

Endogenous Ideas in the non-Marxian Camp

Meanwhile, the search for an endogenous explanation for the transition from precapitalist to capitalist systems developed in the non-Marxian camp. Hicks (1969) produced, perhaps, the most fruitful results of these efforts. According to Hicks, transition is basically the process of transforming pre-capitalist property relations, and namely the creation of the markets for factors of production. According to him, such a transformation is mainly a response to financial, rather than trading, opportunities,. And contrary to Marx, who felt that capital and labour markets were decisive, Hicks argues that the creation of labour and land markets are the key. In specific circumstances it proved to be in the lords's rational self-interest (or the consequences of unconscious actions by lords and peasants (Brenner,1987)) to free their peasants instead of strengthening their extra-economic coercion. They became either free landless tenants or wage labourers. In any case, the direct producers were free from the lords' institutionalized relationship of domination and became also fully separated from their means of subsistence. Tenants became competitive producers (innovating, investing) for exchange, actually market-dependent farmers, ultimately employing wage earners contracted at labour markets and eventually, in the long run, participating in capital markets. As for the landlords either they became an entrepreneurial class of direct producers for exchange or they reorganized and equipped their farms to compete for the best (capitalist) tenant farmers. Hicks (1969, chapter 7) emphasized that as long as the acknowledgement of the fundamental feudal property rights of lords and peasants is only relevant for themselves, with no other interested actor existing, property rights can be defined according to tradition. Financial development made it possible and increasingly appealing for the landowner to borrow. However, credit would be easier if the landlord could mortgage his properties as a warranty for his loan, but traditional rights were a poor guarantee. Being aware of this, the landlord had a rational self-interest to convert his property rights in line with the property concepts of merchants, bearing in mind that the value of his property depended on securing (scarce) labour.

Neo-institutionalism

Neo-institutionalist views on the matter may be seen as an interesting development along Hicksian lines. According to North and Thomas, the transition from feudalism to capitalism is basically the reorganization of institutional structures towards the development of efficient property rights that assured sustained economic growth through the creation of 'an incentive to channel individual economic effort into activities that bring the private rate of return close to the social rate of return' (1973, p. 1), which characterize capitalism. These views would be developed along more theoretical lines in, for instance, North (1990). It is interesting to stress that both Hicks and the neo-institutionalists underline the role of the national state in the context of this process, mainly as a guarantee of property rights.

An Eclectic Attempt

At the same time, an eclectic approach was provided by the work of Fernand Braudel and Immanuel Wallerstein, namely in Braudel (1979), Wallerstein (1976; 1974-1990). Two main aspects of this eclectic approach must be underlined. Firstly, and contradicting all the other classical and modern analyses, 'the market' and capitalism are not seen as two faces of the same coin, but as distinct, and even opposite facts. Thus, Wallerstein could title one of his comments on Braudel work: 'Le capitalisme ennemi du marché' (Wallerstein, 1986). Secondly, the process of transition from traditional economies to (market) capitalist economies is examined in a plurality of relevant spaces : local economies, national economies, and world-economies. We believe that this aspect of this eclectic approach is crucial to overcome, at least partially, the awkward endogenous /exogenous dilemma.

In an admittedly simplified view of Braudel and Wallerstein analyses, several different situations are to be taken into account when considering the transition from traditional economies to (market) capitalist economies:

a) The case of endogenous transformation of traditional economies of the feudal type in the core of the Euro-Atlantic world-economy.
b) The case of partially endogenous, partially exogenously induced transformation of traditional economies of different types in the periphery of the Euro-Atlantic world-economy.
c) The case of partially endogenous, partially exogenously imposed transformation of traditional economies of different types on other world-economies.
d) The case of exogenously imposed transformation of traditional economies of different types on either world or local economies.

Case a) corresponds to what Wallerstein described as the key process in the successful transformation of a redistributive world-system (feudalism or feudal mode of production in the relevant European historical context) into a capitalist world-economy (the modern Euro-Atlantic world-economy in the same historical context). Wallerstein explains this transformation mainly along traditional Marxian lines. Case b) corresponds to what Wallerstein described as another aspect of the same transformation of a redistributive world-system into a capitalist world-economy. The main difference to case a) lies in the fact that systemic interaction with the core of the modern capitalist Euro-Atlantic world-economy transformed according to the lines of case a) led to specific characteristics such as the absence of a strong national state and a strong native bourgeoisie, or the use of unfree (servile or slave) labour that were traditionally (and wrongly, according to Wallerstein) taken as a sign of imperfect or delayed transition to capitalism.

Cases c) and d) correspond to what Wallerstein described as the incorporation of additional external areas into the capitalist world-economies. In case c), redistributive world-systems were able to respond, at least partially, to external challenge. Japan and Russia would appear as the most relevant examples. This ensured an evolution to regulated capitalism and later to market capitalism, consistent with a successful process of take-off into modern economic growth. In case d), either redistributive world-systems, or what Wallerstein calls mini-systems, were unable to provide any significant response to external challenge. This led to formal or informal colonization by the core of the capitalist system, and to significant difficulties in triggering a modern economic growth process.

Moreover, Wallerstein emphasises the extension of the proletarization of labour and the commercialization of land within the expanding capitalist world-economy as an additional element of consolidation of the modern world-system. This allowed the capitalist world-economy to become in the late 19th century a truly world economy. During the 20th century, it faced some challenges, most of which correspond to the war economy schemes and attempts to consolidate socialist centrally planned economies that will be dealt with in the next section. Nowadays, these challenges seem to have been overcome, and the contemporary world economy is engaged in a deepening of its internal articulations through what is usually called the globalization process.

Dismantling of War Economy Schemes and Failure of Attempts to Consolidate Socialist Centrally Planned Economies

Dismantling of war economy schemes and failure of attempts to consolidate socialist centrally planned economies, as transition processes, have remained hitherto unexamined theoretically, especially if we are looking for broader approaches than the discussion of specific issues concerning the current economic theories of the market (see, for instance, Brezinsky, Fritsch, 1997 and Hoen, 1998).

War Economy Schemes and Attempts to Consolidate Socialist Centrally Planned Economies as Challenges to Capitalism

War economy schemes and attempts to consolidate socialist centrally planned economies may be considered as challenges to the contemporary market capitalist economy both as a capitalist system and as a world system. They challenged the contemporary market capitalist economy as a capitalist system, because they replaced market coordination of economic plans and free initiative of economic agents by *ex ante* state coordination of economic plans and state control of economic agents. They challenged the contemporary market capitalist economy as a world system, because they implied a division of the world economy into separate blocks, although this division was seen as transitory. In the case of war economy schemes, the division was seen as transitory, because specific wars would not last forever, and after each war the capitalist world economy would be restored as before. In the case of socialist centrally planned economies, the division was also seen as transitory, because the remaining capitalist economies would not last forever, and would be replaced by a socialist world economy.

In the long run, it may be said that both challenges have been unsuccessful. As a matter of fact, the contemporary market capitalist economy have survived to this day, both as a capitalist economy and as a world economy. This means that transition processes to capitalism in the context of the dismantling of war economy schemes and failure of attempts to consolidate socialist centrally planned economies always occurred against the solid background of the contemporary market capitalist world economy.

Similarities between dismantling of war economy schemes and failure of attempts to consolidate socialist centrally planned economies

It is possible to stress a few crucial similarities between the dismantling of war economy schemes and failure of attempts to consolidate socialist centrally planned economies. Both processes of transition involve restoring market coordination of economic plans and free initiative of economic agents. Restoring market coordination of economic plans implies abolishing *ex ante* state coordination of economic plans. The crucial problem in this context is the inadequacy of the initial prices as a guide for correct economic decisions by economic agents, and the consequent distortion of the allocation of resources (especially those relating to the stock of physical capital and the highly specialized human capital). According to the optimistic mainstream view, once prices are no longer controlled by a central planner, they tend to move quickly to equilibrium levels and any distortions of the allocation of resources tend to be corrected. However, experience seems to show that there are important viscosity phenomena, and inflation usually distorts the whole process. This means that macroeconomic stabilization efforts, especially those related to balancing the state budget and foreign payments, must play an important role in the process.

Restoring free initiative of economic agents implies an abolishing of state control of economic agents. The crucial problem in this context is the existence of a huge state owned sector. According to the optimistic mainstream view, once this state owned sector is privatized, the necessary institutional reforms are performed. However, experience seems to show that economic liberalisation may be disturbed by lack of private capacity to take over public enterprises and further distorted by the absence of what may be called the 'exchange culture' (Granovetter, 1985). This means that deeper (and slower) social transformations may be needed to secure an efficient transition to capitalism. Of course, the problems of viscosity, inflation, lack of private capacity to take over public enterprises and absence of exchange culture are much more serious in transitions from socialist centrally planned economies than in transitions from war economy schemes. This suggests that there are essential differences between means that differences between the dismantling of war economy schemes and the failure of attempts to consolidate socialist centrally planned economies.

Differences Between Dismantling of War Economy Schemes and Failure of Attempts to Consolidate Socialist Centrally Planned Economies

The key difference may be summarised by saying that, while war economy schemes were assumed as a transitory device to fight and win wars, socialist centrally planned economies were seen as the starting point of a new socialist world system. Two implications came out of this difference. Informal institutions such as the already mentioned exchange culture, which take a considerable time to establish and allow an important reduction of transaction costs, were hardly touched during war economy schemes, but severely destroyed during the attempts to consolidate socialist centrally planned economies. On the other hand, dismantling of war economy schemes always occurred in a context of a social consensus about the transitory character of war economy schemes (even if significant sectors of the society might support the idea of converting war economy schemes into the building of socialist centrally planned economies), while the failure of attempts to consolidate socialist centrally planned economies occurred in a context of absence of social consensus about the transitory character of socialist centrally planned economies. These two implications have significant consequences for the credibility of the transition process. Needless to say, this means that dismantling of war economy schemes were easier processes in the institutional and cultural field than dismantling of socialist centrally planned economies.

In what concerns economic stabilization efforts, these differences were not as significant. As a matter of fact, economic stabilization efforts during the dismantling of war economy schemes were usually just as hard and long lasting as in the cases of dismantling of socialist centrally planned economies. However, expectations raised by transition processes may have had some influence in the process. In the cases of dismantling of war economy schemes short run expectations were usually low, while medium and long run expectations were high. On the contrary, short run expectations during the dismantling of socialist centrally planned economies, as far as the increase in the standard of living is concerned, were usually high. This certainly put some pressure on attaining immediate results, and contributed to disturb already uneasy evolutions.

The Combined Dismantling of War Economy Schemes and Socialist Centrally Planned Economies

Mention must be made of a few cases that combined dismantling of war economy schemes and socialist centrally planned economies in a simultaneous process. It is even possible to find cases that combine dismantling of war economy schemes and socialist centrally planned economies in a simultaneous process with restoring links to the world economy deeply destroyed by wars. (On a situation of this type see Fontoura, Valério, 1994).

An Agenda for Research

We argue that the comparison of the three paths to capitalism is essential for those researchers who are interested in studying the emergence of market economies and in discovering a sound basis to deepen theoretical frames for those transition processes. We will try to illustrate this claim with a discussion of a few topics that this approach raises.

A Generalized Marxian Approach

According to the traditional Marxian approach, market capitalism was a new institutional framework needed to overcome the inadequacy of the pre-capitalist institutional framework to the development of productive forces. Marxist doctrine claims that centrally planned socialism is also a new institutional framework needed to overcome a similar inadequacy of the market capitalism institutional framework. However, the failure of the attempts to consolidate centrally planned socialist economies seems to disproof such claims. We believe that it is possible to go further and suggest that market capitalism seems to be the adequate institutional framework for complex economies, except in rather peculiar circumstances.

Let us start from the taxonomy of economic spaces presented in Wallerstein (1976): local economies, redistributive world-systems, and capitalist world-economies and from the taxonomy of economic systems presented in Hicks (1969) routine economies, command economies (with the variants of simple command economies and centrally planned economies), and market economies. Local economies were quasi-self-sufficient small economic spaces. Their economic system was a mixture of routine economy (for the bulk of economic activity) and simple command economy (for exceptional circumstances, such as crises originating in the natural or inter-society context). Redistributive world-systems were large conglomerates of relatively open small economic spaces, linked together by an imperial authority. Their economic system was a complex mixture of centrally planned command (for the activities that involved the imperial authority), routine (for the activities that only mattered for the small economic spaces), and market (for a residual of exchanges among these small economic spaces). Capitalist world-economies have been large inter-related economic spaces. Their economic system is a mixture of market (usually for the bulk of inter-state and intra-state economic activity) and centrally planned command (usually for economic activities where market failures are felt, and exceptionally for the bulk of intra-state economic activity in centrally planned economies and some inter-state economic activity).

According to Wallerstein, there were many false starts of capitalist world-economies throughout the history of mankind, with only one success: the Euro-Atlantic world-economy of the 16th century, which survived and was gradually transformed into the world economy of present. We shall not engage here in a discussion of this proposition. We will just note that this means that the market was absent or played only a residual role in the economic life of mankind until the development of what Wallerstein calls the 'modern world system'. In other words, only a large integrated economic space without a central imperial authority needs market capitalism as its economic system. Conversely, the modern world system developed such a complex economic life that the market, however tarnished by state intervention, became the only economic system which is able to cope with its complexity. This echoes the well known theoretical discussion by the Austrian and Marxist schools on the feasibility of a centrally planned economy (see Mises, 1920 and Lange, 1936-1937). A centrally planned economy is certainly feasible (several countries lived under such a system for decades), but inefficient in the long run (see Kornai, 1992).

The peculiar circumstances that favoured the increase in the importance of central planning may be described as special situations that simplified for a while the social welfare function. In the case of war economy schemes, this is quite obvious as winning the war became a crucial social goal, and it was impossible to rely on the market to achieve it. Thus, command, in the form of state control of the economy, was used as a transitory device to supplement the market. In the case of attempts to build socialist centrally planned economies, two important social goals may be considered as the cause of the shift away from market economy. One is socialism itself, because the suppression of market anarchy, together with the end of exploitation and the improvement of the standard of living of the masses, were basic topics in the early 20th century socialist blueprint. The other was industrialisation and economic growth. Actually, countries attempting to build socialist centrally planned economies were not highly developed countries (as one would expect according to the socialist doctrine of the early 20th century). From a Rostowian perspective (Rostow, 1960), they ranged from pre-take-off to immature industrialized countries.

Market / capitalism

Of course, Immanuel Wallerstein would deny that capitalism implies a market economy. Perhaps he would even stress that, slightly paraphrasing his own words, '*le capitalisme est ennemi du marché*'. However, we do not agree with his idea. Let us briefly explain why. First, central planning capitalism (that is to say, a centrally planned economy with most of economic activities under private ownership), and market socialism (that is to say, a market economy with most economic activities under state ownership) were conscious experiments of the 20th century. Nazi Germany (Bettelheim, 1971; Temin, 1991), and self-management Yugoslavia (Brus, 1986), are perhaps the main cases to be mentioned, respectively. However, they were ephemerous experiments, even more so than the attempts to consolidate centrally planned socialist economies (Kornai, 1991; Nunes, 1997). Second, Wallerstein's (and Braudel's for that matter) arguments are based on the idea that a market economy must be strictly competitive, that is to say, avoiding monopoly and state intervention. However, it is meaningless to say that monopoly is not a market, and state intervention confined within certain limits is not only compatible, but even inevitable, in a market economy (because of market failures). Of course, to a certain degree this becomes a pure semantic issue, but even in that field, we do not believe in the usefulness of too strict a definition of market economy.

A Generalized Smithian Approach

It is also possible to present some generalizations along the traditional Smithian approach. External stimuli to the development of market capitalism were certainly present in the transformation of traditional economies (with the only possible exception of core North-West Europe countries in the early stages of the formation of the Euro-Atlantic economy, according to the eclectic Wallerstein approach presented above). External stimuli to the development of market capitalism were certainly present in the transformation of war economy schemes and previous centrally planned economies. It is even possible to say that the external stimuli came from the same ultimate source, the capitalist world-economy in all cases.

Conclusion

To sum up our proposal for an agenda for research, it may be said that, for an understanding of the economic and social transition processes to market capitalist economies, an historical perspective shows the importance of taking into account two inter-related facts, the ever growing economic complexity of human societies and their ever growing economic integration leading to the on-going globalization process. However hard the (social) resistence of any (partial) society to these processes, in the long run, at different speeds, they are apparent. Thus, the relevance of the distinction between spontaneous transitions to capitalism (viz. the gradual transformation of traditional economies) and government sponsored transitions to capitalism (viz. the dismantling of war economy schemes and the failure of attempts to consolidate socialist centrally planned economies) may be questioned, even if the roles of doctrines, theory and policy seem to have been different in each phase.

Market capitalism has proved to be the most efficient economic system to sustain those processes in the long run. Command, centrally planned economies were quite efficient, probably more efficient, to accomplish a narrow range of human activities for a relatively short time (see Allen, 1998). In the long run, however, the inevitability of both a more complex economy and a higher degree of economic integration showed how difficult it is for centrally planned systems to keep pace with innovation and to built an increasingly complex economy. In any case, endogenous inefficiencies to increase the complexity of the economy and exogenous stimulus within an imposing capitalist world economy have always been the fuel for the transition processes to market capitalist economies.

Of course, this does not mean the 'end of history' proclaimed by Fukuyama

(1992). We even believe that it is meaningful to ask if technological changes or collective needs (e.g. those relating to the environment) will cause planning to play a more important role at a global level in the future, in a replay of Polanyi's 'double transformation'.

References

Allen, Robert (1998), 'Capital Accumulation, the Soft Budget Constraint and Soviet Industrialisation', *European Review of Economic History*, vol. 2, part 1, pp. 1-24.
Berend, Ivan ed. (1994), *Übergang zur Marktwirtschaft am Ende des 20. Jahrhunderts* Südosteuropa-Gesellschaft, München.
Bettelheim, Charles (1971), *L'économie allemande sous le nazisme,* Maspero, Paris.
Braudel, Fernand (1979), *Civilisation matérielle, économie et capitalisme XVe-XVIIIe siècles,* 3 volumes,. Armand Colin, Paris.
Brenner, Robert (1987), 'Feudalism', in *The New Palgrave: A Dictionary of Economics,* edited by John Eatwell, Murray Milgate, Peter Newman, Macmillan Press, London.
Brus, Wlodzimierz (1986), *Histoire économique de l'Europe de l'Est (1945-1985),* La Découverte, Paris.
Brezinsky, Horst; Fritsch, Michael eds. (1997), *The Emergence and Evolution of Markets,* Edward Elgar, Cheltenham-Lyme.
Dobb, Maurice (1946), *Studies in the Development of Capitalism,* Routledge & Keagon Paul, London.
Eatwell, John; Milgate, Murray; Newman, Peter (eds.) *The New Palgrave. A Dictionary of Economics,* Macmillan, London, 1987.
Fontoura, Paula and Valério, Nuno (1994), 'From Self-sufficiency and Planning Towards a Market Economy in Angola: A Case Sstudy on Africa', in Berend, 1994.
Fukuyama, Francis (1992), *The End of History and the Last Man,* Hamish Hamilton, London.
Granovetter, Mark (1985), 'Economic Action and Social Structure: The Problem of Social Embeddedness', *American Journal of Sociology,* vol. 91, pp. 481-510.
Hayek, Friedrich von (1991), 'The Pretence of Knowledge', Nobel lecture delivered in 1976. In *Economic Freedom* Basil Blackwell, Oxford.
Hicks, John (1969), *A Theory of Economic History,* Oxford University Press, London.
Hoen, Herman (1998), 'On the Theory of Economic Transformation', in Hoen, 1998.
Hoen, Herman ed. (1998), *The Transformation of Economic Systems in Central Europe,* Edward Elgar, Cheltenham-Lyme.
Kornai, János (1992), *The Socialist System: the Political Economy of Communism,* Clarendon Press, Oxford.
Kornai, Janos. (1991), 'The Affinity Between Ownership and Coordination Mechanisms. The Common Experience of Reform in Socialist Countries' *WIDER* (United Nations University).
Lange, Oskar (1936-37), 'On the Economic Theory of Ssocialism' *Review of Economic Studies,* vol. 4, Pt. 1, Oct., pp. 53-71; Pt II, Feb., 1937, pp. 123-42. Reprinted in Nove, Nuti, 1972.
Marx, Karl (1967), *Das Kapital* first German edition 1867 (volume I), 1885 (volume II), 1893 (volume III). English translation Capital International Publishers, New York.
Mises, Ludwig von (1920), 'Die Wirtschaftrechnung in sozialistischen Gemeinwesen' *Archiv*

für Sozialwissenschaft und Sozialpolitik, Reprinted in English translation in Nove, Nuti, 1972.
North, Douglass and Thomas, Robert (1973), *The Rise of the Western World. A New Economic History*, Cambridge University Press, Cambridge.
North, Douglass (1990), *Institutions, Institutional Change and Economic Performance*, Cambridge University Press, Cambridge.
Nove, Alec and Nuti, D. M. (1972), *Socialist Economics*, Penguin, Harmondsworth.
Nunes, Ana Bela (1997), 'O modo de organização e funcionamento das economias nacionais no século XX' *Estudos de Economia*, vol. XVI-XVII, no. 3, pp. 253-278.
Pirenne, Henri (1933), *Histoire économique et sociale du Moyen Age*, Presses Universitaires de France, Paris. English Translation, *Economic and Social History of Medieval Europe*, Harcourt Brace & Co., New York, 1937.
Polanyi, Karl (1944), *The Great Transformation- The Political and Economic Origins of Our Time*, New Edition 1957, Beacon Press, Boston.
Rostow, Walt (1960), *The Stages of Economic Growth: a Non-communist Manifesto*, Cambridge University Press, Cambridge.
Schumpeter, Joseph (1974), *Capitalism, Socialism and Democracy*, [1942]. Allen & Unwin, London.
Smith, Adam (1976), *An Inquiry into the Nature and Causes of the Wealth of Nations*, [1776] Clarendon Press, Oxford.
Sombart, Werner (1928), *Der Modern Kapitalismus*, first German edition Leipzig, Duncker & Humbolt, 1902 (volume I + volume II), 1928 (volume III). Castilian translation El apogeo del capitalismo Fondo de Cultura Economica, Mexico, 1946.
Sweezzy, Paul *et al.* (1976), *The Transition from Feudalism to Capitalism*, Left Books, London.
Temin, Peter (1991), 'Soviet and Nazi economic planning in the 1930s' *Economic History Review*, vol. 44 (4), pp. 573-593.
Wallerstein, Immanuel (1974-90), *The Modern World-System*, 3 volumes, Academic Press, New York.
Wallerstein, Immanuel (1976), 'From feudalism to capitalism transition or transitions?' *Social Forces*, vol. 552, pp. 273-83.
Wallerstein, Immanuel (1986), 'Le capitalisme, ennemi du marché? Réflexions sur la thèse de Fernand Braudel' *Revista de História Económica e Social*, no. 17, pp. 1-4.
Weber, Max (1904-5), 'Die protestantische Ethik und der Geist des Kapitalismus' *Archiv für Sozialwissenschaft und Sozialpolitik* English translation 'The Protestant Ethic and the Spirit of Capitalism', George Allen & Unwin, London, 1978 (2nd edition).

Chapter Eight

Friedrich von Hayek's Idea of Spontaneous Social Order and Transforming the Socialist Economy

Janina Godłów-Legiędź

Introductory remarks

The wave of political democratization and economic liberalization that we are going through in the countries of Central and Eastern Europe can be seen as a confirmation of the standpoint presented by the Austrian liberal economists of the 1930s in the famous dispute about the rational character of the socialist economy. The fall of centrally planned economies seems to confirm the thesis formulated by Friedrich von Hayek, that without private ownership and the market, any rational allocation of resources providing for human needs is impossible. The fall of socialist economies on such a large area not only strengthened the economic justification for capitalism, but also added to the moral rehabilitation of capitalism. Without the socialist perspective, it was more difficult to criticize capitalism. And though the moral challenges and dangers that contemporary civilization is facing now, are, in a considerable degree, an effect of the market economy logic and the expansion of market rules to almost all spheres of social life, one cannot deny that the institutions of the market economy are connected with democratic institutions and enable the realization of economic values, as well as the moral values of freedom, equality and participation in social life.

This huge transformation that took place in Poland and in other countries of Central and Eastern Europe at the turn of 1980s and 1990s, had to be a source of satisfaction for the writer who had always kept saying that the market system is not only economically efficient, but it is also the only system that guarantees freedom and justice and favours the development of peaceful and friendly relations between people and nations. But the paradox here is, that when the thesis that rational economic activity without the market is impossible found empirical confirmation, weak points of the doctrine formulated by the author of this prophecy manifested themselves and gradually the enthusiasm for his idea was fading. As long as there was socialism, Hayek's works, not available in the official circulation, were a source of inspiration for the criticism of socialist reality. Hayek's doctrine, both philosophically and economically, was a perfect example of a vision of society and economy being a reverse image of communist ideology and real socialism.

Hayek's doctrine was very powerful and popular among the Polish democratic opposition due to the uncompromising character of his standpoint. The author of *The Road to Serfdom* did not present a liberal attitude characterized by lack of dogmatism, hypothetical character of opinions and readiness to compromise. He was rather one of these liberals who felt an irresistible need to create liberal theory and to formulate what are the assumptions, values and postulates of the 'true' liberalism. He was not in the least degree ready to moderate the thesis that in order to preserve economic freedom and efficiency, it is necessary to respect postulates resulting from the concept of negative freedom and commutative justice. Hayek claimed that a permanent, moral sense of capitalism lies in the fact that it is the only system that can guarantee freedom and prosperity. If capitalist criteria of the distribution of goods and power become the subject of criticism, then it means that people want more than capitalism can give them, but they also want more than humanity can ever achieve. He emphasized that any endeavour of the state to provide the individual with more than liberation from pressure of others and with different participation in wealth than such as is determined by the market, must lead to destruction of economic freedom and efficiency.

Knowledge and the Social Order

The basis for Hayek's enthusiasm for the market system and ruthless condemnation of the idea of central planning and social justice, were the following assumptions:

1) Social phenomena have a very complex nature.
2) Cognitive potential of the human mind is limited.
3) Economic activity is not only a logical problem of using given resources to provide for given ends, but first of all, it is the question of discovering these resources and ends. In short, the economic problem is the problem of applying the knowledge necessary for rational economic activity, which can never be given complete to one person.
4) In the process of social evolution, spontaneous, unplanned social institutions come into being which contain priceless knowledge and help man to solve the economic problem satisfactorily.

Epistemological arguments in favour of the market and the idea of spontaneous social order were the products of Hayek's views on the possibility of introducing economic calculation in socialism. It was the controversy about the rational character of the socialist economy that directed Hayek's interests onto the methodological questions of the social sciences and the question of spontaneously developing social order.

The controversy about the economic calculation in socialism influenced the way Hayek understood the economic problem and the subject of economics. In the first article of the series *Socialist Calculation* (Hayek, 1945) he pointed out that an economic problem such as the allocation of available resources into various applications, is never consciously solved in the capitalism economy, but is solved by the mechanism of competition. In the market system no one consciously defines ends in the macro level, or allocates means centrally. The final hierarchy of purposes and allocation of means is manifested *ex post* as an effect of individual decisions made in individual households and establishments.[1]

Two years later, analysing the concept of economic equilibrium, Hayek emphasized that in the traditional theory of equilibrium, economists assume the permanent character of data, and some also add a condition of perfect knowledge. He warned that what it means is ignoring the key problem, from the economic point of view - how individuals, each equipped with fragmentary knowledge of the conditions of economic activities, are able to create the state of balance which could be a result of conscious actions of one man having at his disposal the collected knowledge of all of them (Hayek, 1937, p. 33).

The problem of knowledge is also dealt with in an important article 'The Use of Knowledge in Society.' Hayek (1945b, p. 519) noticed here that in contrast to the common opinion, the economic problem is not only about the allocation of known resources to known purposes. In this general statement there is an assumption that participants in the economic processes have complete knowledge about the resources of the society and the system of preferences. But the knowledge, which is a starting point for the economic calculation, is never given to one man, but exists in the form dispersed among individuals. The real economic problem, according to Hayek, lies in the proper utilization of this dispersed knowledge and transmitting it to economic subjects, so that they were able to adapt their activities to ongoing transformations. The problem of using this dispersed knowledge is also the basis for the choice of rational economic order.

The market system is the best, due to the fact that the decentralization of economic decisions enables the use of every economic subject's knowledge about specific conditions of place and time, and the prices that are calculated on the basis of competition and the interaction of demand and supply, inform individual economic subjects about their position in the whole economic system.[2]

This idea of knowledge distribution in the market system was later supplemented with one more element - the idea of the rule of law. Moral principles and the rules of law created and developed in an evolutionary process of attempts and mistakes, contain experience of many generations and thus make it easier for the society to best adapt to the environment. Rules of law and morality constitute one more source of knowledge and give better opportunity to anticipate consequences of individual actions (Hayek, 1960, p. 148 a.f.).

Hayek keeps repeating that social institutions, which enable the realization of the distribution of knowledge guaranteeing optimum adaptation of societies to the environment, are not an effect of human plan and reason, but are a product of evolution. Starting from critical rationalism, Hayek finds justification for the free market in the evolution and spontaneity, that is the mechanism of creating a price system and the rules of just conduct. He treats socialism, central planning and state interventionism as symptoms of an incorrect, constructivist attitude, manifested by attempts to shape social organization authoritatively. Hayek believes that the source of the constructivist attitude is excessive belief in the potential of the human mind and improper understanding of social phenomena. People who want central organization, do not understand that individual human beings are the subjects of social actions, and the individuals act according to their own purposes and principles of movement. Only such social systems which let individuals act according to their own, inner principles of movement, have a chance to be successful. Besides, the system must provide individuals, acting according to their individual needs, with conditions enabling them to create an order, where opportunities of every individual and achieved prosperity are maximized.

The market system, containing both individual freedom and order, creates favourable conditions for free society, which, as a whole, can never be oriented on specific ends. Thus, the idea of public good must be changed. Liberalism, with its idea of free society, does not reject - as Hayek emphasizes - the idea of public good. It only rejects the perception of this good as a sum of known results. The essence of common good, that can be realized in the market system, is that voluntary cooperation of free people acting according to the rules of just conduct leads to mutual benefit.[3]

Conclusions for the Process of Transformation

When in 1989, a new direction of changes in political system was settled, Hayek was also referred to in the search for answers to the question of the best way to build the market economy. Depending on the individual views on what the reality should look like, various conclusions were drawn from Hayek's views.

Critics of the idea of introducing 'pure' market economy in Poland, formulated a general conclusion, that Hayek's evolutionary vision shows that fast, radical transformation of the system is impossible. Hayek's concept of rationalistic constructivism became a tool for criticizing the stabilization programme called 'Balcerowicz's Plan.' Government's actions were charged with containing incoherent elements, such as *laissez-faire*-ism in foreign trade and a reluctance to industrial policy on the one hand, and on the other a far-reaching state control in constructing the new system and imposing repressive conditions for economic activity (Kowalik, 1991, p. 39). It was anticipated that 'bringing extreme *laissez-faire*-ism and extreme constructivism together' must lead to deep crisis and will block all the reforms. Constructivism of liberal government was seen in making no allowances for 'humanistic factor' and in 'building the new social order against the opinions of the majority of society and with accepting the political criterion as superior to the requirements of effectiveness" (Ibid., p. 47).

Devotees of the capitalist economy emphasized the beneficial influence of market institutions and believed, irrespective of the criticism, that rationalistic constructivism met with that fast introduction of Hayek's catalaxy rules, will solve basic problems. Economic freedom, competition, price mechanism - these are social institutions whose usefulness confirmed by years of experience that does not have to be copied in the countries of Eastern Europe. The fall of centrally planned economies was an additional, negative evidence that the market economy is the right solution.

Who was closer to Hayek's ideas: constructivistic Polish liberals realizing 'Balcerowicz's plan' or their critics? The answer depends on the answer to another question: was Hayek an evolutionist in the strict sense?

It seems that Hayek would not have called radical market reform constructivism, because he was not an evolutionist in the strict sense. He believed that proper institutional solutions result from spontaneous changes taking place in the social environment which meets certain, preliminary conditions.[4] If Hayek had been an evolutionist in the strict sense, he would not have had to worry about the results of social evolution. His belief in beneficial effect of evolution would have been synonymous with the belief that only beneficial social institutions would appear. Uncompromising criticism of social justice and socialism proves, that his idea of evolutionary development refers to the specific case of spontaneous changes taking place in society, whose members are subject to the discipline of abstract rules of just conduct. Hayek does not leave society with its own logic of evolutionary development. From amongst the transmitted moral tradition he chooses this one, which in his opinion, is the best for the man. He points to private ownership, freedom and personal interests as the principles which let and help societies to develop, and he condemns altruism, group solidarity and aiming at social justice as factors bringing societies to ruin. He does not want to plan society in detail, does not define its specific ends, but he wants to be sure that general rules will be observed and good, tested institutions preserved (Gamble, 1996, p. 40). These principles are necessary for the spontaneously creating order and appearing social institutions to be beneficial. Spontaneity and the long-lasting process of attempts and mistakes are not enough; it is necessary for this process of spontaneous emergence of new solutions to take place within certain framework, and to have certain initial conditions met, such as freedom, private ownership and competition.[5]

In the light of such interpretation, one can say that the very idea of spontaneous social order was questioned. Hayek's critical rationalism and anticonstructivism were questioned as well. This conclusion can be also confirmed by Hayek's opinion, that aiming at social justice is derived from atavistic instincts and in order to save civilisation from extermination being the result of 'morality incapable of living', a rational insight into the principles of social order is necessary, and a rational choice of a moral system adequate to the market economy. If, finally, it is the rational choice that is to decide about survival of capitalism, it means that the idea of uncontrolled, evolutionary choice has been shaken.

It means that Hayek's doctrine is not free from contradictions and thus it is difficult to draw explicit conclusions from this doctrine. It also seems unlikely to draw an explicit conclusion that stabilizing reform and creation of market institutions by the state is a violation of the liberal philosophy. But Hayek's philosophy of market economy makes us realize that the process of political system transformations must be long and difficult. After all, Hayek's doctrine shows that market institutions do not operate in social vacuum. One of the very important elements of a free society is moral tradition, which enables individuals to take responsibility for their freedom. Market cannot function without moral and legal institutions, protecting society from transformation of freedom into anarchy. Freedom is not possible without deeply rooted moral views, and pressure can be minimized only when individuals observe the rules of their own free will (1960, p. 62).

Hayek also emphasizes that the functioning of the market depends on the specific meaning we give to the general rules of private ownership, competition and freedom of agreements. He was warning that adaptation of legal regulations concerning land ownership, patents, copyrights, trade marks, and the right to organize associations, to ongoing transformations, was the necessary condition for preserving and proper functioning of the system based on competition. He admitted that traditional liberal doctrine, not only did not fulfil the task of adapting the law to new problems, but it never created a clear enough project of the legal system that would protect the market system. He even did not hesitate to say that it is the fact of accepting the lack of activity of the state as the fundamental principle of liberalism, and not the policy promoting creation and development of the system of competition, that is equally responsible for the fall of competition as active support of the state for monopolists (Hayek, 1972, pp. 21; 111-117; 1978, p. 145).

If the state in evolving capitalism has to fulfil such important tasks, then it seems obvious that these tasks may be even more serious and difficult in the situation of building the market system from the very beginning. Acceptance of the general rules of just conduct is only the first, initial condition. Hayek does not give definite answers as to what to do later. However, from the point of view of transformation from socialism to capitalism, Hayek's general instructions are of crucial importance. One can point out enumerate drawbacks of the price system, simplifications of the standard description of the market, but from the point of view of society which was functioning within the system of central planning, liberation of prices and making private enterprise possible, is of such benefit, that would be hard to overestimate.

Balcerowicz's plan, whose realization was the key element in the transformation process in Poland after the January 1st, 1990, was a subject of controversy from the very beginning. Discussion focussed on the questions of the rate and the order of the system transformations. Balcerowicz's plan was accused of having a shock character, and the rationality of stabilization without creating institutional conditions for market economy was questioned.[6] The most difficult was the period 1990-1991, when we observed a decline in gross domestic product, increase in unemployment and a severe decline in the population's real income. But, at the same time, positive phenomena manifested themselves, such as: the elimination of shortages and putting the market into equilibrium; liquidation of budget deficit; and increased confidence in the Polish currency. Stabilizing reform began a long-term process of rationalization of economic principles. Beginning in 1993, Poland entered the path of a relatively high economic growth. The average rate of the gross domestic product (GDP) growth in 1993-97, was about 6%, and industrial production grew by 10% annually. The inflation rate was reduced to 13% in 1997. One could also observe technological modernization of fixed assets, considerable growth of labour productivity and better utilization of materials and energy in production processes. There was also growth in real wages recently, and gradual improvement in the situation of individual households. Such a positive balance of the Polish economy has been noted by the economists who were severe critics of the direction taken in 1990 (Sadowski, 1998, p. 9).

In the perspective of 8 years of experience, one must admit that transforming the Polish economy into the market economy brought positive results. The basis for the stabilizing reform was the simplest principle of liberal economy - the principle of price formation based on demand and supply in the conditions of strict budget limitation. Thus, if we can talk about considerable success on the Polish path to efficient economy, it is also a confirmation of the fundamentals of liberal economy.

It does not mean that in Hayek's works we will find solutions to the problems of system transformation, nor that his vision of capitalism is a model to be followed. However, it may justify the inclination of Eastern liberals to the attitude called Marxism *a rebours*. Restoration of private ownership and freedom of entering into agreement do not encompass all political wisdom fill the whole political wisdom but they are necessary. This may explain why even these people who reject communism but are not ready to bet on free market capitalism, are fascinated by Hayek's ideas.

Notes

1. Hayek paid attention to the fact that since there is no market and competition in the centrally planned economy, decisions about the choice of purposes and allocation must be taken centrally. Therefore, in a socialist economy it is necessary to solve problems which do not exist in the market system.
2. In Hayek's opinion, contemporary societies underestimate the price mechanism and overestimate possibilities of central control, and they underestimate the importance of practical knowledge and of economic problems, but they overestimate the scientific knowledge of experts and the importance of technological progress. Hayek emphasizes important contribution of Adam Smith to the discovery that price mechanism is a method which can help the man to overcome his limited cognitive potential and best use the knowledge shared by millions of individuals, see: F. Hayek, 'Competition as Discovery Procedure' in: *New Studies in Philosophy, Politics, Economics and the History of Ideas*, Chicago 1978, p.184.
3. 'The conception of the common welfare or of the public good of free society can therefore never be defined as a sum of known particular results to be achieved, but only as an abstract order which as a whole is not oriented on any particular concrete ends but provides merely the best chance for any member selected at random

successfully to use his knowledge for his purposes. ... The great importance of spontaneous order or nomocracy rests on the fact that it extends the possibility of peaceful co-existence of men for their mutual benefit beyond the small group whose members have concrete common purposes, or were subject to a common superior, and that it thus made the appearance of the Great or Open Society possible.' (F.Hayek, 'The Principles of a Liberal Social Order', in: *The Essence of Hayek,* 1984, p. 366).

4. R.A. Arnold claims that Hayek is a non-theological constructivist, see his 'Hayek and Institutional Reform', in: Friedrich V. Hayek, *Critical Assessments,* vol. III, 1991, p. 227.

5. 'The extension of an order of peace beyond the small purpose-oriented organization became thus possible by the extension of purpose-independent ("formal") rules of just conduct to the relations with other men who did not pursue the same concrete ends or hold the same values except those abstract rules - rules which did not impose obligations for particular actions (which always presuppose a concrete end) but consisted solely in prohibitions from infringing the protected domain of each which these rules enable us to determine. Liberalism is therefore inseparable from the institution of private property which is the name we usually give to the material part of this protected individual domain.' (Hayek, 1984, p. 368).

6. The discussion about the programme of L.Balcerowicz is synthetically described in the work of Edward Aukawera, Z historii polskiej myśl ekonomicznej 1945-95 (*From the History of Polish Economic Thought 1945-95*), Warszawa 1996, p. 69.

References

Ackerman, B. (1996), Przyszłość rewolucji liberalnej (The Future of Liberal Revolution), Warszawa.

Gamble, A. (1996), *Hayek. The Iron Cage of Liberty,* Cambridge: Cambridge University Press.

Hayek, Fredrick von (1984), 'The Principles of a Liberal Social Order' in: *The Essence of Hayek,* Stanford, Stanford University Press.

Hayek, Fredrick von (1972), *Individualism and Economic Order,* Chicago: Chicago University Press.

Hayek, Fredrick von (1968), *New Studies in Philosophy, Politics, Economics and History of Ideas,* University of Chicago, Chicago.

Hayek, Fredrick von (1960). *The Constitution of Liberty,* Chicago: Henry Regnery & Co.

Hayek, Fredrich von (1945a), *Socialist Calculation I: Nature and History of the Problem,* in: *Collectivist Economic Planning,* London.

Hayek, Fredrich von. (1945b), 'The Use of Knowledge in Society' *American Economic Review,* no.4, Sept., pp. 519-30.

Hayek, Fredrich von (1937). "Economics and Knowledge" *Economica* ns 4, Feb., pp. 33-54.

Kowalik, T. (1991), Zmiana ustroju - wielka operacja czy proces spoBeczny (Change of the system - great operation or social process), in: SpoBeczeDstwo uczestniczce. Gospodarka rynkowa. Sprawiedliwo spoBeczna. (Participating Society, Market Economy, Social Justice,) Warszawa.

Sadowski, Z. (1998), Stan gospodarki polskiej w 1997r. i jej perspektywy (The Condition of the Polish Economy in 1997 and Its Prospects), *Ekonomista,* no.1.

Szacki, J. (1994), Liberalizm po komunizmie (Liberalism after Communism), Kraków.

Chapter Nine

Worldly Advice from Other-Worldly Philosophers: Catholic Social Thought and the Problem of Economic Transition

Charles M. A. Clark

> *There is nothing more useful than to look at the world as it really is — and at the same time look elsewhere for a remedy to its troubles.* Leo XIII

Introduction: The Problem of Economic Transition

The policy advice Western governments, international agencies and economists have offered the Central and Eastern European economies attempting to make the transition from central planning to reliance on market mechanisms has been almost exclusively based on neoclassical economic theory. This is an unfortunate situation. Neoclassical economic theory is singularly ill-equipped to understand and give advice on the issues economies and societies undergoing radical transformation face.[1] As many of the papers of this conference attest, it is to the 'Worldly Philosophers', those economists who looked at the economy in its historical and social context, that we should turn, not to the self-attested marginalist theorists.

The problem of economic transition is more cultural, historical and spiritual than it is economic, three factors that neoclassical economic theory cannot, by its very nature and substance, include in its analysis. In this introduction I will explain why I feel the important issues of transition are cultural, historical and spiritual, and not 'economic' in the neoclassical sense. In the second section of this chapter I will attempt to demonstrate why I think neoclassical economic theory is useless for understanding and giving advice on the important issues relating to economic transition. In the third section I will suggest that the Catholic social thought tradition offers a very useful perspective for these issues. This theme is elaborated in the fourth section. The chapter concludes with a plea for a more cultural, historical and spiritual approach to the problem of economic transition.

Culture, History and Spirituality

One of the central points of Karl Polanyi is his assertion that the economy needs to be understood in its historical and social context. This, in fact, is a theme common to all those we would call 'Worldly Philosophers', Robert Heilbroner's term for the great economists. The term is fitting, I feel, because it distinguished those economists who were able to see the big picture, that is those who placed the economy in its historical and social context. The greatest fault of modern neoclassical economic theory is that it has no historical sense; it is unable to view the economy in its historical and social context.

All economies are part of a larger culture and take place in an historical setting: the economy is always embedded in history and culture. A market-based economy certainly has attributes which, if one looks only at the surface and through a certain (neoclassical) lens, gives the impression of an autonomous market — the invisible hand. Yet, even though in those societies in which the market plays an important role, maybe even a dominant one, it is still embedded in a society, in a history and culture. This is necessarily the case and cannot help being otherwise. Markets can only exist if they are created, supported and defined by cultural and social institutions. The market cannot (and never has) generate social or economic order. Market phenomena are social phenomena, they are not natural phenomena. This is true in all cases and at all times. Markets require a great deal of institutional support which comes from, formerly and informally, society, history and culture. One clearly recognized institution needed for markets to function is clearly defined, supported and protected (enforced) property rights. This point has been noted even by neoclassical economists, yet this is no simple point. In order for property rights to be fully secured they have to be an essential aspect not only of the law, but also of the cultural values, hence they come for history and society. The existence of property rights might be a necessary condition for markets to function, but they are never sufficient. The developed values of justice, self control and fairness are of equal importance. There is no reason to expect that markets will, by themselves, be able to establish the conditions necessary for markets to function effectively. Adam Smith knew all this. The self-interested economic actors we meet in *The Wealth of Nations* had already been socialized in *The Theory of Moral Sentiments (TMS)*.

An essential aspect of any society is its spiritual component, even in self professed atheistic societies. This is true for many reasons. As Adam Smith notes in *TMS*, religion is one of the most important devices for socializing the people of a given society into the morals, values and world-view of that society. But religion is also an important aspect of the 'spirit' of the society, a point that has been demonstrated by Max Weber and Richard Twaney, among others. It helps to define the 'good' or 'ideal' of society. This plays an important role in shaping society's goals and ambitions, the direction of its development, what is important for the society. This spirit helps to shape the culture and helps to give direction to its historical development, thus it is an underlying factor in the historical and social context of a given society. Furthermore, religion is what underlies and legitimates society's values, whether it is a revealed religion or a state created 'pseudo-religions' as Maoism became in China or Marxism-Leninism-Stalism became in the Soviet Union.

This is particularly important for a society undergoing rapid and significant transformations. The 'spirit' of the society helps to direct society's energies and efforts, just at a time when the past attitudes and preconceptions are declining and losing acceptance. This was clearly the case when the communist regimes started in Eastern and Central Europe. If this spirit is absent it will be replaced by the guiding spirit of those with power and control. In the case of the Eastern and Central European countries now undertaking a radical transformation, this spirit is being supplied by the ideology and ideals of 'laissez-faire' capitalism and its "pseudo-religion" of neoclassical economics. The ideology of laissez-faire capitalism has many of the qualities of a 'religion'. First off, at its core, neoclassical economic theory is a faith based ideology, based on the belief in the invisible hand and the omnipotence of markets. Although it has the pretense of being a science (i.e. mathematical formalism gives the appearance, but not the substance, of a science) it clearly is a faith based discipline. This can be seen in the fact that neoclassical economic theory: is not an empirically based science (its core assumptions and propositions are not derived from observation); is based on an unrealistic (incorrect) conception of human nature (one psychologists have long since rejected) and society; and is based on an erroneous conception of the structure and functions of prices and markets. These points are readily admitted by the high priests of neoclassical economics in their frequent methodological writings, where, among other confessions, they argue that there is no need for realism in economic theory.

Why Neoclassical Economics is not a Useful Tool for the Problem of Economic Transition

As I stated in the introduction, the problems of economic transition go well beyond economics proper. They require a full understanding of the historical and social context that these countries are in and a vision of a just and humane society as a goal to move towards. Neoclassical economics cannot include historical and social context into its analysis for this would require their abandoning the pretense of being a 'science' on par with physics. In fact, the major thrust of the development of neoclassical economic theory has been the eradication of historical and social context from economic analysis, under the methodological and philosophical assumption that you discover 'universals' by eliminating any analysis of 'particulars'(Clark 1992). Starting with William Stanley Jevons, and moving at a progressively rapid pace, neoclassical economists have narrowed the focus of economic analysis so that they can explain (or at least attempt to explain) all economic activity in terms of autonomous individuals exchanging in a perfect market. The only 'historical' or 'social' factor that is allowed into the analysis is the existence of private property rights, yet even here it is an unhistorical understanding of property rights, as we will see below.

This lack of historical and social context is justified in neoclassical economics by their belief that economic phenomena are, in their essence, 'natural' and not 'social', that is, the result of natural forces and laws (scarcity and human nature) and not the end result of social activity. The laws and theories that make up neoclassical economic theory are consider natural laws, exposing invariant economic forces. Thus they can be applied, the modern neoclassical economist claims, to everything from the medieval manor to contemporary stock markets. What is most important for the transitional societies (historical and cultural factors) is what is not allowed to enter the hard core of neoclassical theory. It is only if one has such a narrow perspective, that one could suggest, after the fall of the Berlin Wall, that all that was needed was to privatize the state sector, establish and enforce property rights and set up a stock market, and the economy (and one supposes society as well) will take care of itself. A decade of experience is more than enough to lead us to question this perspective.

Value and Utility as the Good

Underlying neoclassical economic theory is the marginal utility theory of value. The purpose of value theory in the history of economics is grossly misunderstood. For most economists it is merely an archaic term for price theory, yet value theory is at the heart of all economic theory. As Robert Heilbroner has noted, the theory of value is really about the underlying order of the economy and society. Prices are at best a rather imperfect manifestation of this order, even under ideal conditions, but they are of interest only to the extent that they reflect this order.[2] One of the most important aspects of this order are the 'ideals' of a society, what is the 'good'. Value theory is an expression of what the particular society, or those who are its active force, value. Specifically, what they value enough to carry out in their actions and adjust their behaviour to bring about. In this case, as in all others, the real chases after the ideal.

'In the classical and much of the neoclassical tradition in economics, the maximal satisfaction of wants, notably consumer wants, has been and remains the basic criterion of judgement, the standard of value, the basis on which to distinguish between good and bad, proper and improper, and desirable and undesirable' (Tool 1986, p. 89). Value comes from and is measured by utility.[3] The theory of marginal utility serves both of the functions of value theory: the ordering properties of society and the legitimation and evaluation of ends (Clark 1995). For the neoclassical economist something has value only in so far as it delivers utility to someone through the marketplace. The marketplace sums the total individual utilities of consumers and balances these against the disutilities of producers (demand and supply) and reaches an equilibrium when these are equal. The underlying order of the market (which for neoclassical economics is society) is an expression of society's values. Economist's often note that utility can be had outside of market transactions, but this is seen as a market failure and leads to inefficiencies (not the optimal allocation of utility).

If a society is motivated solely by the search for utility through the marketplace, then neoclassical economics has the possibility of being a realistic depiction of such a society (assuming it could work out all of its other problems, such as the need for complete information, inability to accommodate money or production). If neoclassical economic theory comes to dominate a society, establishing its vision and setting its values as the social norms, then such a society will start to reflect the neoclassical world. This will not be a society in which prices generate economic and social order, merely one that values greed. However, such a society can never fully be created for such a social order is not viable. As James Gordley has recently demonstrated, the world of neoclassical economic theory must, in order to work as an actual economy and society, be populated with citizens who religiously follow the four virtues (prudence, justice, temperance and courage) highlighted in the work of Aristotle and St. Thomas.[4] The problem for neoclassical economic theory is that neither 'markets' as a socializing institution or neoclassical economic theory as an ideology or 'religion' produces such people. Furthermore, their emphasis on greed as a 'good' eats away at such virtues. Thus neoclassical economic theory is itself a threat to social order for it glorifies and legitimates what is essentially anti-social behaviour.

Human Nature

The Neoclassical view of human nature is an outgrowth of their theory of value. This view of human nature is frequently called 'rational economic man'. Although the vast majority of economists will quickly admit that it is a narrow depiction of human nature, overly simplistic and often presented (and accepted) as a caricature, they would also nevertheless claim that it is essential for an understanding of economic activity and market forces.

Economic theory conceives of human nature in utilitarian terms, as a rational utility maximiser, driven solely by self-interest, chained, as Jeremy Bentham so vividly stated, to the twin pillars of pain and pleasure. This mechanical view of human nature comes from, and is necessary for, their mechanistic view of society and creates a truly distorted picture of humans, as has been skilfully and humourously demonstrated by Thorstein Veblen (1919, p. 73-74) when he wrote:

> The hedonistic conception of man is that of a lightening calculator of pleasures and pains, who oscillates like a homogenous globule of desire of happiness under the impulse of stimuli that shift him about the area, but leave him intact. He is neither antecedent nor consequent. He is an isolated, definitive human datum, in stable equilibrium except for the buffets of the impinging forces that displace him in one direction or another. Self-imposed in elemental space, he spins symmetrically about his own spiritual axis until the parallelogram of forces bears down upon him, whereupon he follows the line of the resultant. When the force of the impact is spent, he comes to rest, a self-contained globule of desire as before.

Man seeks pleasure and avoids pain, and every decision comes down to a calculus of costs and benefits, pains and pleasures. Economists will frequently admit that man may be driven by other motives outside their economic life, yet they claim that this depiction of human nature is very useful for developing economic models and theories to explain economic activity. Their deep belief in this view of human nature can be seen by their willingness to use this conception of economic man to explain non-economic behaviour (this being the bases of economic imperialism, the attempt to explain all social phenomena via economic theory), and in their exclusion of all other motives that cannot be reduced to rational self-interest.

One reason economist's hold this view of human nature, as Veblen pointed out long ago, is that their view of society and the economy as an equilibrium system requires deterministic and atomistic behaviour, as does their mathematical models. Yet, rational economic man has no free will. In one of the great ironies of intellectual history, the theory of free markets based on free choice requires that the individuals that make up the economy and society display deterministic behaviour, that is, have no freedom of choice. If one wants to show that a market economy produces optimal equilibrium outcomes, than one has to exclude human choice.

This idea of rational economic man as the view of a universal human nature causes neoclassical economist to expect that policy designed for capitalistic societies will work similarly in post socialistic societies (for the people will behave the same way). They did not fully realize that reacting to market signals in an efficient manner is a socialized response, not fully realized in the most developed capitalistic economy, but non-existent in non-capitalistic economies.

Vision of Society

The atomistic and hedonistic view of human nature leads to a mechanical and individualistic view of society. The individualistic view of society has its roots in the mechanical view of nature, with Isaac Newton as its greatest proponent. In this approach, society is conceived as a collection of individuals. Only the individuals really exist, society as a separate entity is a mental fiction. Mechanics and physics are the primary source of metaphors for displacement into economics for this view of society. Mechanistic social theorists have looked to the individual as the 'final term', meaning that all explanations must be in terms of individual actions and motives. This adoption of 'methodological individualism' stems from the belief that human nature, by itself, includes the necessary drives and propensities that produce social order (equilibrium) and not chaos.

The mechanistic view of society has dominated both classical and neoclassical economic theory. At one level we see this in the extensive use of mechanical and physics analogies and metaphors. The market equilibrium story is a displacement of Newtonian mechanics onto economic activity, with the resultant equilibrium being determined by the balance of individual forces. It is also seen in the necessity to explain all social phenomena as the result of individual human propensities. The net result of adopting the mechanistic view of society is that it forces the theorist to exclude historical and social context from their analysis. The most extreme form of this type of economic analysis is modern general equilibrium theory, in which neither history nor social context exist. In fact, neoclassical economists see this as one of the strengths of their approach. As Werner Stark (1962, p. 56-7) has noted: 'If the social order is likened to an equilibrium system, ... then it is almost certain to be interpreted in a non historical and unhistorical spirit. An equilibrium has no history; its laws do not change with the centuries. The formal equations in which it can be described are of timeless validity, as all purely quantitative propositions must be. Rational mechanics is a branch of mathematics and its students glory in the fact: those social theorists who wanted to model [social theory] on rational mechanics [cannot] admit the reality of developmental change'. As we will see, the Catholic social thought tradition has been extremely critical of the individualism which is at the heart of orthodox economics and the laissez faire philosophy it supports, and rejects this view of human nature and society.

Efficiency

There are two working conceptions of efficiency in neoclassical economics, one micro and one macro. The micro conception is the Pareto principle. This is the notion that any change in the holding of commodities (including money) that makes at least one person worse off is inefficient. This is so because, under the assumptions of neoclassical economics, no one would make such an exchange voluntarily. Furthermore, neoclassical economists do not allow for interpersonal comparisons of utility and make no mention of the original distribution of goods and incomes. All are considered outside the purview of their analysis and thus, by default, all distributions are given equal moral weight. A small number of people or families owning all or almost all of the commodities with everyone else starving or nearly starving is morally equivalent to everyone enjoying a decent standard of living, equal in the sense that neoclassical economic theory is indifferent between the two, that is, cannot, within neoclassical economic theory, chose one over the other.

It is in the macro economic concept of Gross National Product — the price of aggregate output — that the neoclassical view of efficiency has its greatest impact on economic discussion and policy. Here the final criteria is: does it produce economic growth, i.e increases in GNP. This is the most important criteria for neoclassical policy, for GNP is a measure of all the utility consumed in the market place, utility being the neoclassical conception of the 'good'. The limitations of GNP as a measure of social or economic well-being are well known or at least should be. Yet it is worth pointing out that much of the United States economic growth in the past 30 years has been merely social decay by another name, as pollution, the decline of the family, crime and other social ills have generated vast increases in market transactions,[5] but little towards real social improvement.

The limitations of neoclassical economic theory for understanding and guiding economies in transition can be summed up as such: it cannot include historical and social context and it has a morally bankrupt and socially damaging concept of 'good'. It therefore cannot understand the present and cannot help in moving towards a desirable future. The citizens of Eastern and Central Europe need to look elsewhere.

An Alternative Vision: The Perspective from Catholic Social Thought

Unlike neoclassical economic theory, the Catholic social thought tradition is openly and explicitly based on a specific vision and set of value judgements. They are not hidden preconceptions, but instead celebrated pillars upon which all social formations and analysis need to be built. It is a vision grounded in the Old Testament, come to life in the Gospels and it provides the explicit underpinning for the various Encyclicals and other Church documents that make up the Catholic social thought tradition. At the heart of this 'vision' is the belief that 'God speaks to every reality. Whatever we are looking at, whether it is an issue such as world hunger ... or an economic system such as Capitalism, God does have something to say to that reality. Our world either is or is not in accord with God's ideal for it. Consequently it is important for us to come to know what God is saying to whatever reality we are examining. God speaks to these issues or situations in various ways: through the Bible, through the teachings of His Church, through the signs of the times and through the prophets who interpret those signs' (Healy and Reynolds, 1983, p. 5-6).

One bedrock value of this tradition is the assertion of the dignity of all humans. 'The dignity of the human person, realized in community with others, is the criterion against which all aspects of economic life must be measured' (*Economic Justice for All* in O'Brien and Shannon, 1992, p. 584). This is an assertion that runs through the Catholic social thought tradition and its significance cannot be understated, for it calls for a view of society which is not mechanistic and individualistic, as is neoclassical economic theory, or completely organic, as is vulgar Marxism. Both the individual and the community are interconnected and neither can be reduced to the other.

This interconnectedness is at the core of the idea of the common good. Since human nature is defined as social, the welfare of the each individual is connected with that of the community. The common good is not an equilibrium state of affairs. It is a process. 'The common good is a social reality in which all persons should share through their participation in it. It is not simply the arithmetic aggregate of individual goods suggested by the utilitarian formula 'the greatest good for the greatest number'. In a utilitarian understanding, increased aggregate social good (e.g., gross national product) is compatible with the exclusion of some persons from participation in it. Emphasis on the participation of all in the common good is particularly important' (Hollenbach, 1994, p. 193). Pope John XXIII defined the common good as that which 'embraces the sum total of those conditions of social living, whereby men are enabled more fully and more readily to achieve their own perfection' *(Mater et Magistra,* 65). This interdependence was particularly highlighted in the Vatican II document, *Gaudium et Spes*: 'Man's social nature makes it evident that the progress of the human person and the advance of society itself hinge on each other. For the beginning, the subject, and the goal of all social institutions is and must be the human person, which for its part and by its very nature stands completely in need of social life'. John Paul II has recently emphasized that concern for the environment is an essential aspect of the common good, for the obvious reason that man needs more than community to flourish.

In *Economic Justice for All,* the US Bishops stated that six principles must be followed if economic policy is to promote the common good: '1) every economic decision and institution must be judged in light of whether it protects or undermines the dignity of the human person; 2) human dignity can be realized and protected only in community; 3) all people have a right to participate in the economic life of society; 4) all members of society have a special obligation to the poor and vulnerable; 5) human rights are the minimum condition for life in community; and 6) society as a whole, acting through public and private institutions, has the moral responsibility to enhance human dignity and protect human rights' (O'Brien and Shannon, 1992, p. 575).

Economic theory defines efficiency in terms of market transactions and outcomes, profit and loss, underpinned by the mythical entities of utility and disutility. The Catholic social thought tradition asserts a different yardstick. Yet it is not anti-growth or hostile to economic life (both common charges). It is economic growth as an end that is objected to, not economic growth as a means. Catholic social thought offers a different 'vision' of economic development and progress (see *Populorum Progressio*).[6] To follow productivity as a goal, without regard for the context of economic activity and its human dimension, is to follow a false God. As the U. S. Bishops have stated:

> Productivity is essential if the community is to have the resources to serve the well-being of all. Productivity, however, cannot be measured solely by its output in goods and services. Patterns of production must also be measured in light of their impact on the fulfilment of basic needs, employment levels, patterns of discrimination, environmental quality and sense of community (O'Brien and Shannon, 1992, p. 595).

The key distinction that Catholic social thought makes is that humans can never be treated as means to an end, for they are the ends. The treatment of workers as mere commodities to be used to maximize profits is objectionable. We can see a clear statement of this view in *Rerum Novarum*:

> The following duties bind the wealthy owner and the employer: not to look upon their work-people as their bondsmen but to respect in every person his or her dignity and worth. ... They are reminded that ... to misuse people as though they were things in the pursuit of gain ... is truly shameful and inhuman. ... Furthermore, employers must never tax their work-people beyond their strength, or employ them is work unsuited to their sex and age. Their great and principal duty is to give every one what is just. ... to gather one's profit

out of need of another, is condemned by all laws human and divine.... Lastly, the rich must religiously refrain from cutting down the workers' earnings, whether by force, fraud or by unjust dealings ... (RN 16-17) (quoted in Dorr, 1992. p. 24).

And this theme is continued in numerous subsequent documents. Thus for Catholic social thought the concept of efficiency must be defined in terms of the meeting of human needs, regardless of whether these needs are expressed in the market. Furthermore, these needs are not limited to material ones.

The Catholic social thought tradition also has a very different conception of equity. The basis of equity in Catholic social thought is the common gift from God of the earth. Thus the minimum equity criteria is that all have a share in this gift to so that each will meet their basic minimum needs. 'God destined the earth and all that it contains for the use of all people and peoples. Furthermore, the right to have a share of earthly goods sufficient for oneself and one's family belongs to everyone' (Vatican II, in Dorr, 1992, p. 154). This is not a claim for perfect equality, but that all are insured a decent standard of living. This claim is also put forward in the United Nations Universal Declaration of Human Rights.

The Catholic social thought tradition also notes that greater equity is to the benefit of both rich and poor and that there are gains to society from greater equity. 'Excessive economic and social inequalities within the one human family, between individuals or between peoples, give rise to scandal, and are contrary to social justice, to equity, and to the dignity of the human person, as well as to peace within society and at the international level' (*Gaudium et Spes*, 29.3 in Dorr, p. 158). The is not an original observation to the Catholic social thought tradition, Adam Smith recognized it as well.

Catholic social thought has, for the most part, followed a two pronged attack on social justice issues. On the one hand it has noted the many structural issues that lead to the abuse of human dignity and the many social inequities. These issues require structural reform, most often in the form of national or international regulation. Here we would find policies like minimum wage legislation and better terms of trade for the developing countries. Yet equally important for the tradition is the changing of the hearts of individuals. Catholic social thought calls on each of us to look at every person as a fellow child of God, to see Christ in them. This is true for us in our business lives, as owners, managers, workers, consumers and voters, thus it is a call for a new attitude in the micro-aspects of our economic lives.

Advice from Catholic Social Thought

The Catholic social though tradition does not offer an alternative economic theory from which to analyse and understand the problems of transitional economies. What it offers is a 'vision' from which to start such a task, a moral compass to direct researchers and policy makers towards promoting a just society.[7] Many of the concepts developed in the Catholic social thought tradition are of particular interest to transitional economies. This is especially the case since the Catholic social thought tradition originated in the Church's reflection on the social transformations brought about by the industrial revolution. The transformations that the formerly communist countries are undertaking are in many ways analogous to those that the Western countries went through in the last half of the 19th and first half of the 20th centuries. Many of the key principles of Catholic social thought illuminate the problems transitional economies are facing and can serve as a guide for understanding and directing these economic changes. Of particular importance are the principles of: Subsidiarity; Property; Priority of Labour; Solidarity; and the Option for the Poor. This section will briefly review these concepts and what they offer to the understanding of the problems of transitional economies.

Subsidiarity

The principle of subsidiarity relates to the social character of the individual and their natural right to associate with others in general and to organize in the form of groups in particular. It directly contradicts the laissez-faire view of society that states that society is merely a collection of separate individuals. A major thrust of the principle of subsidiarity has been the contention that if a task can be equally carried out by small or large organizations, the smaller one is preferable. It does not assert that larger organizations, such as the state, have no role to play, just that the state should only carry out activities that are beyond the capabilities of smaller organizations. 'In *Quadragesimo anno* Puis XI explicitly makes the principle of subsidiarity the guiding norm upon which the social order is to be restored:

> That most weighty principle, which cannot be set aside or changed, remains fixed and unshaken in social philosophy. Just as it is gravely wrong to take from individuals what they can accomplish by their own initiative and industry and give it to the community, so also it is an injustice and at the same time a grave evil and disturbance of right order to assign to a greater or higher association what lesser and subordinate organizations can do. For every social activity ought of its very nature to furnish help to the members of the body social, and never destroy and absorb them' (quoted in Allsopp, 1994, p. 928).

The underpinning of the principle of subsidiarity is the idea that not only are efficient outcomes necessary, but so also is the process by which they are achieved — the means and ends cannot be separated. Specifically, human dignity asserts that humans participate in their culture and society as fully as possible. Subsidiarity requires that the decisions and activities that affect peoples lives should be carried out by organizations as close to the individuals affected as can be efficiently accomplished. Obviously activities like an aerospace program cannot be carried out at the community level, yet much of what the state does, as well as state enterprises and private enterprises (especially multinationals) can be as effectively (and in many cases more effectively) be carried out by smaller organizations, with greater social participation. The principle of subsidiarity legitimates labour unions and community groups because they exist specifically to provide a means for greater social participation.

In the process of re-creating their economies and society, the transitional economies would be wise to follow the principle of subsidiarity, both in economics and in politics. Social organizations exist to promote human dignity and the common good, and these are best served when those who will be affected by the change are the ones directing and carrying out this change. Domination by the state, IMF or multinational corporations is still domination and the only way to avoid this is to keep decisions and social organizations at a human scale, one that will allow the will of the people to be expressed.

Property

The understanding of property in the Catholic social thought tradition is particularly insightful for the issues raised in transitional economies. This tradition relies heavily of the understanding of property developed by St. Thomas Aquinas. Three themes are strong and constant in this tradition: 1) the necessity to protect private property; 2) the requirement that property be used to promote the common good and 3) the social nature of property. Aquinas' defence of private property is pragmatic. Property tends to be used more efficiently towards the common good when it is held by individuals. According to Aquinas 'the institution of private property is "legitimate," and "indeed necessary for human life" inasmuch as (a) persons are more likely to care for what they possess themselves, (b) "human affairs are more efficiently organized if the proper care of each thing is an individual responsibility," and (3) "peace is better preserved" if persons are content with their own property' (O'Neill, 1994, p. 787). Yet the privateness of property does not remove it from the community, for its use must be for the promoting of the common good. Aquinas argues that it is not immoral for a starving man to steal food to feed himself or his family; in times of scarcity all property becomes common. The defence of private property and the responsibility to use property for the common good go hand in hand as they both stem from the requirement that property be used in a manner that furthers the well being of all in society.

The Catholic social thought tradition recognizes something that neoclassical economic theory ignores almost completely, the social nature of property. The right to private property comes from and through the community and it is both right and reasonable that the community have its interests promoted and protected in this institution. As John Paul II has written, 'It is necessary to state once more the characteristic principle of Christian social doctrine: the goods of this world are *originally meant for all.* The right to private property is *valid and necessary,* but it does not nullify the value of this principle. Private property, in fact, is under a "social mortgage," which means that it has an intrinsically social function, based upon and justified precisely by the principle of the universal destination of goods' *(Sollicitudo*

Rei Socialis, 42).

The issues of property rights in transitional economies are many and varied. One important and contentious problem is the privatization of state property. The argument that this policy will promote greater efficiencies in the operation of these companies is strong and powerful, fully backed up by neoclassical economic theory. Yet one cannot be blinded by ideology here for the issue should be settled on a case by case basis, based on the criteria of whether the common good will be best served with public or private ownership. In most cases the issue of ownership has no real barring with the efficiency of an organization, neoclassical pronouncements to the contrary aside. In the industrialized capitalist economies ownership has long since been separated from the management of the large corporations in any positive sense. Yet there is a negative sense, especially in America, as management is increasingly forced to concentrate on stock values and short term profits in order to please institutional investors. Although many are made wealthy in this casino atmosphere, it is hard to see real evidence that such an environment has promoted the common good.

Another important issue in the move towards privatization is the ethical issue of the distributional effects of privatization. Much of the financial gain that comes from these assets being sold well below their real value and then the physical capital of these enterprises are stripped from the companies and sold, with the profits going to the new owners. To add insult to injury, the citizens are than held responsible for the loans from the west that financed this shell game. Wealth is created on paper but the common good certainly is not being served. The distributional effects of this common form of privatization is an important property rights problem. A good example of this is being played out in Russia. Billions of dollars of loans, from private banks, international agencies and governments have been made to this country, with much of the money ending up in Swiss banks, or in the purchase of Yachts anchored in the French Mediterranean, while the people as a whole are expected to pay back these loans, or to suffer the consequence for their non-payment. Transitional economies would be well served if they emphasized the social nature of property. Here they can follow the middle ground of extreme laissez-faire capitalism and autocratic communism, with most property being in private hands (checking the power of the state) but with the state, through regulation, offering a countervailing power, insisting that the property is used in a manner consistent with the common good.

Solidarity, Priority of Labour and the Option for the Poor

The Catholic social thought tradition has been, in many ways, an attempt to find a third way, an alternative to the excessive individualism and alienation of laissez-faire capitalism and the depersonalization and subordination of communism. It does this by asserting the true nature of society and the individual in a way that protects the dignity of each human and the promotion of the common good. An essential component of this third way is the idea of solidarity. Solidarity is more than a feeling of sympathy or compassion with the poor and marginalised. It is, as John Paul II has said 'a firm and persevering determination to commit onself to the common good'. 'Catholic solidarity' writes Matthew Lamb, 'aimed at transposing pre-modern understandings of natural law, of human beings as essentially social, and of society itself as organic and cooperative, into the modern contexts of industrialized societies with complex exchange economies' (Lamb, 1994, p. 908).

Solidarity calls us to enter into the experience and reality of the 'masses', which in a capitalist economy means the workers. Growing out of the idea of solidarity is John Paul II's assertion of the priority of labour:

> We must first of all recall a principle that has always been taught by the church: the principle of the priority of labour over capital. This principle directly concerns the process of production: In this process labour is always a primary efficient cause, while capital, the whole collection of means of production, remains a mere instrument or instrumental cause. This principle is an evident truth that emerges from the whole of man's historical experience (*Laborem Exercens*, 12).

In many ways John Paul II's understanding of labour and capital is similar to that of Adam Smith and the classical economists, in that capital is seen as past labour. The assertion of the priority of labour over capital is an assertion that people, in this case workers, should not be treated as a means to an end (the capitalist earning profits). Workers create real wealth. Capitalists contribute to the extent that they contribute capital, but their contribution comes from past labour, either their own through savings, or of others through the accumulation of past profits. A third source of 'wealth' or capital comes from finance, a topic which has been neglected in the Catholic social thought tradition. Part of the contributions made by finance stems from the linking up of savers and investors, and here again it is easy to see how labour has created capital. Yet in a modern economy much of the efforts of finance are speculative, with the wealth being created out of thin air (as happens when one has an elastic money supply) or through shifting costs and monopolizing profits. Much of Bill Gates wealth is of this sort. Much of the financial activity going on in the advanced capitalist economies, with the United States as the leading example, involves financial manipulations, such as mergers and downsizing, leveraged buyout and financial re-engineering, derivatives and junk bonds, all geared towards making money, but with little evidence of adding to the real wealth of society, either its productive capabilities, or even more important, the well-being of its members. Furthermore, not only is much of this activity not helpful to the economy, it is often quite damaging. This is especially the case with currency speculators. As a group they have the ability to override government policy and collapse an economy in a very short time period. The state has a responsibility to ensure that such efforts and resources be directed towards the common good.[8]

This leads us to our last principle of Catholic social thought that we will analyse here: the option for the poor. All the principles of Catholic social thought are grounded in the Bible and the message of Jesus, and the option for the poor is a quintessential example. The option for the poor stems from Jesus' injunction that we will be judged based on how we have treated the 'least of our brothers' (Matthew 25). Donol Dorr (1992, p. 3) has noted that there are two aspects of this principle, one at the level of the individual and one at the level of society.

> An option for the poor is a commitment by individual Christians and the Christian community at every level to engage actively in a struggle to overcome the social injustices which mar our world. To be genuine it must come from a real experience of solidarity with the victims of our society. This means that one aspect of an option for the poor has to do with sharing in some degree in the lives, sorrows, joys, hopes, and fears of those who are on the margins of society. Without this, the attempt to serve the interests of 'the poor' will be patronizing— and it will make them feel more powerless and dependent than ever. But an option for the poor is not primarily the choice of a less affluent life-style by individuals or groups. It is a commitment to resist the structural injustice which marks our world. The person who makes such an option is undertaking to work to change the unjust economic, social and political structures which determine how power and resources are shared out in the world .... The aim is to bring about a more just society.

Adopting an option for the poor, in terms of economics, means, among other things, that our first measure of progress is how those on the bottom of the economic ladder are affected. It also means that those at the bottom must be allowed to become agents of their own destinies and be given the support and tools to bring about the transformation of their reality. Thus it is not merely placing them on the dole, or in public housing, or the comprehensive state support that used to be available in the formerly communist countries, but allowing for full social participation, full citizenship. It means not following the dictates of the IMF when they tell you that you have to impoverish millions to pay back loans to rich countries (especially since the loans were not used for the people's benefit). It means not blindly pursuing a policy of privatization which ignores the affects on local communities or workers and their families. It means not selling the countries resources and environment to multinationals who are interested in stripping the country side and leaving with their profits.

Conclusion

Neoclassical economic theory, at a superficial level, is an impressive theoretical structure. Its use of mathematical formalism and its resemblance to the hard sciences, especially physics, has lead many to call it the 'queen of the social sciences'. Furthermore, it has the ability to explain and justify just about anything, something its practitioners are starting to figure out is a weakness rather than a strength. Yet this is all deceiving, for it is an ahistorical and asocial theoretical structure, unable to account for evolutionary change and development. Moreover, it is not an empirical science, it seeks to understand abstract universals, not real particulars, and thus abstracts the real economy away. They follow neither the dictums 'from the particular to the universal' or 'from the universal to the particular', instead remaining at the level of the universal, only descending from these lofty heights to dish out policy advice. But what is most damaging to social development is that it is based on a set of values and a vision which, as the market mentality and neoclassical economic theory spread, infiltrates every aspect of a society's culture. It is an immoral set of values and vision, grounded in extreme individualism and materialism. Not only can it not be the grounding of a good and just society, if its values ever become fully adopted by the population, the social order will certainly dissolve into chaos.

Catholic social thought offers a vision and values which support social order and which directs social development towards a just society. Its roots are deeply embedded in the collective psyche of many of the countries now undergoing an economic transition, thus it is not an alien system of thought. It offers a third way between the extremes of the collectivism and individualistic and economism.

Notes

1. As Warren Samuels has noted, marginal analysis is good only for marginal issues.
2. See Heilbroner 1988 and Clark 1995 for an analysis of the fundamental importance of value theory.
3. As Joan Robinson (1962, p. 47) has noted: '*Utility* is a metaphysical concept of impregnable circularity; *utility* is the quality in commodities that makes individuals want to buy them, and the fact that individuals want to buy commodities shows that they have *utility*'.
4. See James Gordley's 'Economics and the Cardinal Virtues: The Ethics of Profit Seeking' presented at *The Nature and Purpose of the Business Organization within Catholic Social Thought Conference*, August 12-16, 1998, University of St. Thomas, St. Paul, Minn.
5. See 'Mierzenie postepu gospodarczego' ('Measuring economic progress', translated by Janina Rosicka) in *Jakosc Zycia* (Quality of Life), 1998, or 'Progress, Values and Economic Indicators' (with Catherine Kavanagh) in *Progress, Values and Public Policy*, edited by Brigid Reynolds and Sean Healy, (Dublin: CORI) 1996, pp. 60-92.
6. See Dorr, 1992, pp. 180-87, on this new 'Human' vision of development.
7. Since all theoretical activity is necessarily based on 'values' and a 'vision' and since these 'values' and 'Vision' help to shape and form every aspect of the theoretical edifice built upon them, it can be reasonably asserted that adopting the 'values' and 'vision' of Catholic social thought will require either the adoption of an already existent non-neoclassical economic theory or the development of an alternative. Luckily there are many alternatives, with the Institutionalist tradition being particularly attractive in that its underlying value criteria, the instrumental value principle, is very close to the concept of protecting human dignity and promoting the common good.

8. Financiers might argue that the market discipline they impose on countries economic policy curbs excesses and keeps governments honest. Yet what we end up with is neither the governments or financiers having any concern for the common good (although the financiers most likely have faith in the market to bring about the best outcome.

References

Allsopp, Micheal (1994), 'Subsidiary', in *The New Dictionary of Catholic Social Thought*, edited by Judith A. Dwyer, The Liturgical Press, Collegeville, Minn., pp. 927-929.

Clark, Charles M. A. (1998),. 'The Future of Capitalism', *Doctrine & Life*, vol. 48, no. 5, May/June, pp. 258-277.

Clark, Charles M. A. (1995), 'From Natural Value to Social Value', in *Institutional Economics and the Theory of Social Value: Essays in Honor of Marc Tool*, edited by Charles M. A. Clark, Kluwer Academic Publishers, Norwell, MA., pp. 29-42.

Clark, Charles M. A. (1992), *Economic Theory and Natural Philosophy*, Edward Elgar, Aldershot, UK.

Dorr, Donal (1992), *Option for the Poor*, Revised Edition, Gill and Macmillan, Dublin.

Dwyer, Judith A. (ed.). (1994), *The New Dictionary of Catholic Social Thought*, The Liturgical Press, Collegeville, Minn.

Egan, Joe (1998), 'The Image of God and the Practice of Capitalism', *Doctrine & Life*, Vol. 48, No. 5, May/June, pp. 278-290.

Healy, Sean and Brigid Reynolds (1983), Social Analysis in Light of the Gospel, CORI, Dublin.

Heilbroner, Robert L. (1988), *Behind the Veil of Economics*, Norton, New York.

Lamb, Matthew L. (1994), 'Solidarity' in *The New Dictionary of Catholic Social Thought*, edited by Judith A. Dwyer (1994), pp. 908-912.

O'Brien, David J. and Thomas A. Shannon (eds.). (1992), *Catholic Social Thought: The*

O'Neill, William R. (1994), 'Private Property' in *The New Dictionary of Catholic Social Thought*, edited by Judith A. Dwyer, (1994), pp. 785-790.

Documentary Heritage, Orbis Books, Maryknoll, NY.

Riordan, Patrick (1996), *A Politics of the Common Good*, Institute of Public Administration, Maryknoll, NY.

Robinson, Joan (1962), *Economic Philosophy*, C.A. Watts, London.

Smith, Adam (1976a), *The Theory of Moral Sentiments*, Oxford University Press, Oxford.

Smith, Adam (1976b), *An Inquiry into the Nature and Causes of the Wealth of Nations*, Oxford University Press, Oxford.

Stark, Werner (1962), *Fundamental Forms of Social Thought*, Fordham University Press, New York.

Tool, Marc (1986), *Essays in Social Value*, M.E. Sharpe, Armonk, NY.

Chapter Ten

The Promotion of National Prosperity: The Case of Industrial Activities in Portugal in the Transition to Liberalism

Pedro Nuno de Freitas Lopes Teixeira

'The arts, as sciences, go around the world, but only settle where they are well received, and the influence of a good government is always the most powerful cause of their progress'

'It is not by coercive means that agriculture and industry prosper, especially in the cases of introducing new cultures, manufactures or methods, to which people are not used. It is necessary to teach, persuade, and namely stimulate people with the expectation of profit, which is the biggest of all stimuli; to give, prudently, prizes, and the state take a part of the costs, until is needed (...) after these instruments be used, those activities will grow by themselves'

Acúrsio das Neves

Introduction

In the turn to the nineteenth century (and following Adam Smith's writings), self-interest became increasingly seen as a crucial element in the promotion of wealth. Within a certain framework (that Smith would call the system of natural liberty), self-interested behaviour of economic agents would lead to a higher and better productive level, i.e., to a more efficient one (cf. Smith, 1776).

In Portugal, several authors will emphasise the role of self-interest in the promotion of nation's prosperity, and in particularly in the promotion of industrial activities. This discussion will gain importance with the liberal revolution (1820), especially in what concerns the role of the state in the promotion of nation's wealth and the role of the private agents. This debate is linked with the discussion of the transition from an *Ancien Regime* economic system to a Liberal one. In a freer context of discussion, most authors will have the opportunity to criticise the *Ancien Regime* system, its shortcomings, and the possible ways to overcome them.

According to most authors, the existing economic structure (mostly the *Ancien Regime* one) was a serious obstacle to the development and effectiveness of self-interest, and its positive effects in industrial activities. These shortcomings were present either by the persistence of the corporations of arts or by the direct state intervention inherited from the mercantilist period. Therefore, and taking Political Economy as 'a science of the legislator', those authors will make the critique of that environment regulating industry, and will attempt to propose some reforms that could create a sound environment to the development of self-interest and the promotion of prosperity in industrial activities.

Two main groups of authors will be considered in our analysis. One the one hand, we will consider those authors that published already before the revolution (and that will continue after), whose analysis will gain relevance with the regeneration mood brought by the revolution. These are in general more complex and reflected texts. In this group we will find authors like Silva Lisboa, Rodrigues de Brito, Acúrsio das Neves and Solano Constâncio. On the other hand, there are the writings of those authors that will emerge in the midst of the general claim for analyse and discuss nation's economic future, set in motion by the revolution. In this case we are considering a more heterogeneous group of texts. On the one hand, there are more specific and more superficial (in terms of their theoretical background) texts like those sent by individuals or professional groups to the Liberal Courts. On the other hand, there are also the texts of prominent political figures (like Fernandes Tomás or Borges Carneiro), but also the *Textbook of Political Economy* sent by Manuel de Almeida.

The Critique of the Existing Framework Regulating Industry

The situation of industrial activities, in Portugal, around 1820, was not very favourable. In fact, industry was passing through a difficult period since the beginning of the century. Three factors were mainly responsible for this difficult situation. The first factor was the political and economic scenario due to the retirement of the Portuguese court from Lisbon to Brazil.[1] This change led to the break of the colonial pact, opening a period of increased competition to Portuguese manufactured goods in Brazil.[2]

The second factor was the destruction and instability caused by the military events connected with the French invasions. The presence of the French troops (or their expulsion, with the help of English troops), driven the country to a state of destruction and disorder (in both political and economic terms).

The third factor, which was propelled, by the two aforementioned factors, was the increased foreign commercial competition. Indeed, Portuguese manufactures suffered a strong competition of similar foreign products (namely English ones) that competed either in Brazil or in Portugal due to their better quality or to their lower price (in some cases both).[3]

The cumulative effect of these three factors led Portuguese industrial activities to a very difficult situation in the early decades of the nineteenth century. We will frequently find this period being labelled as a crisis. This crisis made part of the more general framework of national crisis that the whole country was living. Therefore, the portrait of the situation of industry at that time would not be very favourable, something that is confirmed by most writers of this period.[4] One of the most commonly used expressions, in order to characterise the situation of industry, is that of decadence. A decadence, whose deepness some impute to the last years of the absolutist regime (Freire, 1821).

The portrait made by most authors of the period follows this same path. The bad situation of industry was visible in the lack of quality (Cardozo, 1821) or in the higher prices of the Portuguese manufactures (Freire, 1820). Hence, Portuguese manufactures faced a high pressure from external suppliers. The foreign competition was generally appointed as one of the major obstacles to the progress of Portuguese industry (Freire, 1820; Cardozo, 1821; C. C. Lisboa, 1821; Acúrsio, 1820). The already mentioned treaty of 1810 (Cardozo, 1821; Acúrsio, 1820) worsened the lack of competitiveness of Portuguese manufactures, which was due to several other shortcomings.

In spite of the beneficial character of an increased freedom of trade, there was a general belief that the changes of the period 1808-10, created an additional (and perhaps unbearable) pressure over the national production. This additional pressure was present not only in the Portuguese territory, but had important consequences in the Brazilian colony, due to the easier access of English production to the Brazilian ports.[5]

However, the crisis of the Portuguese manufactures could not be restricted, according to these authors, to the foreign competition (and especially to the English). It was due to other (structural) problems, that some referred to under the label of backwardness (Tomás, 1820, p. 63); a backwardness in face of the leading industrialising countries, from which (namely Britain) Portugal was suffering increased competition in their national market.

Fernandes Tomás characterised this backwardness by a general lack of everything, Acúrsio das Neves by a lack of many things that he tries to enumerate. Among them was the lack of good raw material, of a technological modernity, and especially by the absence of a good regulating framework (Acúrsio, 1820; 105-6). As far as the regulating framework is concerned, some of the most current complaints are related with the medieval corporations. These were considered to be obsolete, limiting the dynamics of prosperity, by an extensive regulation of the production and commercial activities that was incompatible with the new competitive times (Acúrsio, 1820, p. 117).

The issue of the Corporations

Already an important issue before the revolution, the corporations will become one of the most important ones in the Liberal Courts. By observing the petitions sent to the

Courts, a conflict is visible between those that support their maintenance and those that wanted to restrict or even abolish their privileges.[6]

Facing a decline of their privileges, the corporations of arts will try to seize the political change as an opportunity to reverse this process. Benefiting from an organised and established structure, they will give the more visibility they can to their purposes. This is confirmed by their importance in the petitioner movement. In their petitions, the corporations try to maintain, or even reinforce, their privileges (Pereira, 1992a, pp. 357-364).[7] They claim for a confirmation of their privileges, and that the authorisation of producing similar goods would be restricted to them (Pereira, 1992a, p. 427). At the same time they want a political confirmation of the structure of apprenticeship (Ibid., p. 429), and the extinction of possible instruments of state control over the corporations (Ibid., pp. 441-2).

There is a generalised claim among the corporations upon what they consider to be an unfair competition by the manufactures. These are considered to have great privileges that created a strong pressure over the corporations' production. Amongst these privileges is the privilege of new invention (formalised by the *alvará* of 1809). Although the corporations accept the principle laying behind this privilege, they criticise an extensive use of this possibility, namely to some unsuitable situations such as fraud and foreigners (which would not benefit the national economic interests) (Pereira, 1992a, pp. 431-7).[8]

However, and in spite of their capacity of organisation and lobbying, several voices will emerge in favour of a reduction of their prerogatives, or even their complete extinction. The Commissions of Trade of the two most important cities (Lisboa and Porto) express the preference by the reduction of the privileges of the corporations. The Commission of Lisboa claims for the abolishment of the corporation's preference in the acquisition of some goods (C. C. Lisboa, 1822, p. 39). The Commission of Porto shares this critical viewpoint (giving as an example the situation in the production of silk), and considers it an obstacle to progress. This commission goes even further by proposing a more liberal system, since it does not accept the argument of quality control expressed by the corporations. Moreover, this commission considers that the fact that their production level being below the national needs is an additional element favouring the adoption a more liberal system towards industrial activities (C. C. Porto, 1823, pp. 47-8).

Among those in favour of the extinction we will find Bacelar Chichorro, one important merchant of Lisboa. In spite of denying most of the conflicts imputed to the corporations, and recognising some advantages of their existence (such as the existence of a training system, and a system of control of the production's quality), he proposes their extinction (Pereira, 1992a, p. 438). This proposal is also supported by the Commission of Arts and Manufactures in the Courts (Ibid., pp. 454-5). The extinction of the corporations is justified in the fact that these were considered to be an obstacle to economic liberty, thus an obstacle to the prosperity of industry (and of the nation). At the same time, the period of apprenticeship is consider to be too long (Ibid., p. 494). Another author that considered, following Smith, the corporations as an obstacle to prosperity of industrial activity was Solano Constâncio. Hence, he will also propose their extinction (Constâncio, 1808-42, p. 139).

Still before the liberal revolution, came one of the strongest attacks to the persistence of the corporations from Acúrsio das Neves. He considers that the natural trend of the corporations is to privilege the private interest of their members, and to abuse from their privileges, intending to achieve a situation of monopoly (which was negative to the whole industry) (Acúrsio, 1814-7, p. 176).[9] Accordingly, Acúrsio does not see great benefit in their existence. He gives the example of the system of apprenticeship, which he considered too expensive. Moreover, he recurs to foreign examples, such as the Low Countries, where there are no corporations and the industrial activities prosper (Ibid., pp. 182-4). Hence, the generalisation and persistence of the corporations' system was consider by him as a 'moral disease', which was only supported by their attempt of maintaining political and social power.[10]

Therefore, and since the path towards an increased degree of economic liberty should be continued, in case the extinction of the corporation seemed difficult, the efforts should be addressed to the restriction and prevention of the consequences of their persistence (Ibid., pp. 219-20). Following Acúrsio in most of his criticisms to the corporations system, Manuel de Almeida will also balance between the support of an increased economic freedom (to which he consider them as an obstacle), with the need of a prudent behaviour from the political powers (Almeida, 1821, p. 120).

The target of most of the corporations' criticisms is the *Junta do Comércio*, an institution established by the Marquis of Pombal, in the second half of the eighteenth century, with the purpose of co-ordinating the royal manufactures. This institution represented the manufacture side of the dissension, namely due to the special situation that it ascribed to most manufactures. Its relevance was not even seriously affected by the reduction of state effort of promotion of industrial activity observed after the Marquis of Pombal had left the power. Moreover, the powers of the Junta were increased, namely by its capacity of co-ordinating both the manufactures owned by the state and those owned by private interests. It became a powerful mechanism of co-ordination and promotion of economic activity, under the last decades of the absolutist period, namely in what concerns the industrial activity. Its situation was somehow similar to a Ministry of Economic Affairs at the eve of the liberal revolution (Pereira, 1992a; 360).[11]

There was a general absence of sympathy from the new liberal regime towards the corporation's interests. However, the new political power was not able to define a coherent and articulated economic program (as it also happened in political matters). Accordingly, there was no general policy either restricting or promoting the situation of corporations. In their petitions, the corporations' interests seem to be aware of some hesitation of the political powers towards them, and try to explore it (Pereira, 1992a, p. 431).

The liberal mood did not believe that the traditional structure of the corporations was an effective way of promoting industrial (and nation's) prosperity. However, the fragility of the political support of the liberal courts (expressed by its short period of duration – 1820-23), did not allow a consistent fight against an organised and deeply embedded group as the corporations. Therefore, the conflict between the corporations and the Junta was not solved until 1834, when the second generation liberal regime (winner of the civil war of 1832-4 against the absolutists), decided by the extinction of both the corporations and the Junta. Since the corporations' system was not the best framework of promoting the progress of industry, could the manufactures be considered as an alternative?

The Question of the Manufactures

We already mentioned that the manufactures were part of the so-called mercantilist structure. This kind of state intervention in economic activity was being highly criticised since the late eighteenth century. This critique of a mercantilist approach was not exclusive of the industrial activities, though, this sector was probably the one that concentrated most of these criticisms. It was the sector where this state intervention was more visible (namely by the award of special privileges, such as financial support, special contracts, and tax exemptions). Therefore, this type of state promotion of industrial activities will be under the criticisms of several authors that addressed the mercantilist approach (cf. Cardoso, 1989a).[12]

Already in the first decades of the nineteenth century, previously to the liberal revolution, several authors stressed the need to reform some of the several constraints of the economic activity. Among others, we will find Rodrigues de Brito, Silva Lisboa, and Acúrsio das Neves. All of them recognised the excessive regulations that spread among different economic sectors, and specifically in the industrial activities.

In the case of Rodrigues de Brito, his criticisms made part of a general critique to the mercantile system. In the case of industry, he concentrates on what he considers to be the excessive protection by the state to manufactures in the past, namely in the existence of monopolist situations, which, he believes, in the vested interests. For Brito, monopolist situations were an obstacle to the progress of the nation's wealth. According to him, the protection of the state, leading to a biassed allocation of resources (namely labour), was against the interest of the nation, reducing its potential of wealth.[13]

These criticisms to the mercantile system were shared and deepened by Silva Lisboa in all his main economic writings. For him it was a choice between the benefit of some (when monopolist situations were common), and the nation's prosperity and the general interest (when monopolist situations were generally absent). This opposition between the particular interests and the general interest was present in the case of the privileges conceded to some manufactures and some kinds of trade.[14] Silva Lisboa raises serious doubts about the effectiveness of the progress of industry strictly based in situations of privilege or monopoly.[15] His criticisms envisaged also those cases in which the promotion of manufactures is assumed by the state, by actively funding or organising those activities. Silva Lisboa considered that the direct intervention in economic activity was not the task of the state or of the sovereign (Lisboa, 1804-20), since the question of the allocation of resources should be left to individual judgement. Hence, avoiding the interference of the state by the concession of privileges and monopolies to some particular sector.

This perspective is shared by other important author, Solano Constâncio, which considered that the state should not possess their own manufactures. Moreover, he considered that the past experience showed that these manufactures were generally worst in terms of prices and quality than those owned by private economic agents (Constâncio, 1808-42, p. 136).

Acúrsio das Neves shares most of these criticisms about excessive regulations and privileges. He criticises the role of regulations, special privileges and monopolies affecting the progress of manufactures and commerce. According to Acúrsio, the special treatment of some activities reflected also the prevalence of particular interests over the national interest (Acúrsio, 1820; and Acúrsio, 1814-7, pp. 194-9; 289 and 510).[16]

This path of criticisms towards a strong direct intervention of the state in industrial activities can also be found after the liberal revolution. Some of them will come from the industrial and commercial *milieu*. Among them we will find the claim for the reduction or extinction of the existing monopolies, at the same time it is demanded an improvement in the degree of economic liberty.[17] This claim is supported by the Commission of Trade of Lisboa (C. C. Lisboa, p. 30).

In the midst of criticisms towards the role of the state in manufactures is again the *Junta do Comércio*. This followed an attempt of generalising, as far as possible, the benefits conceded to the royal manufactures. This strategy was criticised either by the treasury (Conselho da Fazenda) or by the Commission of the Corporations. The former, since the exemptions conceded by the Junta reduced significantly its fiscal revenues. The latter, since it considered that it promoted the decadence of the corporations. Nevertheless, the Junta could count with the support of the Court's Commission of Arts and Manufactures, namely in its support of the former workshops that steadily became bigger establishments or manufactures (Pereira, 1992a, pp. 482-7).

Other voices claimed against the policy of the Junta to promote exemptions. Eight members of the Commission of Lisboa will argue in this sense (by writing a separated and additional report to that of the Commission - Voto 8), considering that this policy would only bring benefits to particular interests and not to the general one. Moreover, it created even more difficulties to the already complicated situation of the treasury (Voto 8; 4-6). The Commission of Porto will share this critical stance towards the special privileges awarded to manufactures, namely in those cases that were conceded only to the bigger establishments. Rather, the members of this commission consider that the same conditions should be given to all national producers (C. C. Porto, 1823; p. 36).[18]

As an example of special and unjustified privileges, the Commission of Porto also criticises the exemption of duties over the importation of raw materials (Ibid., p. 35).[19]

Accordingly, a member of the Commission of Lisboa, will propose the replacement of this exemption by the drawback system (Loureiro, pp. 8-9).[20] Disagreeing with these claims will be the Commission of Lisboa, considering positive the exemption of duties over the importation of raw materials, and in the framework of its claim for state support to all economic activities (thus, also to industry), (C. C. Lisboa, 1822, pp. 26-8).[21]

Also criticisable was, for some writers, the excessive presence of the state as a direct economic agent, as far as the industry is concerned. Although some could even recognise the benefits of an initial support, they considered that these establishments should further be transferred to private property (C. C. Lisboa, 30-1).[22] Others will state that there was a need for reducing regulations and privileges, and promoting economic liberty. Hence, the state should adopt a more low profile since the former situation could not satisfy the national needs in terms of manufactured goods, had negative consequences over other sectors,[23] was not justified by the minor relevance of industry to the whole economic activity (Voto 8, 1822; 2-3).

These last points put in question two main aspects: the importance of industry in the national economy, and the role that the state should adopt in this path towards a more liberal economic framework. We will address now these two aspects.

The Place of Industry in the National Economy

The question of the economic vocation of the country was at that time a problematic issue. Moreover, there was a persistent conflict between the agrarian voices and the industrialism ones, which had its consequences also in the administrative structure (Pereira, 1992a, p. 359). The liberal revolution (its discourse of regeneration), enhanced this conflict, namely by discussing if any sector (and in a positive case which one) should be consider as a priority in the promotion of nation's wealth (hence in the attention of the state's economic policy). In the period previous to the liberal revolution, some of the most important authors have already devoted their attention to this issue.

In general, Silva Lisboa advocated an impartial and equal protection of the sovereign to all sectors of economic activity, in order to promote their natural development, thereby the prosperity of the nation.[24] Accordingly, the sovereign should not privilege any particular interest in detriment of the general one. As in the case of monopolies, for Silva Lisboa, the protection to one specific sector was the choice between the wealth of a minority and the wealth of the country, or the choice between short-term benefits and long term ones. The protection and privileges awarded to a specific sector of economic activity (which he calls partiality of the sovereign) promoted the disorder among the economic system.[25]

Hence, Silva Lisboa emphasises the synergetic effects of a promotion of all sectors. Therefore, agriculture would benefit from the prosperity of industry and trade, namely by the application in agricultural work of technological advances developed by the other sectors (Lisboa, 1804-20, p. 68).[26]

Acúrsio did not advocate exclusive promotion of one sector, but rather complementary between manufactures and agriculture. Moreover the former could play a dynamic role in the prosperity of the latter (Acúrsio, 1814-7, pp. 478-9). Therefore, all sectors should receive equal protection of government, because it was their natural combination and progress that promoted nation's prosperity. Acúrsio refers to the inter-related character of all sectors of activity, visible in the need of having low subsistence costs in order to be competitive in the production of manufactures (Ibid., pp. 313-4; and Acúrsio, 1820, p. 80). The liberal revolution renewed the importance of this discussion, namely by questioning the priority between agriculture and industrial activities. Similarly to the authors aforementioned, three possible perspectives emerged.

The first group considered that the priority should be given to agriculture, since the solid and permanent prosperity would come only with its prosperity. For this group, the prosperity of industry was not only superfluous, but also volatile (Anónimo, 1821). Fernandes Tomás (one of the main political leaders of the first liberal period), will visibly assume the defence of a priority given to agriculture as a most effective way to overcome the difficult moment by which the country was passing through (Tomás, 1820, p. 56). Soares Franco (another important voice in the defence of the agricultural activities and its utmost importance for the country's wealth), advocated the superiority of the agriculture activities due to its solid contribution for the nations' future, which was visible in some foreign examples.[27]

A second group, in an attempt of compromise, advocated an equal promotion of all economic activities, namely agriculture and industry. This group was influenced by the idea of an impartial state that did not favour any sector or activity in detriment of another. According to this group only the jointed prosperity of both agriculture and industry promoted general happiness, peace, and national cohesion (with the indirect aim of promoting the solidity of the Monarchy and public good) (Freire, 1820, p. 4). Together, these two activities would promote the eradication of poverty that affected the country, namely due to its current state of decadence (Ibid., pp. 5-13). The same sense of equilibrium in state's behaviour was assumed by the report of the Commission formed by the merchants of Lisbon.[28] According to them, every sector should be recovered of the general state of crisis, therefore no special priority should be awarded (C. C. Lisboa, 1822, p. 3).[29] Advocating a harmonious development of all sectors is also Manuel de Almeida (Almeida, 1821, p. 189). This second group is also representative of the difficulties that characterised the works of the first liberal courts, namely it their definition of priorities, or in the diagnosis of the most difficult problems facing the nation's economy.

Finally, there was the third group, which propelled the promotion of industry as the major task of state's economic policy. In this group is still present the already indicated Acúrsio das Neves, which publishes in 1820 a memory addressing the ways of promoting nation's economic prosperity. In his memory he takes the side of the so-called industrialists, by considering the only possible way of saving the country (cf. Acúrsio, 1820). Another strong author that will try to influence the works of the liberal courts is Henrique Nunes Cardozo. This author, a member of the aforementioned Commission of the Lisbon's merchants, will write a separate report, in order to make clearer his defence of the priority that should be given to industry.[30] Cardozo tries to emphasise the advantages, also for agriculture, of promoting the prosperity of industry, due to its synergetic effects. He claims that, although the industry was a recognised source of prosperity, it was often forgotten or unattended. Moreover, this attention should be stressed, since industrial activities were at an earlier stage of development (Cardozo, 1822).[31] Some commercial interests recognised the need of industry in order to achieve prosperity, leading to a claim for some state support to industrial activities (Pereira, 1992a, p.107).

Although we were far from a unanimous or even clear definition of the priorities for economic policy at that time, industry was recognised, by important sectors of the Portuguese political and economic *elites*, as an important sector. Therefore, some attention should be addressed, by the state, in order to promote its prosperity. The issue was what could be the more effective way of achieving that purpose.

The Role of the State in the Way Towards a Liberal Economic System

We already observed that neither the corporations nor the manufactures were the most suitable way of promoting industry's (and nation's) prosperity. Hence, we would now try to find what should be the economic role of the state, in a framework that most authors claim to be less regulated, less conditioned by particular privileges. Some of the most interesting contributions to this issue are to be found in the years before the revolution, at a time this question was already an important one.

For Rodrigues de Brito the aim of the legislator should be the promotion of the wealth of the nation (Brito, 1803-5, p. 33), namely by a special protection to agrarian activities. The protection of the sovereign does not meant that the other systems (Trade, Industry and Property) would not receive government's attention, since for them he also recommends the protection of the sovereign. However, this protection should not be misunderstood as special privileges.[32]

Silva Lisboa focus his attention in the manufacturer sector that was facing several difficulties at that time. He considers the system of privileges and exclusives, to have quite negative consequences.[33] Therefore, Silva Lisboa doubts of the effectiveness of a mighty powerful state that tries to orient and constrain the individual economic decisions (Ibid., pp. 26-7; 37; 51; 94-5; and 212). He considers that industry[34] should not be awarded with special privileges, in spite of some slowness in its progress. The sovereign should be patient and not force the natural development of that activity, since the progress could only be achieved through *natural ways*. This perspective is clear in his assertion that the manufactures that adapted to the conditions and state of development of the country should not fear the future (Ibid., pp. 265-6; 337-8; 342-4 and 376).³⁵ Therefore, the most reasonable way of promoting industry would be through export taxes' exemption, because it enlarges the market and eases the consumption of these products. A special case is that one of the manufactures crucial to the defence of the country, which should receive special attention because the country should not depend of foreign supply (Lisboa, 1804-20, p. 400).

In spite of his criticisms to the situations of privilege and monopolies, Acúrsio das Neves presented a *nuanced* perspective on special protection and on the role of the state in some particular economic activities. In fact, he has a favourable evaluation of the efforts of the Marquis of Pombal, a typical man of the mercantile system. In one of his most important works (Variedades...), he departs from an evocation of the mercantilist times (D.José I and Pombal), and of their capacity in overcoming difficulties and obstacles, namely in what refers to manufactures (Acúrsio, 1814-7, pp. 116-7). Moreover, he enhances the importance of some stimulus by the state to promote the development of manufactures in an early state,³⁶ namely in the case of technical achievements (Ibid., pp. 128; 130 and 187).

Acúrsio's approach demands more liberty to economic activity but with some protection to national interests (Pedreira, 1988, p. 78). This ambivalence was based in his conviction that the industrial (and commercial) activities had an important advantage over agriculture.³⁷ Those activities had not other limits than those of nations' behaviour, while agriculture faced the limitations imposed by the fertility and extension of land. Thus, he often emphasises the crucial importance of industry in the promotion of wealth.

For the promotion of industry he requires a freer framework for economic activity and the help of a good government. Essential characteristics of a good government are stability and persistence in the efforts of promoting industry and a simple administration with enough knowledge on the subject (Acúrsio, 1820, pp. 71-2; 98; 113 and 122). Other important conditions to the development of industry were the existence of good raw materials and the introduction of machinery. Furthermore, the author emphasises the importance of introducing machinery, because of its improvement on production levels, turning all activities more productive (Ibid., pp. 106 and 138; and Acúrsio, 1814-7, pp. 343; 358 and 360). As far as this aspect is concerned, he blames the backwardness of the country in the use of machinery. In fact, importance of machinery to economic activity is an important feature in his writings (Castro, 1980, p. 81).³⁸

In the role of the state in industry, Acúrsio will address some specific and relevant issues, such as the already mentioned privilege of new invention. He considers it a necessary stimulus to the promotion of prosperity, since the making and adoption of new inventions make industry more productive (Acúrsio, 1814-7, p. 125).³⁹ This prize was for him a sort of compensation by the investment made by the author of the invention (in time, or material resources), that was needed in order to promote technical progress. Moreover this privilege was time-limited, hence, would not conflict with his claims of increased economic liberty (Ibid., p. 148). This exception is justified by the importance that Acúrsio awarded to technical progress, one of the critical issues in his writings on industry (Cf. Almodovar, s/d1). It was by the application of knowledge to industry that its productive potential was improved. Therefore there was the need to promote both spaces of discussion and diffusion of new techniques,[40] but also possibilities of development and adoption of these applications that confirmed their usefulness (Acúrsio, 1814-7, pp. 349-58 and 393). Hence, it emerged an important role to the state, by promoting education and the enlightenment of society (Ibid., p. 355). Despite this exception of the new inventions, he considers, based in common sense and experience, that the prosperity and the promotion of manufactures could only be achieved through 'a release of the private economic agents', the extinction of monopolies, and by the reduction of excessive and useless regulations (Ibid., pp. 194-9).

Although some restrictions could be founded in respectable purpose, they were not the most suitable way of promoting industry. Rather, they promoted particular interests, instead of the general one. However, it was the general one that should be pursued, though sometimes some private interests could suffer (Ibid., pp. 224-6). Among these respectable interests was the claim for prohibiting the importation of foreign manufactured goods. Acúrsio criticises this purpose, since it will create a monopoly to national producers, which was unfavourable to national general interest (Ibid., p. 510). Another understandable, but erroneous, measure were the obstacles raised to the exportation of raw materials. These would limit the development of agriculture, hence of industry. On the one hand, because the great prosperity would come only by the cumulative prosperity of all sectors.[41] On the other hand, this led to higher prices of raw materials, which would not favour industry (Ibid., p. 314). This was another example of what he considered to be the tight complementary of all economic sectors (Ibid., p. 477).

Therefore, the promotion and stimulus of industrial activities should be achieved by several other instruments rather than privileges and restrictions. Much more useful than these was a good legal framework, suitable to the multiplicity, variety, and flexibility of economic activity (Ibid., p. 223). If the state wanted to promote prosperity, it should take care of the security of people and property. It should also promote an impartial and effective exercise of justice, namely by fighting against fraud (Ibid., pp. 224 and 500).[42]

Writing mostly at the same time as Acúrsio, another important author of this period, Solano Constâncio, will share most of his viewpoints. Constâncio advocates the promotion of both agriculture and industry, namely by easing the fiscal charge and by promoting instruction (Constâncio, 1808-42, p. 35). He also considers the possibility of attracting technicians from other countries (Ibid., p. 39). In order to achieve prosperity, the state should guarantee three crucial conditions: justice, property, and individual freedom (Ibid., p. 37). Constâncio shows his mistrust either by the mercantilist practices of monopolies and exclusives (or by the ineffective volunteerism of the Junta do Comércio), but also by the effectiveness of free trade policies proposed by Smith (Ibid., pp. 41; and 66-71). Thus, the promotion of industry should be attained by the social valorisation of producers (Ibid., p. 136),[43] by the reduction of the obstacles to economic activity, and by the promotion of machinery and new techniques that improved the capacity of industry. Moreover, these would lower industrial goods' prices, propelling consumption and employment (Ibid., pp. 116-7 and 124).[44]

The attention of a government interested in the promotion of industry should be devoted to the adoption of generic and homogeneous rules to the economic activity, to the exemption of duties over the importation of raw materials, and the reduction of obstacles over the exportation of raw materials (Ibid., pp. 135-6).[45] The importance he gives to machinery, leads him to propose that it should be awarded a temporarily privilege to the owners of new inventions (Ibid., p. 139).

As far as the external trade is concerned, he suggests a balance of the different interests in question. Therefore, he takes some distance from Smith, by accepting the adoption of some duties over the imports, as far as they were adapted to the country's situation and its stage of development of industry (Ibid., p. 142).[46] This empathy towards a moderate protectionism will be further enhanced in the late thirties. When commenting the work of Louis Say, he will share his criticisms to the free trade doctrines of Smith and the British Political economists.

The ambivalence shown by Acúrsio das Neves towards the role of the state, as far as industrial activities are concerned, is also visible in the early years of the liberal revolution. The defence of a state support balances between a certain nostalgia of the mercantilist achievements[47] and the claims for something resembling to a liberal system (Cf. Pereira, 1992a, p. 55). This aspect is observable in the consultation made by the Junta de Comércio to the local commissions of trade. This consultation, which is quite representative,[48] confirms, also, the mix between the commercial and industrial interests.[49] The consultation of the Junta expresses some of the divergence pervading the main economic agents related to industry, about the role of the state. On the one hand some will argue for an entrepreneurial state, that in the absence of private initiative should advance and make the investments required to the establishments of industries. The role of the state could be either a financial one, providing financial support (Pereira, 1992a, pp. 234; 242-4; and 261), or as a direct investor establishing new plants (Ibid., p. 185). This visible role of the state would be justified by the importance of this activity (that some consider as 'the productive by excellence') (ibid.).

For those arguing for a more visible place, the role of the state could also be translated in an exemption of duties to exports (Ibid., pp. 117; 145; and 158), exemption of duties to imported raw material and machinery (Ibid., pp. 145 and 246), the reduction of the fiscal charge faced by industry (Ibid., p. 425), the exemption of military service to those workers of the industrial establishments (Ibid., p. 426), or the attraction of technicians from other countries (Ibid., p. 245).[50] They also frequently claim for a strong power capable of overcoming the obstacles faced by industry (Ibid., pp. 523-4), and for a strong pressure over the foreign competition as a way of protecting agriculture and industry (C. C. Porto, 1823, p. 39).

Frequently indicated as a possible way of promoting industrial societies were the diffusion of techniques, and the development of the best conditions to industry (C. C. Lisboa, 1822, p. 33). Accordingly, others recognised the need of enlightenment and education in order to achieve material progress (cf. Brito, 1821, p. 59).[51] Another claim addresses the need of an improvement in the physical and legal framework affecting internal circulation (C. C. Lisboa, 1822, p. 82; and C. C. Porto; 1823, pp. 37-8). On the other hand, others will claim for an increased liberty for industrialists (Pereira, 1992a, p. 116), with a reduction of the bureaucratic and administrative obstacles (Ibid., p. 246). At the same time they advocate the extinction of the privileges awarded to some establishments, a position that is even shared by one of the industrialists favoured by them (Ibid., pp. 258-60).[52]

Manuel de Almeida, will generally support this second perspective. Influenced by the writings of Smith, he considered that the role of the state consisted mainly in the promotion of liberty (namely that of circulation of people and capital), security (the protection of the country and its citizens), the providing of public goods (such as a good communication's network), and a good legislative framework (Almeida, 1821, pp. 128 and 190-1).[53] Nevertheless, and though he proposes liberty and security for industry (as well for agriculture), rather than proportion and protection (that he proposes for trade), there were some situations that justify some intervention of the state in the industrial milieu (Almeida, 1821, pp. 87 and 190). Among these situations were the fight against prejudice, the stimulus of the preference for common goods rather than for luxury ones, and the promotion of a large population (which he, in a neo-mercantilist approach, associates with prosperity) (Ibid., pp. 87-8).

The need for a period of experience, and his doubts about foreign trade (by considering that commercial treaties should only be signed by nations with the same economic force), give some space for a more visible role of the state, namely in the protection against foreign competition (Ibid., pp. 192-3). In fact, and though he recognises the need of competition among industrial activities, he supports the establishment of some limits to the importation of foreign goods (Ibid., pp. 193-6). Moreover, he considers that internal trade should be preferred to external one (Ibid., p. 207). The vestiges of a mercantilist tradition became more visible when goes to more detail, as far as the role of the state in industrial activity. Hence, we observe that his technological and productive framework is somehow obsolete, with references to the royal manufactures, older legislation, and training process based on something resembling with the corporation's masters (Ibid., pp. 203-4).[54]

What About the Private Economic Agents - The Release of the Private Economic Activity

The criticisms of these authors to the mercantile system, with its multiple regulations, are followed by a steady demand for increased liberty aiming the development of economic activity.

For Brito, there is a real need for more liberty among economic activity (Cardoso, 1988, p. 103). Moreover, he considers that the liberty requested by several authors (such as Silva Lisboa) is compatible with the tasks of the sovereign (Brito, 1803-5, p. 211). In his argumentation the example of the Physiocrats is frequently used (Ibid., p. 207).

These claims for a much more free economic activity are a recurrent issue in Silva Lisboa's writings. In several moments Silva Lisboa emphasises the need of the state promote an increased level of liberty within the economic activity, aiming the promotion of national wealth. Freedom of trade is, according to Silva Lisboa (and using Smith's *Wealth of Nations*), the best way of promoting production. Nevertheless, he recognises the existence of criticisms to this idea, and tries to refute them. In this framework, the decision of allocating resources would be preferably left to the individual judgement. According to Silva Lisboa a higher degree of freedom would lead the nation to a wealthier state, because economic decisions are self-interested. Within this framework of increased liberty, competitiveness played a significant role, motivating the individual economic agents to do the best allocation of resources, thus leading to the promotion of the general wealth. There are also several references about the reliability of self-interest, acting in a more free economic space, as a driving force to nation's wealth (Lisboa, 1804-20, pp. 99; 172; 178 and 232). The writings of Smith are used as a way of enhancing all these aspects.

Acúrsio das Neves shares with Silva Lisboa the most of these considerations about the role of increased economic freedom as the right way to prosperity (Cardoso, 1988, pp. 93-5). Acúrsio emphasises strongly the need to reduce the constraints affecting the economic activity in general, enhancing a higher degree of freedom within economic activity. According to this idea there are specific references to the case of the circulation of information and intellectual exchange, to the corporations of arts, and to the allocation of capital resources (Acúrsio, 1814-7, pp. 117; 194; 227; 231 and 281; and Acúrsio, 1820, pp. 79; 83 and 128).

The role of private agents was crucial, since, and following Smith, the general prosperity was built by the composition of individual prosperity. This was the result of the individual effort of improving material conditions, stimulated by self-interest, and enhanced by the division of labour (Acúrsio, 1814-7, pp. 343-4). Hence, Acúrsio assumed self-interest as the main engine in the path towards prosperity (Ibid., p. 480). An important additional element in the achievement of prosperity was the parsimonious behaviour of private agents (Ibid., p. 348).

In spite of the important role of self-interest and competition in order to promote economic progress, the author recognises the difficulties and the obstacles in achieving the natural order through increased economic liberty. These obstacles and difficulties came mainly from the particular interests of those that benefited from economic privileges and monopolies, resisting to adapt to a new and more liberal and competitive framework. Therefore, this path could be enhanced by the constancy and persistence of the sovereign in the support of economic activities (and especially of industry) (Ibid., pp. 217; 340; 344; 348; and Acúrsio, 1820, p. 118).

Manuel de Almeida considered that in the countries where there is a good system of Political Economy established, the working and the determination of the main economic variables (such as the rate of interest), was set by the interaction of the private agents, and not by a legal intervention of the state (Cf. Almeida, 1821, p. 100). The same type of reasoning favouring the role of self-interest can be found in Solano Constâncio. This author considers that if the governments wanted to promote prosperity, they should let the individuals pursue their material interests. Hence, the economic legislation could be almost resumed to the principle of free competition (Constâncio, 1808-42, p. 257). Some will argue for the private role in the investment decisions. According to them, the allocation of resources to the industrial activity should be left to the material motivations of the private sector. An example is given by one of the local commissions of trade: 'we believe that government should not establish manufactures, because the private will do in case they see by the prosperity of others that this is of their interest' (Pereira, 1992a, p. 277).

In most of the writings of the liberal period, namely to those sent to the Courts, there are scarce references to the role of individuals. There are some general claims advocating an increased degree of economic liberty, and specially a reduction in the restrictions and privileges awarded to other economic agents. However, and at the same time, almost all sectors want a special attention from the political powers to their problems, that frequently would be translated in a new situation of preference (cf. the claim for protection from the foreign competition).

Concluding Remarks

Although industry was not the most important sector at that time, it contained a sample of the most important debates on the economic role of the state. Furthermore, it would become the critical sector in the new century. Hence, its analysis provided some interesting insights upon the Portuguese experience of transition towards liberalism.

Since the late eighteenth century, and especially in the first decades of the nineteenth century, there was an increased critique towards the regulatory framework of the economic activity, with particular attention towards industrial activities. This critique addressed the existence of excessive and/or inadequate regulations that promoted individual or class interests, instead of the general prosperity.

In the case of industry the main criticisms will be devoted to the corporations of arts and the royal manufactures. According to most authors the former were an absurd restriction to economic initiative, leading to blockages in the introduction of new products or new processes of production. According also to those authors, the negative environment to private initiative was also due to the special privileges and conditions that benefited manufactures for a long time. Both cases led to a claim for an intervention of the state in order to promote more favourable conditions to economic activity in general, and specifically to industry.

Therefore, we could easily found a re-definition of the economic role of the state. Accordingly, the state should promote a clear and stable definition of the economic rules, avoiding as possible the establishment of special conditions or privileges that benefited only some of the private agents (as it was the case of those regulating the Corporations and most of the manufactures). This re-definition of the state intervention in economic activity would leave the main decisions of resource allocation to private sphere, reducing significantly the degree of direct economic intervention (as it occurred frequently in the past through the direct investment or funding of new production units).

The liberal regime will try to promote some changes, based in most of these criticisms upon the existing framework regulating industry and the type of state economic intervention. This attempt to build a new order will be founded on the canons of the classical political economy, namely in Smith's system of natural liberty. However, this will be much more visible in the destruction of some existing regulations and restrictions of the economic activity, rather than in the establishment of a new type of relationship between the state and the economic activity, especially with industry.[55]

Classical Political Economy, namely Smith and Say (which were the most relevant influences for the Portuguese case), was clearly more persuasive in the destruction of the *Ancien regime* framework, rather than in its replacement by something resembling to classical proposals. Notwithstanding the abstract claims for economic liberty and prosperity that echoed at the eve and during the first liberal period, soon these will give place to a nostalgic neo-mercantilist claims for a more decisive and active role of the state that could miraculously overcome the difficulties and the backwardness faced by industrial activity. If the financial difficulties of the treasury would not allow an active role of the state, it could (and indeed was interested) promote some protection by adopting higher duties over imports.[56]

Several previous signs of this progressive disenchantment with the classical approach to the economic role of the state (namely in the Smith-Ricardo version), will be consolidated in the thirties. Ferreira Borges, the author of the commercial code (1833) and one of the most prominent liberal politicians at that time, recognised the fragile industrial activity, showed both by the persistence of the corporations (until 1834), and by the low profile of the private initiative (cf. Brandão, 1990, p. 142).

Under the pressure of aggressive and more competitive European counterparts, suffering the consequences of a traumatic and hesitant transition from the *Ancien Regime* towards the new liberal order (which included the civil war and the independence of Brazil), and with a hesitating and heterogeneous new political power, Portuguese industry will develop a divergent path from the liberal canon.

Notes

1. These were escaping from the French troops that were invading the country.
2. Accordingly, the ports of Brazil were opened to the English boats in quite favourable conditions (during a certain period paying duties below those paid by the Portuguese ones). This favourable situation to the English interests consolidated by the political and commercial treaty signed in 1810 between Portugal and Brazil. This treaty settled a much easier access of English products to Portuguese and Brazilian markets, following the path defined already in 1808.
3. The difficulties faced by Portuguese industrial products were increasing since the turn of the century, due to the growing competitiveness of the leading industrial European countries, such as England or France. Their productive structures were clearly ahead the Portuguese one in technological and commercial terms. Moreover, England, as the traditional ally and most important commercial partner, benefited for a long time of more favourable trading conditions than the other countries trading with Portugal.
4. Moreover, and with the occlusion of the liberal revolution, they will write in a period in which there was a general belief of regeneration or reconstruction. These labels were frequently used at that period (cf. Verdelho, 1981), since the liberal revolution opened the possibility of discussing the future path for the country, in a new political framework. To a certain extent, there was a feeling that everything, or almost, could be questioned, discussed, and that a 'new start' was possible. Hence, there was a need of knowing which were the problems faced by the national economy, or more specifically, by each sector of activity, including industry. That was the time for diagnosis, for re-evaluating, for finding the weak points, identifying problems and obstacles to the progress of nation's wealth.
5. Some figures confirm that the Brazilian market become, in the early years of the nineteenth century an important market for national production. It absorbed almost whole exported manufactures, representing one third of the total trade between the metropolis and the colony (cf. Pedreira, 1994).
6. This conflict was not new, and gained relevance since the second half of the eighteenth century: At that time, and integrated in the more general program of promotion of manufactures, by the Marquis of Pombal, were made the first serious attacks against the corporations' structure. Further legislation strengthened the conflict between the corporations, whose position was being menaced, and the manufactures, which represented a serious competition to the corporations, namely since manufactures were not submitted to the same kind of regulations as the corporations.
7. In the analysis of the petitioner movement sent to the first Liberal Courts, we will use the most valuable anthology recently organised by Miriam H. Pereira (1992a).
8. In some cases the corporations' interests will even claim by a generalisation of the privileges awarded to manufactures to them (Pereira, 1992a; 440).
9. In his argumentation against the corporations, Acúrsio will frequently recur to the writings of Smith, either in the analysis of their origins and evolution an institution, or in the critical points. (cf. Acúrsio, 1814-7, p. 178 and following pages, namely 196-8).

10. This political and social power was shown in another of Acúrsio's examples. It was the attempt, at the time of Louis XVI, of extinguish the corporations in France. Unfortunately, and since these were old and resistant institutions, embedded in the social network, the good purpose failed and the French sovereign had to reverse his decision of abolish them (Acúrsio, 1814-7, pp. 199-217).
11. This divergence of visions and interests between the corporations and the manufactures, led by the Junta, was present even when addressing a common menace: the external competition. The corporations required an administrative intervention of the new liberal regime, by fighting against smuggling or legally restraining the access of foreign products (Pereira, 1992a, p. 367). The approach of those related to manufactures was different. They concentrated in technological issues, the promotion of the consolidation of the internal market, the prohibition of importing manufactured goods similar to those produced in the country, or the possibility of a financial support provided by the state (Ibid., pp. 371-4 and 421). These last aspects are quite interesting, since it indicates the persistence of the so-called mercantilist tradition of state financial support to the manufactures' activity.
12. One of the most claimed issues among industrial interests is the accomplishment of what was established in the *alvará* of 1809, namely in what refers to the privilege of new invention and the promotion of the introduction of new machinery in industrial activities (Pereira, 1992a, pp. 414-8 and 511-2). The Commission of Lisboa (C. C. Lisboa, 1822, p. 27) will also support this purpose, which we already know that was quite controversial at that time.
13. In his argumentation, Brito uses the example of Adam Smith (following the French translation of the *Wealth of Nations*) in his criticisms to the mercantile system (Brito, 1803-5, pp. 35 and 71).
14. Situations of special privileges, regulations and monopolies are referred to as the dominance of a minority interest over the general interest of the nation. According to this author this policy of monopolies, for being against common sense, demanded administrative and political fuzziness, which were unnecessary if particular interests were not attended (Lisboa, 1804-20, pp. 255; 265; 276 and 311). Moreover, situations of monopoly promoted a non-natural division of labour, which is the case of the colonies, namely of Brazil, with negative effects to the wealth of the metropolis (Portugal) and to the colonies (Brazil).
15. In his argumentation against the monopolist situations, the author refers the criticisms of David Hume about its negative consequences (Lisboa, 1804-1820, pp. 35; 54; 83; 200 and 246).
16. In his criticisms to the mercantile system, Acúrsio recurs to the support of Smith and Say's work (Acúrsio, 1814-7, p. 438).
17. They specify their claim with one of the most criticised monopolies at that time, that was the case of the production of soap (Pereira, 1992a, pp. 413-5).
18. This is shared by the Commission of Lisboa, and enhanced by some of its members (C. C. Lisboa, 1822, p. 28; Voto 8, 1822, pp. 12-3).
19. This exemption is also criticised by the already mentioned eight members of the Commission of Lisboa (Voto 8, 1822, p. 3).
20. This more liberal stance of this author will lead him to criticise also the strong duties applied to foreign competition (Loureiro, 1822, pp. 1-5).

21. Although they consider that the preference should be given to those industries dealing with raw materials available in the country (C. C. Lisboa, 1822, p. 27).
22. A process that already occurred in the late seventeenth century, after the displacement of Pombal from the political arena.
23. The negative effects related to trade, and mainly to agriculture. As far as the latter is concerned, it is criticised the obstacles raised to the export of raw materials, as a way of promoting industry (C. C. Lisboa, p. 33).
24. According to him: 'all system of preferences and restrictions blocked, instead of promoting, the opulence of any nation' (Lisboa, 1804-20, p. 106).
25. Silva Lisboa shared with Rodrigues de Brito the conviction that the privileges and preferences exhibited by the state authority promoted a distortion in the *correct* allocation of the national resources. Moreover, the privileged sectors received more capital and more labour that they should at expense of the non protected sectors (Lisboa, 1804-20, pp. 18; 44; 72 and 106). The sovereign should always choose the general interest (by equally protecting all sectors) and not a particular interest (by giving special treatment to one specific sector). With the system of liberty, state promoted the equilibrium and the order among the economic activity, as well the above mentioned prosperity (Ibid., pp. 95; 101; 276; 336 and 381).
26. Nevertheless, for strictly equal conditions, Silva Lisboa established a hierarchy of common individual preferences: first agriculture, then manufactures, internal trade and then external trade (Lisboa, 1804-20, pp. 262; 336; 399; and 213).
27. In fact, the main political attention of this period will be devoted to the agriculture and land issue, since it was there the basis of the *Ancien Regime* structure. Thus, this was more interesting for those searching for effective political ways of damaging the power of the absolutist groups. These issues were much less relevant in the case of industrial activities.
28. However this was not unanimous within the Commission. The eight members already mentioned, considered that the prevalence should be given to trade and agriculture (which was the country's economic vocation). For these members, industry was not nation's priority, hence foreign products should not be blocked. Moreover the importation of foreign goods, since it can increased the degree of competition, could stimulate national industrial producers. In fact, they consider that current state of protection not favoured national industry, visible for them in the worst quality and price of the national production (Voto 8, 1822, pp. 4-10). The Commission of Porto (C. C. Lisboa, 1822, p. 27) also sustains this aspect.
29. A special reference is given to internal trade, which is considered the sector capable of promoting, with its prosperity, all the others. This is understandable, since only merchants formed this commission.
30. His report, as well as others written by other members of that commission, indicate the diversity, or even the contradictions, present in this period, as far as the priorities of economic policy are concerned. That is the so even in a small and professionally homogeneous group like this commission.
31. Cardozo uses here an argumentation inspired in the French author Chaptal. This author would later influence List, namely in his theory of stages of development and in the arguments in favour of the protection of industrial activities at their earlier stage.

32. The protection of the sovereign is much more important due to the state of stagnation of agriculture and manufactures (Ibid., pp. 9; 36; 41; 47; 56; 58; 76 and 79-80). However, the protection of manufactures should not be confounded with the award of special privileges, which, as we already saw, Brito considers to be negative to the general interest (*manufacturer volunteerism*) (Ibid., p. 71).

33. Once again is referred the need of leaving allocation decisions to the individual judgement, without artificially promoting, through state support, the development of manufactures (Lisboa, 1804-20, pp. 338; 342 and 364). This not only did not have the desired effects, but would also affect the equilibrium and the natural order of the economic system, 'disturbing, more or less, the right allocation of resources, funds...' (Ibid., p. 101).

34. The concept of industry of Silva Lisboa, is sometimes similar to that of popular industry (common in the economic writings of the second half of eighteenth century), i.e., that of an activity complementary of the agricultural activity and benefiting of the free time left by the latter (Lisboa, 1804-20, p. 340). Therefore when he addresses the problems of industrial activity his reference is essentially a pre-modern industry (namely manufactures).

35. Furthermore, Silva Lisboa presents some requisites to the prosperity of industry, such as the availability of capital, raw materials and labour resources, an internal demand, competitiveness in relation with external products, diffusion of knowledge, freedom of economic activity and the promotion of technical advances by the award of prizes and privileges. The importance of promoting technical advances is enhance by references to Say or to legal documents (the already mentioned *alvará* of 1809). Thus, we can found references to the doctrine of Say about the privileges on patents and technological achievements (Lisboa, 1804-20, pp. 345-353; 356-60; 376; 235).

36. As he states 'for where go the capitals, go also population and industry' (Acúrsio, 1820, p. 92).

37. In some moments Acúrsio shows his ambivalence towards mercantilist practices. Although he criticises the excesses of regulation: 'trade and arts escape from where they are oppressed and go to where they can freely breadth' (Acúrsio, 1814-7, p 224); he does show some nostalgia by the mercantilist times, namely by the strength shown at that time by state's power (Ibid., pp. 341 and 546-551). This is visible when he states that past state support to the manufactures was along term investment, either by the financial support provided, or by the setting of manufactures by the state itself (Ibid., pp. 128 and 481-93). This ambivalence is also shown when he considers that industry would be promoted 'neither by excessive freedom, nor by excessive regulation' (Ibid., p. 224).

38. In this aspect becomes evident the transition of Acúrsio from a *Smithian* industrialism to a more modern one, following Say's writings (Almodovar, 1995, p. 90). Departing from a pre-modern industrial reference (namely manufactures), Acúrsio will be increasingly concerned with technological advances (namely by the introduction of machinery) and its impact in the improvement of production.

39. Before, he will devote some time to the analysis of the legislation on that subject, available at that time in Portugal, Britain, France and USA. Accordingly, he concludes that more flexibility should be awarded to the concession of patents, in the Portuguese case (Acúrsio, 1814-7, pp. 130-147).

40. He will emphasise at this moment the creation of the Royal Academy of Sciences of Lisboa (Acúrsio, 1814-7, p. 355).
41. This affiliates in his defence of the composed system of economic activity, in which he shows the influence of Smith's work (Acúrsio, 1814-7, p. 476).
42. Again we observe the influence of Smith and Say, authors that he explicitly mentioned in this issue.
43. In which he shows his affiliation to Chaptal (Constâncio, 1808-42, p. 110).
44. At this point he criticises Sismondi's scepticism about the effects of machinery on employment (Constâncio, 1808-42, p. 124).
45. The agreement with Acúrsio is visible. Constâncio considered that the effect was the opposite of what was intended. Although the obstacles to this exportation aimed the promotion of industry, it had negative consequences over agriculture, leading to a low consumption of agrarian classes (also of manufactured goods), which blocked industrial production (losing instead of winning with this measure) (Constâncio, 1808-42, p. 135).
46. Once again, the influence of Chaptal's work.
47. The mercantilist flavour of some of the measures claimed is confirmed by the evocation of the former role of Colbert, or Pombal, in the protection of industry (Pereira, 1992a, pp. 241-2).
48. There are available 53 reports of the 56 commissions consulted (Pereira, 1992a, p. 9).
49. This can also be consider to be characteristic of a pre-modern economic system, where the separation between agents of different sectors of activity is still scarce.
50. There are some other odd claims, such as that of the promotion of schools and exams inside the manufactures, which shows a sort of mixture between the manufacture size and the corporation's regulations (Pereira, 1992a, p. 257).
51. This author (João Rodrigues de Brito), one of the more prominent liberals at that time, shows a visible influence of Say's writings.
52. Borges Carneiro, one of the more prominent political figures of the early Liberalism, brings one interesting example of this second approach. Focussing on the need of regenerating the national economy, he considers that the state should promote liberty and security. Hence, it would be promoting the national manufactures, and with their prosperity it also promoted the increase of the fiscal sources (Carneiro, 1820, pp. 34; 45-6; Carneiro, 1820a, p. 98). This promotion of liberty and security, was the pursuit of *Common Good*, the task of the state: this contrasted with the past experience of favouring particular interests and of arbitrary expenditures (1820, pp. 26, 40; 1820a, p. 89). These arbitrary and negative measures would lead to a strong financial charge that was unfavourable to the development of economic activities (1820, p. 33). As most of the writings of this period, Carneiro shows a scarce theoretical background as well as the loosely association between political and economic liberalism (Castro, 1980, pp. 87-8).
53. A good economic legislation should promote prosperity, security and equality, and take into account the specificity of the economic activity (namely by being clear, concise, systematic, coherent, and exhaustive (Almeida, 1821, pp. 172 and 175).
54. Although he gives the English example as one that should be emulated, namely the ability of English industry to adjust to consumers, and the help given by the English government, with wise provisions, he does not specify what should they be. At the

same time he is not very explicit about the meaning to him of competition and freedom (Almeida, 1821, pp. 107-8).
55. Legislation was one of the most used instruments, corresponding to liberal's belief in law as a powerful instrument of changing society (cf. the example of Mouzinho da Silveira in 1832-34, in Brandão, 1990, p. 133).
56. The spread mistrust towards free-trade, will steadily became a generalised protectionism unanimity, that pervade most of the economic writings and the economic interests, specially those related with industry (cf. Bonifácio, 1991).

References

Almeida, Manuel (1821), 'Compêndio de Economia Política', in *Colecção de Obras Clássicas do Pensamento Económico Português*, Banco de Portugal (1993).

Almodovar, António (1995), *A Institucionalização da Economia Política Clássica em Portugal*, Edições Afrontamento, Porto.

Almodovar, António (1993), '*Introdução*', in *Escritos Económicos Escolhidos de Silva Lisboa*.

Almodovar, António (1992), 'Portugal e Brasil: a Economia Política em Dois Continentes', in Cardoso, José Luís and António Almodovar (Eds.) (1992) - *Actas do Encontro Ibérico Sobre História do Pensamento Económico*, CISEP, Lisboa.

Almodovar, António (1990), 'Caminhos para a Economia Política em Portugal (1789-1836)', in *Estudos sobre o Pensamento Económico em Portugal*, edited by Almodovar, António, Faculdade de Economia do Porto.

Almodovar, Antònio (1988), 'O Pensamento Económico Clássico em Portugal', in *Contribuições Contribuições para a História do Pensamento Económico em Portugal*, edited by Cardoso, José Luís, Dom Quixote, Lisboa.

Almodovar, António (1988?), 'Estudos introdutórios', in *Acúrsio das Neves*, Obras Completas, Vols 1° e 3°.

Almodovar, António (1988), 'Texto e Contexto: A Questão dos Privilégios de Novo Invento em José Acúrsio das Neves', in *Acúrsio das Neves*, Obras Completas Vol 4°.

Anónimo (1821), *Carta Política de certo Amigo da Corte de Lisboa a outro de Paris*, Off. De J. M. F. Campos, Lisboa.

Bonifácio, Maria de Fátima (1991), *Seis estudos sobre o Liberalismo Português*, ed Estampa, Lisboa.

Brandão, Maria de Fátima (1990), 'A Via Legislativa para a Mudança: Reflexões em torno de Acúrsio das Neves, Mouzinho da Silveira e Ferreira Borges' in Almodovar, António (Ed.) (1990) *Estudos sobre o Pensamento Económico em Portugal*, Faculdade de Economia do Porto.

Brito, João Rodrigues de (1821), *Cartas Economico-Politicas*, Imprensa Nacional, Lisboa.

Brito, Joaquim José Rodrigues (1803-1805), Memórias Políticas Sobre as Verdadeiras Bases da Grandeza das Nações 1803-1805', *Colecção de Obras Clássicas do Pensamento Económico Português*, Banco Portugal (1992).

Cardoso, José Luís (1991), '*A legislação económica do Vintismo: economia política e política económica nas Cortes Constituintes*', *Análise Social*, vol XXV, pp. 112-113.

Cardoso, José Luís (1989), *O Pensamento Económico em Portugal nos Finais do Século XVIII (1780-1808)*, Editorial Estampa, Lisboa.
Cardoso, José Luís (1989a), '*Os Agentes Económicos, e a Mudança na Sociedade Portuguesa de Antigo Regime (1780-1808)*', in *O Comportamento dos Agentes Económicos e a Reorientação da Política Económica*, CISEP, Lisboa.
Cardoso, José Luís (1988), 'A Influência de Adam Smith no Pensamento Económico Português (1776-1811/12)', in *Contribuições para a História do Pensamento Económico em Portugal*, edited by Cardoso, José Luís, Dom Quixote, Lisboa.
Cardozo, Henrique Nunes (1822), *Exposição*, in C. C. Lisboa.
Carneiro, Manuel Borges (1820), *Portugal Regenerado, 1° Ed*, Typographia Lacerdina, Lisboa.
Carneiro, Manuel Borges (1820a), *Portugal Regenerado, 3° Ed*, Typographia Lacerdina, Lisboa.
Castro, Armando (1980), *O Pensamento Económico no Portugal Moderno*, Biblioteca Breve, ICP, Lisboa.
Castro, Armando (1980), 'Estudos introdutórios', in Acúrsio das Neves, *Obras Completas* (Vols 1° and 3°).
Constâncio, Francisco Solano (1808-1842), *Leituras e Ensaios de Economia Política, Colecção de Obras Clássicas do Pensamento Económico Português*, Banco de Portugal (1995).
C. C. Lisboa (1822), *Memoria dos Trabalhos da Comissão para o melhoramento do Comercio nesta Cidade de Lisboa*, Typographia Rollandiana, Lisboa.
C. C. Porto (1823), *Resultados dos Trabalhos da Comissão do Comércio do Porto*, Typ. Viuva Alvarez Ribeiro & Filhos, Porto.
Freire, João António (1820), *Memoria sobre o melhoramento da Nação*, Impressão de Alcobia, Lisboa.
Lisboa, José da Silva (1804-20), *Escritos Económicos Escolhidos, Colecção de Obras Clássicas do Pensamento Económico Português*, Banco de Portugal (1993).
Loureiro, João (1822), 'Parecer Autonomo', in C. C. Lisboa.
Neves, Acúrsio das (1817), 'Variedades Sobre Objectos Relativos Às Artes, Comércio e Manufacturas, Consideradas Segundo os Princípios da Economia Política, Tomos I e II (1814-7)', *Obras Completas, Vol. 3°*, Edições Afrontamento, Porto.
Neves, Acúrsio das (1820), 'Memória Sobre os Meios de Melhorar a Indústria Portuguesa, Considerada nos Seus Diferentes Ramos', in *Obras Completas, Vol. 4°*, Edições Afrontamento, Porto.
Pedreira, Jorge Miguel (1994), *Estrutura Industrial e Mercado Colonial Portugal e Brasil (1780-1830)*, Difel, Lisboa.
Pedreira, Jorge Miguel (1988), 'Agrarismo, Industrialismo, Liberalismo. Algumas Notas Sobre o Pensamento económico Português (1780-1820)', in Cardoso, José Luís (Ed.) (1988) *Contribuições para a História do Pensamento Económico em Portugal*, Dom Quixote, Lisboa.
Pereira, José Esteves (1992), '*Introdução*', in *Memórias Políticas* de Rodrigues de Brito.
Pereira, José Esteves (1988), 'Mentalidade e Economia: o Pensamento de Joaquim José Rodrigues de Brito', in Cardoso, José Luís (Ed.) (1988) *Contribuições para a História do Pensamento Económico em Portugal*, Dom Quixote, Lisboa.
Pereira, Miriam Halpern (1992a), *Negociantes, Fabricantes e Artesãos entre Velhas e Novas Instituições - Estudos e Documentos (1821-2)*, Edições João Sá da Costa, Lisboa.

Smith, Adam (1976) [1776], *An Inquiry Into the Nature and Causes of The Wealth of Nations,* Liberty Press, Indiana.

Tomás, Manuel Fernandes (1821), *Relatório Sobre o Estado e Administração do Reino,* Seara Nova (1974), Lisboa.

Verdelho, Telmo (1981), *As palavras e as ideias na Revolução Liberal de 1820,* INIC, Lisboa.

Voto 8 (1822), *Voto em separado de 8 membros da Comissão do Comércio de Lisboa,* in C.C. Lisboa.